BEHOLD
THE
MESSIAH

BEHOLD THE MESSIAH

Robert J. Matthews

BOOKCRAFT
Salt Lake City, Utah

Library of Congress Catalog Card Number: 94-73504
ISBN 0-88494-966-4

First Printing, 1994

Printed in the United States of America

Contents

Why This Book Was Written

This material was prepared to be used primarily by members of The Church of Jesus Christ of Latter-day Saints. I do not feel that another exhaustive commentary detailing the earthly ministry of our Savior Jesus Christ is needed. Such has been gloriously accomplished by President J. Reuben Clark, Jr., Elder James E. Talmage, and Elder Bruce R. McConkie, whose individual works total thousands of pages. Other writers, not of General Authority status but with years of experience in languages, culture, travel in the Holy Land, and spiritual insight, have given us other thousands of pages of commentary and historical material. All of these authors are firm in testifying of the divine mission of the Lord Jesus Christ.

Ahead of any of the foregoing published materials, the Bible itself must stand as a basic source for the earthly ministry of Christ, especially the Latter-day Saint edition of the Bible published in 1979, which contains numerous study helps, chapter summaries, language clarifications, a dictionary, footnotes, a topical guide, cross-references to the other standard works, and excerpts from the Joseph Smith Translation. This book about the New Testament is designed to be used with that publication of the Bible.

The reader will already have observed that this is not a large book. It does not purport to cover all the events spoken of in the sacred records of Jesus' earthly ministry. This book has no busy-work, nor lengthy explanation of cultural, geographical, or historical information. It is a collection of useful information about the New Testament and of Jesus' ministry obtained primarily from the scriptures and as made clearer by the teachings of the Prophet Joseph Smith and his translation of the Bible. It contains summaries, observations, and condensations that are designed to give a reader direction and insight quickly without his having to analyze large numbers of pages. If the book has a virtue, it is perhaps its brevity and simplicity.

It has been a lifelong endeavor with me to understand the mission and personality of the Savior. My joy in Jesus' words has not come from study of the Bible alone. Many years ago I began to realize that the Prophet Joseph Smith had a refreshing and bold understanding of the Savior. Through both his public teachings and his translation of the Bible I caught a viewpoint, a vibrancy, and an assertiveness about Jesus that I found nowhere else. It is that blessed viewpoint, coupled with my own studies and testimony, that produced this book. I love the Jesus that the Prophet Joseph Smith knew and about whom he spoke and wrote.

It is my absolute and firm conviction that a complete concept of the Savior cannot be obtained from the New Testament alone. Such can be obtained only from studying latter-day revelation to learn how to evaluate and interpret the Bible. I do not believe any person can know enough about the real Jesus without knowing what the Book of Mormon, the Doctrine and Covenants, the Pearl of Great Price, and the Joseph Smith Translation[1] have to say. These sources, when joined with the New Testament and a personal witness from the Holy Ghost, provide understanding about Jesus that without them will remain hidden to mankind.

I have written this book with a conscious gratitude to the Prophet Joseph Smith and to others who have taught me the

---

1. For a brief description and history of Joseph Smith's translation of the Bible see Bible Dictionary in LDS edition of the Bible, 1979, p. 717.

gospel. Likewise, I hope that this work will lead its readers to a wider appreciation of the life and ministry of the Savior. What would any of us give to understand the scriptures as Joseph Smith knew them? Would we be willing to study carefully what he has said about Jesus and discover how he understood the various utterances and events of Jesus' mortal life?

Furthermore, in the midst of increasing skepticism, secularism, disbelief, and dissension in the world, there is always room for a voice in defense of the truth that Jesus Christ is the literal Son of God, the only Savior of mankind. Not only is our society sick with a skepticism about religion but also so many of those who do believe in Christ have so misunderstood his true character that they regard him as weak and colorless. Even many professing Christians, both lay members and clergy, do not see Jesus as divine. The world needs the true Christ and his sound doctrine, because Jesus alone can rescue man from total destruction. This work is intended to reflect the clarity and boldness of the JST and the teachings of Joseph Smith and the other scriptures in defending the great truth that Jesus is literally the Son of God.

This book is designed to give readers a viewpoint from the scriptures that testify of Jesus' earthly ministry. It centers primarily on the books of Matthew, Mark, Luke, John, and Acts, the latter-day revelations that pertain thereto, and the teachings of the Prophet Joseph Smith.

This work is not an official publication of the Church. I alone am responsible for the views it expresses.

ROBERT J. MATTHEWS
June 1994

Acknowledgments

No one reaches maturity without an indebtedness to many individuals and institutions for information, example, and assistance. Throughout my life I have received much that was beneficial from parents, five brothers and a sister (all older than I), Church leaders, teachers, friends, and for forty years colleagues in the Church Educational System. Brigham Young University has been generous in enabling me to teach and research for twenty-five of those forty years. Several General Authorities, past and present, have inspired me with their friendships, discourses, writings, and examples of courage. I am indebted to Richard Lloyd Anderson, long-time friend and colleague, for his testimony, faith, and scholarly diligence in many gospel subjects, including the New Testament. Robert L. Millet, Dean of Religious Education, has also emphatically encouraged me in the production of this work. A heartfelt thanks is due also to Marilyn Whitchurch and Kristin Gerdy of the BYU Religious Education Faculty Support Center for typing the manuscript. Finally, I thank my wife, Shirley, and our four children (Camille, Daniel, Robert D., and Tricia) and their families for making life enjoyable and productive. Without the help of all those mentioned above, and many others, this book would not have been possible.

Abbreviations

Citations from the standard works of scripture of The Church of Jesus Christ of Latter-day Saints are shown in the usual way. Some other source titles are abbreviated, as follows:

Antiquities   "Antiquities of the Jews." William Whiston, trans. *The Life and Works of Flavius Josephus.* Holt, Rinehart and Winston, N. Y., n.d.

CR   Conference reports of The Church of Jesus Christ of Latter-day Saints.

DNTC   Bruce R. McConkie. *Doctrinal New Testament Commentary.* 3 vols. Salt Lake City: Bookcraft, 1965–73.

JD   *Journal of Discourses.* 26 vols. Photo Lithographic Reprint. Los Angeles: General Printing and Lithograph Co., 1961.

JST   [Joseph Smith Translation of the Bible]. The Holy Scriptures: Inspired Version. Independence, Mo.: Herald Publishing House, 1970.

KJV   The King James Version of the Bible.

TPJS   Joseph Fielding Smith, comp. *Teachings of the Prophet Joseph Smith*. Salt Lake City: Deseret Book, 1976.

Titles of works cited only once are not abbreviated, and in each case the complete bibliography is given in the text.

PART I

The Essential Doctrinal Background

Part I deals with events that occurred long before there was any New Testament, even long before this earth was created, and hence before the human race began on the earth with Adam and Eve. The purpose is to give enough information to project a clear perspective of why there is a New Testament. Latter-day Saint doctrine asserts that mankind had a pre-earth life in a spirit existence wherein conscious preparation was made for the life we now live. In the words of Elder John Taylor: "The principles that we believe in reach back into eternity. They originated with the Gods in the eternal worlds, and they reach forward to the eternities that are to come." (*The Gospel Kingdom*, G. Homer Durham, ed. [Salt Lake City: Bookcraft, 1964], p. 14.)

This Part deliberately is not an elaborate presentation, but extensive writings are available, if desired, that would support the concepts discussed here. This is designed as an orientation on the fundamental things about the purpose of the Creation, the role of Jesus Christ, and the origin and destiny of man and of the devil, thus establishing a framework of reference for understanding the New Testament. In particular, it ensures a predefined understanding about who Jesus is, why he came to earth, and what he needed to accomplish. Likewise, when we consider the Twelve with whom Jesus associated, or any other

1

scriptural characters, or the people of any time (including our-selves), we know they came from a premortal life to work out their salvation upon the earth as part of the Father's great plan.

CHAPTER 1

A Unique Doctrinal Emphasis

The Church of Jesus Christ of Latter-day Saints asserts as a unique doctrinal emphasis that every human being had a long, individual, conscious, active, and intelligent existence in spirit form before being born into this world. This earth was created as a place where these premortal spirits could come and obtain a body of flesh and bones as a second step in their eternal progression. As all mortals eventually die, the body then returns to the earth and the eternal spirit enters a third stage, the postmortal spirit world. It stays there until the time of resurrection, when it is reunited with the elements of its physical body and thus enters the fourth and final stage. These four stages or estates of the eternal spirit personage can be spoken of as (1) unembodied state, (2) embodied state, (3) disembodied state, and (4) re-embodied state.

Every stage of existence has its particular opportunities and characteristics, and in each stage we have a direct relationship to the Redeemer and his atonement. We knew Christ in the premortal world. In the present world we are in the second or embodied state, whereas Jesus Christ himself has reached his fourth or final stage. Likewise there are millions of spirits waiting to be born; also millions who have entered the postmortal, disembodied realm, awaiting the resurrection. The Savior's work will not be finished until everyone and everything connected with this earth, and even the earth itself, has reached its final destiny.

The degree of emphasis that is placed on this long journey of man's eternal spirit sets The Church of Jesus Christ of Latter-day Saints apart from all other churches. It projects a more detailed and comprehensive reason for the creation of the world, explains more clearly what is meant by the fatherhood of God and the brotherhood of man, and gives a wider view of the work of redemption of Jesus Christ than does any other religious organization. Thus when a person who knows the plan reads of Jesus' earthly sojourn, he "sees" principles and "hears" echoes harking back to man's premortal existence.

Perhaps this wider perception and appreciation for the scope of the Lord's ministry is best illustrated by a comparison I made of four substantial works written about the life of Jesus Christ by four authors representing four different backgrounds. These four are:

—Frederic W. Farrar, *The Life of Christ*, first published in 1874, consisting of 744 pages. Cannon Farrar was a high-ranking clergyman of the Church of England.

—Cunningham Geikie, *The Life and Words of Christ*, first published in 1880, consisting of 1,257 pages. The Reverend Geikie had a doctor of divinity degree, and was of a Protestant background.

—Giuseppi Ricciotti, *The Life of Christ*, first published in 1947, consisting of 703 pages. G. Ricciotti is a scholar and member of the Roman Catholic Church.

—James E. Talmage, *Jesus the Christ*, first published in 1915, consisting of 804 pages in current editions. Elder Talmage was an ordained Apostle in The Church of Jesus Christ of Latter-day Saints.

Each of the above works has had wide distribution among students of the New Testament. I have read all of them and have made extensive comparisons of the content. All are favorable to the mission of Christ, and all are supportive of the New

Testament reports of his ministry. However, it was quickly apparent that Elder Talmage not only presented everything about Jesus Christ that the others included but in addition he elaborated at length on eight topics that the others either failed to mention or did so in a very brief manner. These topics, as shown by chapters in the table of contents of Elder Talmage's *Jesus the Christ*, are:

2 Preexistence and Foreordination of the Christ. (11 pages)
3 The Need of a Redeemer. (15 pages)
4 The Antemortal Godship of Christ. (10 pages)
36 In the Realm of Disembodied Spirits. (8 pages)
39 Ministry of the Resurrected Christ on the Western Hemisphere. (24 pages)
40 The Long Night of Apostasy. (13 pages)
41 Personal Manifestations of the Eternal Father and His Son Jesus Christ in Modern Times. (22 pages)
42 Jesus the Christ to Return. (14 pages)
Total = 117 pages

The significant points of difference in Elder Talmage's work represent the particular doctrinal foundation of The Church of Jesus Christ of Latter-day Saints as compared to the other religious organizations. This is not to say that others do not believe or know some of these subjects, but it is to say that there is a lack of emphasis and focus on these subjects in the other books.

Additional and impressive evidence of the doctrinal basis by which the Church interprets the New Testament is seen in the monumental volumes published by Elder Bruce R. McConkie, member of the Quorum of the Twelve Apostles. From 1978 to 1982 he published a total of six volumes that are popularly called the Messiah series, and which consist of the following: *The Promised Messiah; The Mortal Messiah* (4 books); and *The Millennial Messiah* (Salt Lake City: Deseret Book Co.). These six volumes total 3,155 pages of print. The first volume, *The Promised Messiah*, presents 453 of its 615 pages in detailed discussion about the calling, activities, and glory of the Lord Jehovah (who is Jesus Christ) in the premortal life. As the series progresses to the four books of the *Mortal Messiah*, chapter 109 gives 15 pages of the Lord's ministry in the realm of departed spirits between his crucifixion and resurrection, while his body lay in the tomb. The final book of the series, *The Millennial Messiah* consists of a 711-page discussion of the future activities and work of the Messiah when he returns to the earth as King and Lord.

The entire scope of these volumes is dependent upon the doctrinal foundation that is laid by latter-day revelation that came through the Prophet Joseph Smith. Without that, neither Elder Talmage's nor Elder McConkie's works could have been written.

CHAPTER 2

Importance of the Premortal Life

The revelations given to the Church, primarily through the Prophet Joseph Smith, have provided considerable information about the premortal existence. The value of such knowledge is that it gives us the correct perspective about our present lives, background on the Lord Jesus Christ, and the origin of the devil. In 1909, the First Presidency of the Church issued a formal exposition on the origin of man, from which the following are excerpts:

> Adam, our progenitor, "the first man," was, like Christ, a pre-existent spirit, and like Christ he took upon him an appropriate body, the body of a man, and so became a "living soul." The doctrine of the pre-existence—revealed so plainly, particularly in latter days—pours a wonderful flood of light upon the otherwise mysterious problem of man's origin. It shows that man, as a spirit, was begotten and born of heavenly parents, and reared to maturity in the eternal mansions of the Father, prior to coming upon the earth in a temporal body to undergo an experience in mortality. It teaches that all men existed in the spirit before any man existed in the flesh, and that all who have inhabited the earth since Adam have taken bodies and become souls in like manner. . . .

. . . Jesus, however, is the firstborn among all the sons of God—the first begotten in the spirit, and the only begotten in the flesh. He is our elder brother, and we, like Him, are in the image of God. All men and women are in the similitude of the universal Father and Mother, and are literally the sons and daughters of Deity.

> Joseph F. Smith,
> John R. Winder,
> Anthon H. Lund,
>> First Presidency of The Church of Jesus Christ of Latter-day Saints. (As quoted in *Encyclopedia of Mormonism* [Macmillan, 1992], vol. 4, pp. 1668, 1670).

Since "all men and women are in [that] similitude," obviously there were both male and female spirits in heaven. Elder James E. Talmage wrote:

> We affirm as reasonable, scriptural, and true, the eternity of sex among the children of God. The distinction between male and female is no condition peculiar to the relatively brief period of mortal life. It was an essential characteristic of our pre-existent condition, even as it shall continue after death, in both disembodied and resurrected states. . . . [The] scriptures attest a state of existence preceding mortality, in which the spirit children of God lived, doubtless with distinguishing characteristics, including the distinction of sex, "before they were [created] naturally upon the face of the earth." ("The Eternity of Sex," *Millennial Star*, 24 August 1922, p. 530.)

In the Grand Council in Heaven the Savior was chosen as the central figure in the Father's plan for his children. We read in Moses' record:

> And I, the Lord God, spake unto Moses, saying: That Satan, whom thou hast commanded in the name of mine Only Begotten, is the same which was from the beginning, and he came before me, saying—Behold, here am I, send me, I will be thy son, and I will redeem all mankind, that one soul shall not be lost, and surely I will do it; wherefore give me thine honor.

But, behold, my Beloved Son, which was my Beloved and Chosen from the beginning, said unto me—Father, thy will be done, and the glory be thine forever.

Wherefore, because that Satan rebelled against me, and sought to destroy the agency of man, which I, the Lord God, had given him, and also, that I should give unto him mine own power; by the power of mine Only Begotten, I caused that he should be cast down;

And he became Satan, yea, even the devil, the father of all lies, to deceive and to blind men, and to lead them captive at his will, even as many as would not hearken unto my voice. (Moses 4:1–4.)

The Prophet Joseph Smith assured us of our participation in that Grand Council: "At the first organization in heaven we were all present, and saw the Savior chosen and appointed and the plan of salvation made, and we sanctioned it" (TPJS, 181). Other appointments too were made in premortal councils. Said Joseph Smith at another time: "Every man who has a calling to minister to the inhabitants of the world was ordained to that very purpose in the Grand Council of heaven before this world was. I suppose I was ordained to this very office in that Grand Council." (TPJS, 365.)

From Abraham's writings we learn of the implementation of the Father's plan in the creation of the earth:

And there stood one among them [among the spirits] that was like unto God, and he said unto those who were with him: We will go down, for there is space there, and we will take of these materials, and we will make an earth whereon these may dwell;

And we will prove them herewith, to see if they will do all things whatsoever the Lord their God shall command them;

And they who keep their first estate shall be added upon; and they who keep not their first estate shall not have glory in the same kingdom with those who keep their first estate; and they who keep their second estate shall have glory added upon their heads for ever and ever. (Abraham 3:24–26.)

As we saw from Moses' record, another critical actor in the plan rebelled against the Father and thereby chose himself for the leading negative role. Because of Satan's rebellion, he will never have a physical body. We quote Joseph Smith again: "We came to this earth that we might have a body and present it pure before God in the celestial kingdom. The great principle of happiness consists in having a body. The devil has no body, and herein is his punishment." (TPJS, 181.) "And this was the case with Lucifer when he fell. He sought for things which were unlawful. Hence he was sent down, and it is said he drew many away with him; and the greatness of his punishment is that he shall not have a tabernacle. This is his punishment." (TPJS, 297.)

The foregoing statements give us a starting point from which we can more fully appreciate our Lord's entry into mortality. He was on the Father's errand and came by appointment, and as he said, "I came down from heaven, not to do mine own will, but the will of him that sent me" (John 6:38). Thus we gain a better view not only as to why the Savior came but also as to who we are, and why we are here, for we also were schooled and prepared for earth life during that long premortal period. We likewise learn something of who the devil is and why he is an archenemy of Christ. Who are the evil spirits or devils we read about in the New Testament? They are among those who followed Satan in the premortal life and were cast out with him (Revelation 12:4–9; D&C 29:36–38). Without this background the New Testament does not reveal its full message to us. With this information we learn that the same individuals who were present and active in the premortal life are now found upon the earth—the same characters, but in a different environment. For a succinct treatise on additional aspects of premortality see Neal A. Maxwell, *A Wonderful Flood of Light* (Salt Lake City: Bookcraft, 1990), chapter 3.

CHAPTER 3

The Need for a Redeemer

When the Lord created the physical earth and all things in it there was no death. The earth was physical and real; Adam and Eve had bodies of flesh and bone (no blood), the animals likewise. Because there was no death, all created things would have forever remained just as they were (2 Nephi 2:22–25). Furthermore, all things were in the presence of God, meaning that there was no spiritual death.

The Fall and Its Consequences

The Fall of Adam and Eve brought a great change not only to themselves but also to the entire earth. It brought two kinds of death: first, spiritual death, for Adam and Eve now were shut out of the presence of God; later came physical changes and ultimately physical death, death of the body. Adam and Eve personally experienced both these deaths as a consequence of their transgression. Also, all their children were born mortal and fallen, and this has been the case for all generations—children are born innocent, but mortal. As explained by Samuel the Lamanite: "All mankind, . . . by the fall of Adam being cut off from the presence of the Lord, are considered as dead, both to things temporal and to things spiritual. But behold, the resurrection of Christ redeemeth mankind, yea, even all mankind, and bringeth them back into the presence of the Lord." (Helaman 14:16–17.)

Because all mankind have inherited the effects of the Fall, every person sins in some way. No one else had any responsibility in Adam and Eve's transgression, yet we all inherit its consequences, being subject to the two deaths. The atonement of Jesus Christ automatically redeems all mankind from those consequences. That is, every person who ever lived or will yet live will rise in the resurrection with the same physical body he or she had on earth, and every person, after being resurrected, will return to the presence of God for a judgment concerning his or her own sins.

Thus from the fall of Adam we will all be unconditionally redeemed. From our own "fall" occasioned by our own sins committed after arriving at the age of accountability, we are saved on condition of our obedience to the gospel of Jesus Christ.

The power of death over the whole creation is visible on every hand. Children, born innocent in the sight of God, are nevertheless mortal and subject to death. If Jesus had been a mere mortal he too would have been subject to death and thus unable to save either himself or others. The physical Jesus was born of Mary, a mortal woman; but he was the literal, biological son in the flesh of God the Father, from whom he received power over death (see John 5:26; 10:17–18). Thus by his atonement Jesus conquered death—both physical death and spiritual death—for himself and all mankind. His life and his death on earth was not as the natural man, but as a God. When he was sacrificed it was the death of a God, infinite and eternal (Alma 34:9–11).

The Fall has such a strong hold on mortal man and death (both the physical and the spiritual kinds) is such an "awful monster," that if there had been no Christ and no atonement every mortal being would have become a devil, miserable forever (2 Nephi 9:7–9, 11).

The Redeeming Power of Christ

We need to know all the above things about Jesus and about the origin of death and sin on the earth. Only in the revelations do we find answers as to "the human predicament," as philosophers call it. If we know about the premortal life, the purpose of creation, the conditions of creation, and the effects of the Fall upon all the human family, we begin to see why Jesus came, why he was born as an infant, and why he was the Only Begotten of the Father in the flesh. Thus the New Testament takes on a dimension and a meaning that those without that background cannot see.

The scriptures teach us that Jesus is the only true Redeemer, that the gospel of Jesus Christ is the only plan that will work and is the only plan authorized by the Father. They further attest to the fact that there is no salvation—that there are no conditions nor ways nor means for salvation—except through Christ (Mosiah 3:17; 4:8; 5:8).

The uniqueness of Jesus Christ and the seriousness of man's situation without the Redeemer leads us to catch a glimpse of just how dependent upon Christ we really are. If there were no atonement by Christ nothing anyone or everyone could do would make up for the loss. We are completely unable to save ourselves in any degree without that atonement. As Jesus said: "I am the vine, ye are the branches . . . without me ye can do nothing" (John 15:5). Sever a branch from the vine and how quickly it withers! On the other hand, because of Christ, mankind can progress to eternal glory and become even as God, as he said: "For behold, this is my work and my glory—to bring to pass the immortality and eternal life of man" (Moses 1:39).

CHAPTER 4

Premortal Jesus Christ Was a God

Prerequisite to even a small degree of appreciation for the Savior's mortal life and ministry and indeed to an understanding of the scriptures is the knowledge that premortally he was a God with power, glory, and wide experience; that he was also a God when he lived on earth; and that he came to earth by the Father's appointment to do a particular work that no other person could do.

It is necessary also to realize that when Jesus was in his mortal ministry he knew exactly who he was, who he had been in the premortal life, and what he must accomplish while on earth. Jesus' entire mortal life conformed to the purpose for which he came. Everything he said and did was directed toward the fulfillment of that plan.

A succinct summary of the Lord's high status is given by Elder Bruce R. McConkie:

> As far as man is concerned, all things center in *Christ*. He is the Firstborn of the Father. By obedience and devotion to the truth he attained that pinnacle of intelligence which ranked him as a God, as the Lord Omnipotent, while yet in his pre-existent state.

As such he became, under the Father, the Creator of this earth and of worlds without number; and he was then chosen to work out the infinite and eternal atonement, to come to this particular earth as the literal Son of the Father, and to put the whole plan of redemption, salvation, and exaltation in operation.

Through him the gospel, all saving truths, and every edifying principle have been revealed in all ages. He is the Eternal Jehovah, the promised Messiah, the Redeemer and Savior, the Way, the Truth, and the Life. By him immortality and eternal life become realities, and through his grace and goodness salvation is possible for all who will believe and obey.

He was born into this world as the Son of Mary (inheriting from her the power of mortality) and as the Son of Man of Holiness (inheriting from him the powers of immortality). In this life he received not of the fulness at the first, but went from grace to grace until, in the final triumph of the resurrection, he gained the fulness of all things; and all power was given him both in heaven and on earth. He has all truth, all power, all knowledge; he comprehends all things, is infinite in all his attributes and powers; and he has given a law unto all things. . . .

If the sectarian world, or even the spiritually unenlightened in the Church, had the slightest concept of the dominion, exaltation, and pre-eminence of our Lord both in pre-existence, during his mortal ministry, and now that he has returned to his Father, it would seem little short of direful and presumptuous blasphemy to them. Words, either written or spoken, cannot convey such a realization; it can only come by the revelations of the Spirit. (*Mormon Doctrine*, 2d ed. [Salt Lake City: Bookcraft, 1966], pp. 129–30.)

Jesus as Creator

We do not know how many worlds Jesus has created under the direction of the Father, but it is a very large number. "Innumerable are they unto man; but all things are numbered unto [God]" (Moses 1:35). We gain a glimpse of the immensity of that number from the following exclamation by Enoch: "And were it possible that man could number the particles of the earth, yea, millions of earths like this, it would not be a beginning to the number of thy creations" (Moses 7:30). The drama is increased when we remember that Jesus himself came to earth to be born and walk upon one of the earths he had created. In its final destiny this earth will become a celestial world, and Jesus will dwell here with other celestial beings (D&C 88:17–20, 25–26; 130:9; Articles of Faith 1:10).

Jesus as God of This World

Jesus was the God of ancient Israel and of the prophets before Israel, even back to Adam. Jesus appeared to Adam, Enoch, Noah, Abraham, Isaac, Jacob, Joseph, Moses, Isaiah, Daniel, and other Old Testament prophets. He appeared also to the Jaredite and the Nephite prophets. They all worshipped him and received direction and salvation from him. It was Jesus, as Jehovah, who gave the law to Moses and who led Israel for so many centuries.

All the true prophets from Adam to John the Baptist knew that their God would come to earth and be the Messiah, Redeemer, and Savior and that he would bring to pass the resurrection of mankind. This has always been the message of all true prophets. (Jacob 7:11–12; Mosiah 13:33–35.)

A definitive statement of the superior position of Jesus Christ was issued by the First Presidency and the Council of the Twelve on June 30, 1916. A portion of that solemn and official declaration reads:

> Among the spirit children of Elohim the firstborn was and is Jehovah or Jesus Christ to whom all others are juniors. . . .
>
> There is no impropriety, therefore, in speaking of Jesus Christ as the Elder Brother of the rest of human kind. That He is by spiritual birth Brother to the rest of us is indicated in Hebrews: "Wherefore in all things it behoved him to be made like unto his brethren, that he might be a merciful and faithful high priest in things pertaining to God, to make reconciliation for the sins of the people" (Hebrews 2:17). Let it not be forgotten, however, that He is essentially greater than any and all others, by reason (1) of His seniority as the oldest or firstborn; (2) of His unique status in the flesh as the offspring of a mortal mother and of an immortal, or resurrected and glorified, Father; (3) of His selection and foreordi-

nation as the one and only Redeemer and Savior of the race; and (4) of His transcendent sinlessness.

Jesus Christ is not the Father of the spirits who have taken or yet shall take bodies upon this earth, for He is one of them. He is The Son, as they are sons or daughters of Elohim. So far as the stages of eternal progression and attainment have been made known through divine revelation, we are to understand that only resurrected and glorified beings can become parents of spirit offspring. Only such exalted souls have reached maturity in the appointed course of eternal life; and the spirits born to them in the eternal worlds will pass in due sequence through the several stages or estates by which the glorified parents have attained exaltation. (Cited in James E. Talmage, *Articles of Faith*, Salt Lake City: The Church of Jesus Christ of Latter-day Saints, pp. 471–73.)

This same exalted Being who was born in Bethlehem, who led the ancient Saints, and who conquered death and sin in Gethsemane and on the cross, who rose from the grave in eternal splendor—this is the same Jesus who with the Father came to Joseph Smith in the Sacred Grove in western New York in 1820.

It is in the light and perspective of the special doctrinal background given to the Latter-day Saints that this book on the mortal ministry of the Savior is written. I verily believe that the New Testament alone, in its present condition, is inadequate to convey the proper understanding of Jesus Christ. The additional light and knowledge given through the Prophet Joseph Smith moves us to greater heights of understanding, so that we too can say, with Andrew, "We have found the Messiah" (John 1:41).

PART II

The New Testament Records

The New Testament is the chief source of information about the earthly ministry of Jesus. However, the books of Matthew, Mark, Luke, and John were each written for a different audience, and each emphasizes some aspect of our Lord's life that the others do not. Each book is unique and is uneven in its coverage, but there is also a large amount of sameness about them. They unitedly proclaim that Jesus Christ is a God, hence much more than a mortal man; that he is assuredly the divine Redeemer of mankind.

The New Testament books themselves contain some apparent chronological contradictions, but this is of minor concern since they are of the nature of testimonials rather than biographies.

It is a cardinal tenet of The Church of Jesus Christ of Latter-day Saints that the New Testament records have not been preserved intact; some parts are missing and other parts have become blurred through error of transcription and translation. The major deficiencies of the New Testament result from persons, inspired by the devil, having deliberately removed plain and precious parts so as to render the Testament less effective (1 Nephi 13:20–41; Articles of Faith 1:8). For that reason we find it desirable to verify, supplement, interpret, and also correct portions of the New Testament text with revelation God gave the Prophet Joseph Smith. It is noteworthy that for various New Testament situations a comparison with latter-day revelation frequently shows that the New Testament tells us *what* occurred and latter-day revelation adds *why*.

CHAPTER 5

Sources of Knowledge About Jesus' Earthly Ministry

There is no substitute for reading the scripture itself. To learn of Jesus' mortal life we should begin by reading the books of Matthew, Mark, Luke, and John, which will give us a fairly accurate (though incomplete) account of Jesus' life among the people of ancient Palestine, and will expose us to his teachings and doings. Traits of his personality shine through the record, and when reading the holy word one cannot help but be inspired with his kindness and spiritual greatness.

New Testament Manuscripts

No original manuscripts of the New Testament are available today, nor have they been since the second or third centuries A.D. It is certain that presently available manuscripts differ somewhat from the originals (1 Nephi 13:21–29), just as later copies differ from earlier ones.

Early manuscripts were not divided into chapters and verses, although they contained a type of paragraphing. The particular chapter and verse designations we find in the Bible today were developed for ease of reference and use with a concordance, and were first employed in Greek and Latin Bibles. The first English Bible to employ this verse system was the Geneva Bible of 1560. The Geneva Bible also used a ¶ symbol to indicate subject-matter changes in the narrative. The King James Version of 1611 borrowed this symbol (for example, see Matthew 1:18; 2:11, 16, 19), and also the chapter and verse system.

The Records Are Testimonies

In Bibles that are published today each of the books of Matthew, Mark, Luke, and John (commonly called the four Gospels) is titled, "The Gospel According to. . . ." Scholars tell us, however, that these titles were added sometime around the fourth century A.D., and that before that time probably only the name of the writer appeared; that is, only the name of Matthew, for example.

It has become customary to speak of these books as though they were histories, and in one sense they are, but they are not so much biographies or histories as they are testimonies. In the Joseph Smith Translation, each of the four records is titled with that word: "The Testimony of St. Matthew," and so on. This is a more accurate description of the content and purpose of each of these books than to style them, "The Gospel According to. . . ." They do not offer a detailed biography or life history of Jesus, nor is the gospel of any private interpretation. These books are testimonies about Jesus: they tell who he was, what he said, what he did, and why that is important. Because of the influence of the JST, in this book I have purposely avoided calling the books of Matthew, Mark, Luke, and John "Gospels." Rather, I refer to them throughout as Testimonies.

If we examined the four Testimonies, removed the duplications, and placed each event on a timeline, we would find that only thirty to thirty-one days of Jesus' thirty-three-year life are delineated on a day-by-day basis. There is some detail of his birth and the early weeks, then brief mention about his being taken to Egypt as a child, and later his returning to Palestine. A few paragraphs tell us something about him at age twelve, his baptism at age thirty, his temptations in the wilderness, and various journeys throughout Palestine, with emphasis generally surrounding the annual feast days. Sometimes the record skips weeks or even months between events. The events of the last ten days of his life are given in considerable detail—the most detailed portion we have of any part of his life.

The largest number of column inches of printing space given to any one day of Jesus' life is for the Tuesday in the last week of his mortal life. Matthew devotes from chapters 21:18 through 26:16 to that one day alone. In the medium-sized print of the 1979 Bible published by the Church, this one day consists of 116 column inches of print. About no other single day in Jesus' life do we have so much column length or so much information.

On the other hand, beginning in John 5:1 Jesus is in Jerusalem in April at the time of the feast of the Passover. Long discussions follow on the same day. Chapter 6 gives a record of three major events over a period of the next six months in Galilee. Chapter seven is back in Jerusalem in October at the time of the feast of Tabernacles, with long discussions in chapters 7, 8, 9, and part of chapter 10 centered at that same time. Without warning, in chapter 10:22, it is suddenly late in December at the feast of Dedication. In these chapters nine months' time (270 days), from April to December, are covered in 112 $\frac{1}{2}$ column inches, which is a little less than the space that was given for just one day in the example from Matthew. The point is obvious: coverage is uneven. But this doesn't matter. The writers were forging neither biographies nor histories. They were bearing testimony of what Jesus said and did. There is no contradiction in this, just an example of different writing styles and different emphases.

Why This Perspective Is Important

What is the practical importance of knowing that the records are not intended to be complete biographies? First, the image that the world has about Jesus and the Twelve is almost that they were vagabonds, with no fixed home, rootless, and always on the move. A more careful examination of the sources makes it obvious that we need not view their ministry in that way. Travelling considerably—yes. Travelling always—without time for home or family—no. Nothing in the record strictly requires us to believe that Jesus and the Twelve were itinerant preachers, always away from home and family, and always on the move. When Jesus said "Foxes have holes and birds of the air have nests; but the Son of man hath not where to lay his head" (Luke 9:58) he may have meant that the temple—the house of God—had been defiled by the people and hence was no longer the sacred sanctuary it once had been (see *History of the Church* 2:414–15).

Second, it is abundantly clear that the Bible does not contain all the words or deeds of Jesus. It is such a partial record that it is simply unthinkable to the reasonable mind that this sketchy record contains all his teachings, or that he never said anything new or worthwhile on those other days. John makes reference to this when he says: "And there are also many other things which Jesus did, the which, if they should be written every one, I suppose that even the world itself could not contain the books that should be written" (John 21:25).

In this connection one is reminded of Paul urging his friends from Ephesus "to remember the words of the Lord Jesus, how he said, It is more blessed to give than to receive" (Acts 20:35). It is clear that Paul knew this as a particular statement by Jesus, yet nowhere in the four "testimonies" is Jesus represented as saying that.

Even though the Testimonies of Matthew, Mark, Luke, and John in the New Testament are the basic sources for a record of Jesus' earthly ministry, these records are supplemented and clarified by other sacred records such as the Book of Mormon and the Doctrine and Covenants. Furthermore, though we have been warned that the Bible has been deliberately altered, and depleted by the removal of many plain and precious things, we can profit from the clarifying and restorative work of the Prophet Joseph Smith in his translation of the Bible, which makes clear and meaningful many things that otherwise are cloudy, vague, incomplete, or sometimes completely lacking in all other Bibles.

To these scriptural sources we add the teachings of Joseph Smith and other prophets of this last dispensation who have known Jesus by revelation and have spoken with a personal understanding of spiritual things.

CHAPTER 6

A Look at
the Four Testimonies

The Testimonies written by Matthew, Mark, Luke, and John are the basic sources of information about Jesus' earthly ministry. These are supplemented by references in the book of Acts and in the epistles written by the early leaders of the Church. The writers of the New Testament are of two classes:

1. Those who had known Jesus personally and were among the original Twelve chosen by him (such as Peter, John, and Matthew).
2. Those who were not of the original Twelve but who became leaders in the Church after Jesus' ascension to heaven (such as Mark, Luke, and Paul).

Although none of the original manuscripts of the New Testament are available today, there is more tangible evidence for the authenticity of the New Testament than for any other ancient book. Manuscripts of the New Testament are more numerous and are of much earlier date than those of the great classical Greek writings. Available manuscripts for these classics are few in number and most do not go back earlier than the ninth century A.D., although the histories they relate are very old. By comparison, there are thousands of New Testament manuscripts available that date much earlier than the ninth century. Several complete manuscripts date to within three hundred years of New Testament times, and there are fragments reaching to within a hundred years. (See F. F. Bruce, *The New Testament Documents: Are They Reliable?* 5th ed. [Grand Rapids: Wm. B. Eerdmans Publishing Co., 1965], pp. 15–17.)

In addition to the manuscript evidence for the New Testament there are the records of latter-day revelation (such as the Book of Mormon, the Doctrine and Covenants, the Pearl of Great Price, and the Joseph Smith Translation of the Bible) that the Church of Jesus Christ recognizes as sacred scripture. These books confirm the authenticity of the New Testament in general content as well as in many specific instances. We can therefore be secure in the knowledge that the New Testament, though incomplete, is a reliable record.

A Comparison of the Four Testimonies

Each of the Testimonies gives an account of the thirty-three years of Jesus' earthly life; yet each has some peculiarities and unique features of its own. Some material can be found in all four of the records, some in three, some in two, and some in only one.

The following chart shows the percentage of information that is common to all the records and the percentage that is particular to an individual writer.

Book	Exclusive Material	Common Material
Matthew	42%	58%
Mark	7%	93%
Luke	59%	41%
John	92%	8%

From the above we see that 93 percent of the material in Mark is included in the other records, while only 8 percent of the information in John is included in the others, and so forth.

Matthew

Main emphasis is toward the Jews:
a. Apparently written to and for Jewish readers.
b. Places great emphasis on fulfillment of Old Testament prophecy, and presents Jesus as the fulfillment of that prophecy.
c. Note Matthew's use of the Old Testament:
    Matthew 2:15—"Out of Egypt. . . ."
    Matthew 2:17–18—"spoken by Jeremy [Jeremiah]."
    Matthew 2:23—"He shall be called a Nazarene."
    Matthew 27:9—"Thirty pieces of silver."
d. Has several lengthy discourses. Examples: Sermon on the Mount (chapters 5–7); instruction to the Twelve (chapter 10); rebuke to the Pharisees (chapter 23); the Second Coming (chapter 24).

Some material exclusive to Matthew:
a. Visit of the wise men; a star in the east. (Matthew 2:1–12)
b. Flight into Egypt. (Matthew 2:13–14)
c. Slaying of the Bethlehem children. (Matthew 2:16–18)
d. Sermon on the Mount. (Matthew 5, 6, 7)
e. Ten parables that the others do not have.

Some peculiarities of the book of Matthew:
a. He alone mentions the circumstances of Jesus' paying tribute to the tax collector of Capernaum. (Matthew 17:24–27)
b. He alone mentions "sealing the stone and setting a watch" at the tomb. (Matthew 27:66)
c. Concerning Matthew's feast for Jesus and some publicans, both Mark 2:15 and Luke 5:29 indicate that it was Matthew who gave the feast, but Matthew's account tends to keep him anonymous. (Matthew 9:9–13)

Mark

Main emphasis is on the doings of Jesus:
a. Written to Gentile (most likely Roman) members of the Church.
b. Apparently used Peter as a chief source of information.
c. Emphasis is upon acts rather than upon teachings and discourses. No long sermons.
d. Great emphasis upon miraculous events.
e. Seems to emphasize the Galilean ministry rather than Jesus' ministry in Judea.

Some material exclusive to Mark:
a. One exclusive parable. (Mark 4:26–29)
b. A young man wearing a sheet. (Mark 14:51–52)
c. Signs that follow believers. (Mark 16:17–18)

Some peculiarities of the book of Mark:
a. Explanation of Jewish terms and phrases. These explanations are not found in corresponding passages in Matthew or Luke. (Mark 7:2; 7:34; 5:41; 2:26; 7:2–13) This is probably because Mark wrote to non-Jews who, without some explanation, would not understand Jewish phrases, geography, and culture.
b. An anonymous reference to himself? (Mark 14:51–52)
c. Emphasis upon Jesus' physically resting. Eleven places mention Jesus resting; this is more than in any other record.
d. The only one to mention that Jesus was a carpenter. (Mark 6:3)

Luke

Main emphasis is on the universality of Jesus' teachings:
a. Written to Theophilus, a Gentile Christian acquaintance. (Luke 1:1–4)
b. Emphasis upon Jesus' teachings, especially the parables.
c. Apparently used Paul as a major source of information.

d. Has a strong Gentile appeal, as contrasted with the Jewish emphasis in Matthew.

Some material exclusive to Luke:
a. Visits of Gabriel to Zacharias and to Mary. (Luke 1)
b. Births of John the Baptist and Jesus, circumcision, Anna, and Simeon's prophecies. (Luke 1, 2)
c. Jesus at the temple at age 12. (Luke 2:41–52)
d. Twelve parables that the others do not have.
e. Only one to mention the Seventy. (Luke 10:1–25)
f. Only one to tell of Jesus' sweating blood. (Luke 22:44)
g. Jesus' discussion with a thief about paradise. (Luke 23:39–43)
h. Jesus eating fish and honey after resurrection. (Luke 24:41–43)

Some peculiarities of the book of Luke:
a. Special attention to illness and medical terms—circumcision, Jesus sweating blood, withered *right* hand, leprosy, healing of Malchus's ear.
b. Emphasis on prayer. More frequent mention of prayer than in any of the other records.
c. More attention to women and stories about women than any of the other records.
d. An emphasis on individual salvation, and the salvation of Gentiles, as contrasted to the salvation of the house of Israel.

John

Main emphasis is on such spiritual fundamentals as Jesus being the Son of God:
a. Probably addressed to both Jewish and Gentile audiences—a general tract.
b. The main purpose was to emphasize that Jesus is the Son of God. (John 20:30–31) (Yet, surprisingly, John makes no mention of the virgin birth.)
c. An emphasis upon Jesus' ministry in Judea as well as in Galilee.

d. Several long discourses, such as the bread of life (chapter 6), the Holy Ghost (chapters 14, 16), prayer in the Garden (chapter 17).

Some material exclusive to John:
a. The call of four early disciples, wedding at Cana, Nicodemus's visit to Jesus, an early clearing of the temple, the woman at the well in Samaria, curing the nobleman's son, curing the lame man at the pool. (John 1:35 to 5:24)
b. Discourses on the bread of life, on the light of the world, on the living water, healing a man born blind, the raising of Lazarus. (John chapters 6–11)
c. The only one to mention the washing of feet at the Last Supper, discourse about the Holy Ghost, prayer in the Garden, piercing of Jesus' side, Thomas the doubter, promise of John's tarrying. (John 13 to 21)
d. No true parables, but two allegories: John 10 (the good shepherd) and John 15:1–8 (the vine and the branches).

Some peculiarities of the book of John:
a. Anonymous references to John himself? (John 13:23; 20:1–11; 21:20–24)
b. Emphasis on Philip. (John 1:43–45; 12:21–22; 14:8–9)
c. Emphasis on Thomas. (John 11:16; 20:24–29; 21:2)
d. The testimony of John is notable for what it omits as well as for what it contains. There is no reference or allusion to Jesus' forty days in the wilderness, the parables, calming the storm at sea, the Mount of Transfiguration, casting out of devils, the Sermon on the Mount.

Some variations in the Testimonies:
a. The genealogy of Jesus given in Matthew 1 and Luke 3. Matthew's account runs from Abraham down to Christ in the style of the Old Testament genealogies. Luke's account runs in the other direction from Jesus back to Abraham and then continues to Adam. This direction is said to be consistent with Greek genealogies. Thus each of these is consistent with the purpose of the book in which it is found.
b. Healing of two who were possessed of a devil. Mark and

Luke say one man; Matthew says there were two men
thus possessed. (Mark 5:2; Luke 8:27; Matthew 8:28)

c. Triumphal entry into Jerusalem. Matthew reads that
Jesus rode two animals; Luke, only one. (Matthew 21:1–7;
Luke 19:28–36) This situation is corrected by the JST in
Matthew.

d. Varied statements of the inscriptions on the cross.
(Matthew 27:37; Mark 15:26; Luke 23:38; John 19:19)

e. Angel at the tomb (one or two angels?) (Matthew 28;
Mark 16; Luke 24; John 20) This is corrected by the JST to
read consistently that there were two.

f. Names of the Twelve (alternate names and also some
grouping into pairs). (Matthew 10:2–4; Mark 3:16–19;
Luke 6:13–16; Acts 1:13)

Help from Latter-day Revelation

The *Book of Mormon* is very helpful in clarifying and supple-
menting numerous concepts and events in the New Testament.
This is particularly noticeable in the Savior's sermon to the
Nephites (3 Nephi 12, 13, 14), which is similar to the Lord's instruction to the Twelve (Matthew 5, 6, 7). Considerable light is
given in the Book of Mormon concerning which part of the sermon is applicable to the world, or even to the Church in general, and which parts are for special chosen disciples only. For
example, 3 Nephi 13:25–34 makes it plain that the command in
Matthew 6:25–34 that one should "take no thought for tomor-
row, for food or clothing" is not a command for the whole
world, or even for Church membership in general, but for the
Twelve only.

Likewise, valuable information is given in the Book of
Mormon account concerning the Beatitudes (compare 3 Nephi
12 with Matthew 5). Also, much valuable information is given
about the sacrament (3 Nephi 18) and the meaning of the "other
sheep" mentioned in John 10:16 (3 Nephi 15:11–24).

The Book of Mormon confirms that Jesus is a God of
miracles and that he performed many mighty miracles among

the people of Palestine during his mortal ministry (Mosiah 3:5–10; Mormon 9:16–18). To these may be added the following items in which the Book of Mormon refers to and supports specific events that are recorded in the New Testament:

Work of John the Baptist (name not specified):
a. A prophet to prepare the way for Christ. (1 Nephi 10:7; 11:27)
b. To baptize Christ with water. (1 Nephi 10:9–10; 11:27; 2 Nephi 31:4–8)
c. To bear witness of Christ. (1 Nephi 10:10)
d. Not worthy to unloose Christ's shoe latchet. (1 Nephi 10:8)
e. The place of baptism. (1 Nephi 10:9; compare John 1:28)

Jesus Christ (named beforehand by prophecy—2 Nephi 10:3; Mosiah 3:8):
a. Jesus, God of the Old Testament. (3 Nephi 15:4–5; 1 Nephi 19:7–10; Mosiah 3:5–11; 7:27)
b. Baptized. (1 Nephi 10:9–10; 11:27; 2 Nephi 31:4–8)
c. Received the Holy Ghost (sign of the dove). (1 Nephi 11:27; 2 Nephi 31:8)
d. Rejected by the people. (1 Nephi 11:28–32; Mosiah 3:9)
e. Sweat blood. (Mosiah 3:7)
f. Crucified. (1 Nephi 10:11, 11:33; 2 Nephi 10:3; Mosiah 3:9)
g. Buried, rose the third day. (2 Nephi 25:13; Mosiah 3:10)
h. The first to rise in the resurrection. (2 Nephi 2:8)
i. Chose twelve Apostles from among the Jews. (1 Nephi 11:29–36; 12:9; 13:24, 26, 39–41; Mormon 3:18–19)
j. Performed many miracles (in Palestine). (1 Nephi 11:31; Mosiah 3:5; 3 Nephi 17:7–8)
k. His Apostles also performed miracles (in Palestine). (Mormon 9:18)
l. Fulfilled the law of Moses. (3 Nephi 15:5–8)
m. Ended the law of circumcision. (Moroni 8:8)
n. Ascended to heaven (from Palestine). (3 Nephi 11:12)
o. There is no other name in which to trust for salvation besides the name of Christ. (2 Nephi 31:21; Mosiah 3:17, 5:8)

Mary, mother of Jesus (named beforehand by prophecy—Mosiah 3:8; Alma 7:10):
   a. A virgin. (1 Nephi 11:13–20; Alma 7:10)
   b. To live at Nazareth. (1 Nephi 11:13)
   c. Mother of the Son of God. (1 Nephi 11:18)

Other items:
   a. One of the Twelve to be named John. (1 Nephi 14:27)
   b. John to have writings in the book of the Jews (1 Nephi 14:23)
   c. John not to taste of death. (3 Nephi 28:6–7; compare John 21:21–23)
   d. Record of the Jews to consist of the writings of the prophets and also the records of the Twelve Apostles (Old and New Testaments). (1 Nephi 13:38–41)
   e. Jerusalem to be destroyed after Christ's ministry. (2 Nephi 25:14; 6:9–10)
   f. The Twelve Apostles to judge Israel. (1 Nephi 12:9; Mormon 3:18–19; compare Matthew 19:28)

The *Doctrine and Covenants* also gives much information about the New Testament, particularly confirming its authenticity. References include the following:

Persons:
   a. John the Baptist. (27:7; 84:27–28; 133:55)
   b. Zacharias, father of John the Baptist. (27:7)
   c. Peter, James, John. (27:12)
   d. Paul, an Apostle. (18:9)
   e. Nathanael, a man without guile. (41:11; compare John 1:47)

Events:
   a. Mount of Transfiguration. (63:21; compare Matthew 17)
   b. Washing of feet. (88:140–41; compare John 13)
   c. Holy Ghost (in the sign of a dove) descending upon Jesus. (93:15; compare John 1:32)
   d. Parable of the ten virgins. (45:56; compare Matthew 25)
   e. Parable of the wheat and tares. (86:1; compare Matthew 13)

    f. The Mount of Olives. (133:20)
    g. Crucifixion of Jesus. (20:23)
    h. Resurrection of Jesus. (20:23)
    i. A white stone. (130:10–11; compare Revelation 2:17)
    j. A sea of glass. (130:6–7; 77:1; compare Revelation 4:6)

In addition to the numerous references from the Book of Mormon and the Doctrine and Covenants, many references could be cited from the Pearl of Great Price that sustain and support the general thesis of the New Testament.

CHAPTER 7

Using Latter-day Revelation to Understand the New Testament

We value the spirit and the content of the New Testament because we can feel its truth as it bears witness of the Lord Jesus Christ. However, we have been amply warned in both the Book of Mormon and the eighth Article of Faith that many plain and precious truths and many covenants of the Lord have been taken out of our current versions of the Bible. But despite these deletions the Book of Mormon assures us that the Lord will not leave the world to grope in the darkness and stumble because of any inadequacies in the biblical record (1 Nephi 13:32–34). The promise was that the Lord would bring forth other books that would testify to the truth of the Bible and would also "make known the plain and precious things that have been taken away" from it (1 Nephi 13:39–40). These "other books" surely must include the Book of Mormon, the Doctrine and Covenants, the Pearl of Great Price, and the Joseph Smith Translation of the Bible. As was noted earlier, in many instances the Bible tells us some parts of *what* happened, but often it is only from latter-day revelation that we find *why* it happened.

Since there is only one Redeemer of mankind, and since the plan of redemption was presented in the Grand Council before the world was created and there is only one way for man to be saved, we can be assured that the Lord has not had multiple plans and systems in operation among mankind. His plan is one. Variations from that plan are man's doing, not the Lord's. Hence we feel a sense of security in knowing that the pattern established in other scriptures such as the Book of Mormon and the Doctrine and Covenants can and does contribute to an understanding of the New Testament, and can help bridge the gaps occasioned by a loss of biblical information. Following are a few items in which latter-day revelation helps to stabilize our thinking on otherwise unsettled New Testament ground.

Church Organization

It is certain that the Church in the New Testament was not fully organized at first. Probably there were no bishops, deacons, and so forth during the three years of Jesus' ministry. The more complex organization may have taken place during the forty days of Jesus' ministry with the Twelve after his resurrection (see Acts 1:3). This seems likely, because of the experience in our own dispensation, in which it was five years from the time the Church was formally established on 6 April 1830 until a complex organization was in place in 1835. During those first years the various offices (bishops, First Presidency, and so forth) were added one at a time as the need arose.

Written Records

The Lord has always commanded his servants to keep records. This is true of Adam, Enoch, Abraham, Moses, Nephi, the Nephite Twelve, and the Lost Tribes as well as with the Prophet Joseph Smith. We can see no reason why it would have been any different with the New Testament Church. While the present New Testament gives very little clue to such things, given the pattern disclosed by records of other dispensations mostly revealed in the latter days we would suppose the establishment of basic records for the New Testament Church from the very start, including an official central history of the Church that contained sermons by the Lord, instructions, revelations, minutes of meetings, and such things. Such a record could have formed the core of the books of Matthew, Mark, Luke, and John, and also the later preaching of the Apostles. We are specifically told in the Book of Mormon that John the Beloved was a writer, and that some of his writings would be in the record of the Jews—the Bible (1 Nephi 14:14–28). Furthermore, the angel told Nephi that the book of the Jews contained "the records of the twelve apostles of the Lamb" (1 Nephi 13:41). This is a strong suggestion that these Apostles were writers, and that their writings, although depleted somewhat, are in the New Testament.

For whatever it is worth, two of the books of the New Testament most questioned as to authorship today by textual scholars are the book of John and the book of Revelation. However, in latter-day revelation there is strong support for John's authorship of these two works (D&C 88:3 and 88:139–41 for the book of John, and 1 Nephi 14:14–28 and D&C 77 for the book of Revelation).

John the Beloved—Clarification of Status

Most textbooks on the New Testament that were authored by non-LDS writers speak of the death of John the Apostle in Ephesus around A.D. 110. There is an old tradition to that effect. Doctrine and Covenants 7 and 3 Nephi 28 leave no doubt that the tradition is false, and that John is still alive, in keeping with the Lord's promise in John 21:20–25.

The Mount of Transfiguration

The experience on the Mount of Transfiguration is spoken of in Matthew 17, Mark 9, and Luke 9, but in none of these, either separately or combined, is the whole story told, nor do any of them tell the main point of what happened on the Mount.

They tell us where, who, and approximately when, but not *why*. To understand the significance of this event we must know what the purpose was. From the Prophet Joseph Smith we learn that the keys of the priesthood were there given to Peter, James, and John (TPJS, 158). From Doctrine and Covenants 63:20–21 we learn that these three also saw a vision of the earth as it will appear when it is glorified. The similarity of the experience on the Mount of Transfiguration with that of Joseph Smith and Oliver Cowdery in the Kirtland Temple suggests a set way for keys and authority to be passed on from past dispensations to the current one. It also shows that the priesthood of the New Testament era is the same as Moses and Elijah had, and as we have now. This is a unifying concept.

Parables

The parable of the ten virgins is explained in Doctrine and Covenants 45:56–58 and 63:53–54. That of the wheat and the tares is explained in Doctrine and Covenants 86, with an interesting reversal in the order of the gathering. Both of these parables are shown to have reference to the last days.

The Holy Ghost Before the Day of Pentecost

Because of the statement that the Holy Ghost "was not yet given because Jesus was not yet glorified" (John 7:37–39), many have thought that the Holy Ghost was not enjoyed in any degree by anyone before the day of Pentecost spoken of in Acts chapter 2. There is sufficient in the Bible to determine this is not so, but it is made far more clear in latter-day revelation, which shows that the ancient Saints and prophets had both the power and the gift of the Holy Ghost from the days of Adam (Moses 6:64–66; 1 Nephi 10:17–19; D&C 20:26–27). The meaning of John 7:37–39 is that the *gift* of the Holy Ghost had not been received in that local area of the country in that dispensation among the Jews, where Jesus was in person. But they did enjoy the *power* of the Holy Ghost, which gave them testimonies. The Nephites at this same time had both the power and the gift.

The foregoing are a few of the many clarifications that latter-day revelation offers to readers of the New Testament. Others will be encountered in the subsequent pages of this book.

PART III

John the Baptist: A Burning and a Shining Light

"Among those that are born of women, there is not a greater prophet than John the Baptist." (Luke 7:28). "John . . . bare witness unto the truth. . . . He was a burning and a shining light: and ye were willing for a season to rejoice in his light" (John 5:33, 35). With many such words the Lord Jesus praised the work of his friend John the Baptist.

Part III is a discussion of the things that made John great. His privileges exceeded those of any other prophet. His was the one-time-only honor of preparing the way before the ministry of the Lord himself; of baptizing the Son of God; of announcing to the Jewish nation that their Messiah was at that very moment among them; and of identifying the Lord in person to the people. He was also the teacher and tutor of several future Apostles.

John was born to trouble. As a child of promise his life was almost immediately threatened by the head of state. He grew to maturity in the harshness of a semi-tropical desert. His public ministry occupied less than a year, and was followed by months of imprisonment and torture in the dreariness of a dungeon cell. His violent death in his early thirties was due to a weak and lustful king's being manipulated by an infuriated, scheming queen and a charming dancing girl.

John filled every responsibility of his mission. He alerted and aroused a nation to an awareness of their Messiah, and introduced the New Testament dispensation. His short life bridged two dispensations: he was at once the embodiment and great representative of the law of Moses and the first prophet of the dispensation of the meridian of time.

Perhaps John's outstanding service is scantily appreciated because his life is overshadowed by the presence of the Son of God. Such obscurity was perfectly acceptable to John, who also said as much. However, here we will attempt to illustrate the elements of John's true magnificence.

CHAPTER 8

John: Forerunner and Herald of the Messiah

J ohn the Baptist is one of the great figures in sacred literature. Though his brief mortal ministry was limited in time and travel to a small portion of the Holy Land during the New Testament period, he is widely acclaimed in scripture and spoken of in all four standard works. He was in effect the last prophet of the Old Testament and the first of the New, and a necessary participant in the dispensation of the fulness of times.

A Child of Promise

Most of us know two things about John: He baptized Jesus Christ in the Jordan River, and he ordained Joseph Smith and Oliver Cowdery to the Aaronic Priesthood near Harmony, Pennsylvania on the banks of the Susquehanna River. Although in our eyes these may be the two most significant things he did, there is a great deal more that is interesting and even thrilling concerning his life, character, and ministry. His mission was important enough that it was made known to prophets and seers hundreds of years beforehand. His forthcoming birth was announced by the angel Gabriel and attended by miraculous circumstances showing him to be an unusual child of promise. During his life he was emphatically and singularly eulogized by the Lord Jesus Christ himself.

The work of John is spoken of by Isaiah (40:3–5; compare Matthew 3:1–3) and Malachi (3:1; compare Luke 7:27), and Lehi (1 Nephi 10:7–10) and Nephi (1 Nephi 11:27; 2 Nephi 31:4, 8). Although these prophecies do not mention him by name, there can be no mistaking that John's mission is the topic. He is acknowledged in all four New Testament testimonies as having baptized multitudes before he baptized Jesus, and he is praised by the Savior for the diligence of his ministry and the importance of his work. Jesus described him as a "burning and a shining light" (John 5:35); an unexcelled prophet (Matthew 11:7–15); and an example of righteousness whose testimony would condemn in the day of judgment all who refused to obey what he taught (JST Matthew 21:32–34; JST John 5:34–36).

In praise of John the Baptist the Prophet Joseph Smith said: "he had his authority from God, and the oracles of God were with him, and the kingdom of God for a season seemed to rest with John alone. . . . John was a priest after his father, and held the keys of the Aaronic Priesthood, and . . . was a legal administrator; . . . for no man could have better authority to administer than John; and our Savior submitted to that authority Himself, by being baptized by John" (TPJS, 272–73).

After he baptized Jesus, John saw the Holy Ghost descend as a sign that Jesus was the Messiah (John 1:32–34). He also heard the voice of the Father proclaim Jesus as his beloved Son in whom he was well pleased (JST Matthew 3:45–46; D&C 93:15–16). This personal experience with all three members of the Godhead made John one of the most able of witnesses.

Extensive Knowledge of the Gospel

Latter-day revelation projects a much broader and deeper appreciation for John's preaching than we are able to obtain from the KJV alone. We learn that John's knowledge of the gospel was far more extensive than is usually accredited him.

The JST takes special note of this and states that John "came into the world for a witness . . . to bear record of the gospel through the Son, unto all" (JST John 1:7). He taught personal righteousness, emphasizing repentance, confession, baptism, prayer, fasting, and receiving the Holy Ghost. He discussed brotherly kindness, generosity, honesty, moral virtue, and justice. John likewise spoke of the gathering of Israel, the conversion and adoption of the Gentiles into Israel, the second coming of the Messiah, the resurrection of the dead, the keys of the kingdom, the fulness of time, and the day of judgment. From the following JST passage we learn something of the extent of John's knowledge and understanding:

> And he came into all the country about Jordan, preaching the baptism of repentance for the remission of sins.
>
> As it is written in the book of the prophet Esaias; and these are the words, saying, The voice of one crying in the wilderness, Prepare ye the way of the Lord, and make his paths straight.
>
> For behold, and lo, he shall come, as it is written in the book of the prophets, to take away the sins of the world, and to bring salvation unto the heathen nations, to gather together those who are lost, who are of the sheepfold of Israel;
>
> Yea, even the dispersed and afflicted; and also to prepare the way, and make possible the preaching of the gospel unto the Gentiles;
>
> And to be a light unto all who sit in darkness, unto the uttermost parts of the earth; to bring to pass the resurrection from the dead, and to ascend up on high, to dwell on the right hand of the Father.
>
> Until the fulness of time, and the law and the testimony shall be sealed, and the keys of the kingdom shall be delivered up again unto the Father;
>
> To administer justice unto all; to come down in judgment upon all, and to convince all the ungodly of their ungodly deeds, which they have committed; and all this in the day that he shall come;
>
> For it is a day of power; yea, every valley shall be filled, and every mountain and hill shall be brought low; the crooked shall be made straight, and the rough ways made smooth;
>
> And all flesh shall see the salvation of God. (JST Luke 3:3–11.)

Not only does the above passage attest to John's wide knowledge of the gospel but also it clearly shows that John understood the difference between certain events that would occur in the meridian of time and those of the fulness of time. The day of judgment, the day of power, bringing low the mountains and the valleys being filled, was to occur at the time of Jesus' second coming. The way these verses are presented in all other Bibles makes it appear that John thought those events were for his time. The JST clarifies this matter and at the same time gives a glimpse of John's extensive knowledge.

Significance of John's Mission

John singlehandedly challenged the network of priestcraft and apostasy that existed among the Jewish hierarchy and was given the divine appointment "to overthrow the kingdom of the Jews and to make straight the way of the Lord before the face of his people, to prepare them for the coming of the Lord" (D&C 84:28). John was an Elias, which means he was the forerunner, a preparer of people, and the proclaimer of the Messiah.

Being the forerunner was neither a simple task nor an honorary title. Difficult and dangerous work needed to be done. We learn from the Book of Mormon that priestcrafts and iniquities at Jerusalem in the time of the Savior made that generation the worst in the world (2 Nephi 10:3–5). Into this maelstrom John, a mere mortal—armed with the Aaronic Priesthood, a divine commission, personal righteousness, the truth of God, and a huge amount of courage—was launched on his ministry to prepare the way for the Son of God. What John was called to do placed his life in jeopardy.

The term *forerunner* is descriptive. Forerunners anciently would run before the chariot of the king and clear the path of rocks or other obstacles, and loudly proclaim the coming of the ruler. This practice is referred to in 1 Samuel 8:11, 1 Kings 1:5, and Isaiah 62:10. Both Saul and Rehoboam kept "runners" for this purpose.

John was both a forerunner and a proclaimer of Jesus. He was the divinely appointed herald. These two roles are reflected in the scriptures. The records of Matthew, Mark, and Luke tell of John's vigorous preaching to "prepare the way" for the Lord, whereas John's record emphasizes that John the Baptist came to "bear witness" (John 1:6–7) and to identify the Messiah in person among the people. These different points of emphasis are complementary to one another. The difference between them is that Matthew, Mark, and Luke deal with the preaching of John *before* he baptized Jesus, hence the emphasis that the Messiah *will* come (Matthew 3, Mark 1, Luke 3), whereas John the Apostle's Testimony deals with the preaching of John *after* he baptized Jesus, hence his emphasis that the Messiah has come (John 1). Jesus' forty-day experience in the wilderness took place between these two phases of John's testimony of Christ.

Multitudes recognized the magnificence of John. He was so successful that there "went out to him Jerusalem, and all Judea, and all the region round about Jordan, and were baptized of him in Jordan, confessing their sins" (Matthew 3:5–6). Many sought his counsel, among whom were the publicans and the soldiers. We read the following: "Then came also publicans to be baptized, and said unto him, Master, what shall we do? And he said unto them, Exact no more than that which is appointed you. And the soldiers likewise demanded of him, saying, And what shall we do? And he said unto them, Do violence to no man, neither accuse any falsely; and be content with your wages." (Luke 3:12–14.)

An understanding of the way that taxes were collected in those days makes the foregoing passage more meaningful. The publicans were not popular as tax collectors because they were Jewish persons collecting taxes for the Roman government. Jews were naturally reluctant to pay taxes to the enemy, and to have a Jewish collector at one's door made it worse. But what was still worse was that the tax collector was given a quota from each area, and anything he could collect above that amount was his to keep. This was an incentive to collect all that was possible. For that reason the collector—that is, the publican—would have a Roman soldier accompany him, so as to lend authority to his request. The soldier also received a cut of the surplus tax. Citizens were less likely to refuse to pay when an armed soldier stood in the doorway. Hence John said to the publicans "exact no more than is appointed you"; and to the soldiers he said, "Be content with your wages."

Popularity of John

John the Baptist was an excellent preacher and soon became very popular. Not only did he have a wide range of doctrinal and scriptural knowledge but also he preached by the power of the Holy Ghost. He had a timely message to give. For the first time in four hundred years there was a prophet in the Holy Land. Within six months or so from the beginning of his ministry he had roused and alerted the Jewish nation, and raised their anticipation that a Messiah was soon to come among them. He was so successful that the people thought that he was the Messiah. "And . . . the people were in expectation, and all men mused in their hearts of John, whether he were the Christ, or not" (Luke 3:15). When they began to think that, John was very careful and quick to inform them that he was not the Messiah, but was his forerunner (Luke 3:16; John 1:25–28).

John met all the requirements of a forerunner and a herald. He preached repentance, spoke against the evils and wrongdoing of the people (including the adulterous and incestuous marriage of Herod Antipas and Herodias), proclaimed the imminent arrival of the Messiah, and identified him personally and publicly when he arrived. John fulfilled his ministry with dignity and thoroughness, and while not everyone obeyed him, those who heard him knew that he was a preacher of righteousness and a proclaimer of the Messiah. After his death people were heard to say: "John did no miracle; but all things that John spake of this man [Jesus] were true" (John 10:41).

Likewise, Jesus left no doubt in people's minds of his great admiration and love for John. While John was confined in Herod's dungeon, Jesus sent angels to minister to him (JST Matthew 4:11). When two of John's disciples travelled the long distance from the prison to see Jesus in Galilee, the Lord received them graciously and bade them return to John with a reassuring message. The reassurance was more for the disciples than for John, for he already knew exactly who Jesus was, having had unmistakable witness at the baptism. After the two disciples of John had departed out of Galilee, Jesus spoke to the multitude concerning John's unshakable character and unique status:

> What went ye out into the wilderness for to see? A reed shaken with the wind?
>
> But what went ye out for to see? A man clothed in soft raiment? Behold, they which are gorgeously apparelled, and live delicately, are in kings' courts.
>
> But what went ye out for to see? A prophet? Yea, I say unto you, and much more than a prophet.
>
> This is he, of whom it is written, Behold, I send my messenger before thy face, which shall prepare thy way before thee.
>
> For I say unto you, Among those that are born of women there is not a greater prophet than John the Baptist. (Luke 7: 24–28.)

Many Bible commentators have thought that John himself was wavering while in prison, wondering and even doubting whether Jesus was the Messiah, and therefore had sent these two disciples to enquire. That is not likely, however, since John knew by revelation who Jesus was. Furthermore, Jesus' own words, just cited, declare that John was not a "reed shaken with the wind," which he would not have said if John had been wavering.

The Prophet Joseph Smith explained John's greatness:

> How is it that John was considered one of the greatest prophets? His miracles could not have constituted his greatness.
>
> First. He was entrusted with a divine mission of preparing the way before the face of the Lord. Whoever had such a trust committed to him before or since? No man.
>
> Secondly. He was entrusted with the important mission, and it was required at his hands, to baptize the Son of Man. Whoever had the honor of doing that? Whoever had so great a privilege and glory? Whoever led the Son of God into the waters of baptism, and had the privilege of beholding the Holy Ghost descend in the form of a dove, or rather in the *sign* of the dove, in witness of that administration? . . .
>
> Thirdly. John, at that time, was the only legal administrator in the affairs of the kingdom there was then on the earth, and

holding the keys of power. The Jews had to obey his instructions or be damned, by their own law; and Christ Himself fulfilled all righteousness in becoming obedient to the law which he had given to Moses on the mount, and thereby magnified it and made it honorable, instead of destroying it. . . . These three reasons constitute him the greatest prophet born of a woman. (TPJS, 275–76.)

A Tutor of Future Apostles

John's responsibility to prepare the way before Christ went beyond teaching the multitudes. He soon attracted those individuals who would later become the Apostles and special witnesses of the Lord. Andrew was a disciple of John and brought his brother Peter to meet Jesus, because of John's teaching (John 1:40–42). It appears that John the Beloved was also a disciple of John the Baptist, for most likely he was the "other disciple" mentioned in company with Andrew (John 1:35–40). Peter's instructions to the Church (after the resurrection and ascension of Jesus) concerning the selection of a new member of the Twelve in place of Judas, suggests that many if not all of the Twelve had been tutored by John before becoming disciples of Jesus: "Wherefore of these men which have companied with us all the time that the Lord Jesus went in and out among us, beginning from the baptism of John, unto that same day that he was taken up from us, must one be ordained to be a witness with us of his resurrection" (Acts 1:21–22). These future members of the Twelve received their first earthly lessons in the gospel from the faithful, capable, knowledgeable, and trusted servant, the legal administrator of the kingdom, John the Baptist.

John's Three-Fold Mission

Having first prepared the way and aroused a nation, and second, having publicly identified the Messiah among the people, John then began the third phase of his ministry: to persuade his converts to leave him and follow Jesus. John's humility and his loyalty to Jesus were dramatically illustrated when some of his disciples brought him the news that Jesus was even more popular than he (John) had been, and that many of his converts were now following Jesus (John 3:25–26). John's response was clear and to the point: "Ye yourselves bear me witness, that I said, I am not the Christ, but that I am sent before him. He that hath the bride is the bridegroom: but the friend of the bridegroom, which standeth and heareth him, rejoiceth greatly because of the bridegroom's voice: this my joy therefore is fulfilled. He must increase, but I must decrease. (John 3: 28–30.)

It is to be understood that there was not a competitive attitude or rivalry between John and Jesus. Leaving John and following Jesus did not require any change in doctrine or belief. John taught the true gospel. His converts were actually disciples of Jesus Christ.

John had now completed the fundamental tasks of his earthly appointment. His public ministry would diminish, while Jesus' would rise and enlarge. John would soon be cast into prison, be executed, go into the world of spirits, be resurrected, and await the fulness of times, when he would participate in the restoration of the gospel again upon the earth.

Why John Was of the Lineage of Aaron

The Prophet Joseph Smith explained: "The Spirit of Elias was a going before to prepare the way for the greater, which was the case with John the Baptist. . . . The spirit of Elias is to prepare the way for a greater revelation of God, which is the Priesthood of Elias, or the Priesthood that Aaron was ordained unto. And when God sends a man into the world to prepare for a greater work, holding the keys of the power of Elias, it was called the doctrine of Elias, even from the early ages of the world" (TPJS, 335–36).

In order for John to fulfill his divinely designated role as the Elias, forerunner and witness of the Messiah, some careful selections had to be made. First, to hold the keys of the Aaronic Priesthood he had to be of the firstborn lineage among the sons of Aaron (D&C 68:16–18). Second, to be the one designated to use that priesthood to prepare the way for and baptize the

Messiah requires a pre-earth appointment, as the Prophet Joseph Smith said: "Every man who has a calling to minister to the inhabitants of the world was ordained to that very purpose in the Grand Council of heaven before this world was" (TPJS, 365). Third, John's mission was to be the living embodiment of the law of Moses—which was the "preparatory gospel" functioning under the Aaronic Priesthood (see D&C 84:26–27). John was to do as a man, literally, what the law of Moses was to do as a statute, and that was to prepare the way for the presence of the Lord by teaching the first principles of the gospel and performing baptisms as called for in the law of Moses. John was the world's finest example of the powers and purposes of the priesthood of Aaron and the law of Moses. It was absolutely essential that John come to earth through the lineage of Aaron.

Selection of the mortal lineage through which John's foreordained spirit would come to earth was governed by ancient law and procedure, in order for him to be legally entitled to the priesthood of Aaron. The rule given by the Lord to Moses read: "And thou shalt anoint Aaron and his sons, and consecrate them, that they may minister unto me in the priest's office" (Exodus 30:30). And concerning the sons of Aaron: "And thou shalt anoint them, as thou didst anoint their father [Aaron], that they may minister unto me in the priest's office: for their anointing shall surely be an everlasting priesthood throughout their generations" (Exodus 40:15).

Commenting on this procedure, the Prophet Joseph Smith explained: "Here is a little of law which must be fulfilled. The Levitical Priesthood is forever hereditary—fixed on the head of Aaron and his sons forever, and was in active operation down to Zacharias the father of John" (TPJS, 319).

Provisions of the law of Moses, especially with regard to the qualifications of the priests and their functions in the offering of various animal sacrifices, were designed by revelation to prefigure and typify the Messiah and to bear witness of him. Heavy penalties were affixed if sacred rites and duties were performed without the proper authority (Numbers 16:1–40; 1 Chronicles 13:7–10; 2 Chronicles 26:16–21). It was therefore essential, when the Messiah was about to come to earth in person as the Lamb of God, that John, the forerunner, the herald and witness of the Lamb, must be of the proper lineage to qualify him for the mission. Since it was necessary for a priest to be of the lineage of Aaron in order to labor with the sacrificial symbols, which were only prefigures of the Messiah, how much greater the necessity that John, the forerunner of the Messiah in person, be of the proper priestly lineage and authority!

The Lord therefore chose Zacharias, a priest of the family of Aaron, and Elisabeth, his wife, one of the "daughters of Aaron" (Luke 1:5), to be the mortal parents who would provide the right lineage to complete the inheritance—to bring about the proper combination of body and spirit. As the son of Zacharias and Elisabeth, John was fitted and qualified by earthly lineage to be the forerunner, proclaimer, and baptizer of the Messiah. He was also qualified by preappointment and foreordination. When John was eight days old at the time of his circumcision and naming, Zacharias was inspired by the Holy Ghost to pronounce a father's blessing upon him and outline his great work (Luke 1:68–79). This blessing is today popularly called the Benedictus, and a part of it reads as follows:

> And thou, child, shalt be called the prophet of the Highest: for thou shalt go before the face of the Lord to prepare his ways;
> To give knowledge of salvation unto his people by the remission of their sins,
> Through the tender mercy of our God; whereby the dayspring from on high hath visited us,
> To give light to them that sit in darkness and in the shadow of death, to guide our feet into the way of peace (Luke 1:76–79).

When Zacharias was visited by the angel Gabriel nearly a year before, he had been struck dumb, and maybe also deaf (Luke 1:62–63). All the people in the temple and all of Zacharias's family and friends knew he had seen an angel, and they knew he had become dumb, and now they knew he could speak. John was a child of promise, and his entry into this world was accompanied by signs and wonders. The people said in their hearts, "What manner of child shall this be!" (Luke 1:66).

John was the right person to be the final representative of the law of Moses in its capacity as a schoolmaster to bring men to Christ. He bridged two dispensations by being the last legal representative of the law of Moses and at the same time being the preappointed one to specifically introduce and prepare the way for the coming of the Lord.

It was further specified in the law of Moses that a Levite or priest should begin his priestly ministry at age thirty (Numbers 4:3; 1 Chronicles 23:3). Therefore, when John was about that age the word of God came to him in the wilderness and authorized him to begin his work (Luke 3:1–3; John 1:29–34). Through the years the Holy Ghost had been preparing John's mind for his ministry. He had the Holy Ghost from the time of his mother's womb (D&C 84:27; Luke 1:15), and no one can receive the Holy Ghost without receiving revelation (TPJS, 328). John was "baptized while yet in his childhood," and received a setting apart to his mission from an angel when only eight days old (D&C 84:28). He later would receive the full powers of the Aaronic Priesthood, which includes the keys of the ministering of angels (D&C 13). Having such keys, it follows that John would receive the visitation of angels during these preparatory years. Elder James E. Talmage wrote: "He had been a student under the tutelage of divine teachers; and there in the wilderness of Judea the word of the Lord reached him; as in similar environment it had reached Moses and Elijah of old (*Jesus the Christ* [Salt Lake City: Deseret Book Co., 1948], p. 122).

The training of this great herald and forerunner of the Messiah required the finest and most effective spiritual education possible and included study of the scriptures, lessons in Israel's history, the workings and revelations of the Holy Ghost, and the ministry of angels. When John came forth preaching at the age of thirty, he was ready. He knew what his mission was and what he must do, and he had the authority to go about it.

The Closing Events of John's Public Ministry

John preached and baptized for about six months before he baptized Jesus. He then continued about six to nine months afterward until he was imprisoned by Herod Antipas. During the imprisonment John was probably tortured, scourged (Matthew

17:12–13), and bound with chains, for such was the ancient custom. After nine to twelve months in the dungeon, John was beheaded at the order of Herod, who in his lust for Salome, a dancing girl, had fallen prey to a murderous scheme of Herodias to destroy John (Mark 6:17–29).

The scriptural record does not mention Salome by name, nor does it say where the prison was located, but Josephus the Jewish historian identifies her and places the prison in Herod's castle at Machaerus near the northeastern border of the Dead Sea (Antiquities XVIII, v, 1–2, 4).

The story of John, Herod, Herodias, and Salome, and the events that eventually culminated in John's execution, is so important it needs to be recited here.

In the summer months following the baptism of Jesus, John was baptizing at Aenon, near Salim, "because there was much water there" (John 3:23). Many people came and were baptized. It was apparently also at Aenon that John gave his last recorded testimony of Christ and urged his disciples to follow Jesus in preference to himself (John 3:25–31). But even though John always faithfully bore witness that Jesus was the Messiah and testified that he himself was much inferior to Jesus, some of John's disciples showed a reluctance to leave him. It is not known with certainty today just where "Aenon near to Salim" was. Several locations have been proposed by scholars. While it probably does not matter much to us today where the ancient site was, it might have meant something very particular to John, since he may have gone there not only because of its much water but because he needed a place to go outside of the domain of Herod. Subsequent events show that John had incurred the envy of the Pharisees and also of Herod, and it is reasonable to conclude that he sought a place of refuge where he would be out of Herod's reach and yet where he could continue his preaching and baptizing. Since Herod's political domain at this time consisted of Galilee and Perea, John would be relatively safe in the wilderness areas of either Judea, Decapolis, or Samaria.

Nothing is recorded from May to December regarding either John or Jesus beyond the mention that Jesus was baptizing in Judea with his disciples and that John was baptizing at Aenon near Salim, for he had not yet been cast into prison (John

3:22–24). It was, however, a time of turmoil and trouble for both John and Jesus, and the hatred of the Jewish rulers was particularly intense. The JST gives emphasis to the envy of the Jews:

> When therefore the Pharisees had heard that Jesus made and baptized more disciples than John,
> They sought more diligently some means that they might put him to death; for many received John as a prophet, but they believed not on Jesus (JST John 4:1–2).

This proved to be John's last summer of freedom. He had begun his preaching and baptizing about a year or so earlier in Judea near the region of the Jordan River, and had baptized Jesus after perhaps about six to nine months of his ministry. Sometime during the late summer or autumn he fell into disfavor with the Judean ruling family. He particularly offended Herodias, the wife of Herod Antipas, by his insistence that it was not right for Herod to have her, since she was legally the wife of Herod's half-brother, Philip. This angered Herodias to the point that she would have killed John if she could, but because John was a prophet Herod looked upon him with awe and for a time protected him (Mark 6:17–20.)

Herod's marital situation, to which John objected, was somewhat complex. Herod was originally married to the daughter of Aretas, the king of Arabia, but on a visit to Rome he stayed with his half-brother Philip and had an interest in Philip's wife, Herodias. This was an opportunity for Herodias. Her husband, Philip, had no title and ruled no province. In her estimation he was a "nobody" and, while married to him, she was simply a housewife. As Herod's wife she would be a queen. So she agreed to marry Herod on condition that he divorce his first wife. With her daughter Salome, Herodias left Philip and their residence in Rome and became the wife of Herod Antipas the King, ruler of Galilee and Perea.

To further complicate the relationship, Herodias was not only Herod's sister-in-law, but also his niece, being the daughter of Aristobulus, Herod's half-brother. She was married, therefore, first to one uncle and now to another uncle. Such close-relation marriage was forbidden in the law of Moses.

Meanwhile, as this situation was developing, Herod's first wife became aware of it and fled to her father, King Aretas, in Arabia, whereupon, for this and other reasons, Aretas in due time raised an army and five years later made war upon Herod and defeated him.

John's Arrest

Of the arrest of John the scriptures simply state that "Herod had laid hold on John, and bound him, and put him in prison" (Matthew 14:3; also Mark 6:17; Luke 3:19–20).

There are some interesting circumstances associated with both the reasons for and the mechanics of John's arrest. Somewhat conflicting reports are given as to the cause of John's imprisonment. According to Mark, John was imprisoned because he had infuriated Herod and Herodias by questioning the validity of their marriage (Mark 6:17–19). However, Josephus says that John was imprisoned because he was becoming so popular and commanded such a following that Herod feared his political power. Although Josephus confirms the matter of Herod's unlawful marriage, he does not associate it as a factor in John's imprisonment (Antiquities XVIII, v, 1–2).

Whatever the reasons, the sources agree that John was imprisoned at the command of Herod. It may be that both causes were contributory: the political factor may have been the initial cause of his imprisonment, so far as Herod was personally concerned. Pretending to be primarily concerned about the domestic issue may have been Herod's way of placating the insistent Herodias.

The Pharisees may have collaborated with Herod in the capture and arrest of John. First, the Pharisees were antagonistic to John (Luke 7:20–30) and openly denied the legitimacy of his baptism. Second, the KJV says that John was "cast" into prison (Matthew 4:12), but the meaning of the Greek word in this instance is more than "cast": It carries the sense of being "delivered up" and it so appears in the texts of the American Standard Version, the Confraternity (Catholic) Bible, and the Syrian manuscripts translated by Lamsa. Each of these contains the statement that John was "delivered up" into prison. Third, when John was "delivered up and imprisoned" Jesus immediately left the area, and went to Galilee, possibly for the safety of himself and his disciples (Matthew 4:12).

That it was really the Pharisees, and not Herod only, who were the "enemy" is seen by the fact that Jesus went into Galilee, which was still under Herod's jurisdiction. If Herod had been the real enemy, Jesus would still have been in danger in Galilee. But while Galilee was still Herod's domain, it was somewhat out of reach of the Judean Pharisees who were repeatedly laying snares to catch John and/or Jesus. Possibly John had become a victim of the devices of the Pharisees and somehow had been lured by them into Herod's area and delivered into Herod's custody; then perhaps Jesus, knowing what had happened, left Judea and went into Galilee, where the situation was less tense. This idea is strengthened by the Lord's observation to Peter, James, and John that the Jews "have done unto him [John] whatsoever they listed" and that "likewise shall also the Son of man suffer of them" (Matthew 17:12–13). Since it is known that the Pharisees were active in the arrest and crucifixion of Jesus, the Savior's statement suggests that they "likewise" were agents in the arrest and imprisonment of John.

This assumption is further supported by a subsequent encounter in Galilee between Jesus and a delegation of the Pharisees. In this instance the Pharisees—who are never identified as friends of Jesus—came to him in Galilee and said, "Get thee out, and depart hence: for Herod will kill thee" (Luke 13:31). Although it is remotely possible that these particular Pharisees were honestly concerned for the welfare of Jesus and that this warning to him was prompted by a genuine interest for his bodily safety, it seems more likely that the Pharisees were only feigning friendship for Jesus and that their real motive was to lure Jesus out of Galilee and back into Judea, where Herod had no jurisdiction but where Jesus would fall into the hands of the Jewish rulers. The Lord's reply to them is instructive. The Pharisees and Herod had little in common, except a dislike for Jesus; yet Jesus' reply indicates that he knew that the Pharisees and Herod were in communication with one another. Said he, "Go ye, and tell that fox . . . I must walk to day, and to morrow, and the day following: for it cannot be that a prophet perish out of Jerusalem" (Luke 13:32–33). Such a reply not only gave notice to the Pharisees that Jesus was not about to buy their supposed act of friendship, but also gave a message to them—and to Herod—that Jesus' death, when it did occur, would not be in Galilee but in Jerusalem, and he did not fear what they could do to him in Galilee. It is likely that these clever Pharisees, who had successfully plotted with Herod in the capture of John, were now attempting the same kind of strategy (in reverse) to capture Jesus.

Another passage that further attests to the collusion between the Pharisees and Herod is found in Mark 3:6, which states that the Pharisees plotted with the Herodians to destroy Jesus. Hate makes strange bedfellows. The Jewish rulers had no love for the Herodians. The Pharisees hated Herod and all who supported him; but they hated Jesus even more, and were willing to unite with their national enemies, the Herodians, to destroy him.

The wisdom of God is always greater than the craftiness of men or the cunning of the devil, and had heaven so desired, the machinations of evil men could never silence a prophet of God. But sometimes the righteous are permitted to be slain after they have completed their missions, that they might be honored and the wicked condemned (compare Alma 14:11–13; D&C 136:39).

John's Imprisonment

Herod's castle at Machaerus near the north-eastern border of the Dead Sea where John was imprisoned was some fifty miles east and a little south of Jerusalem. How long John was imprisoned is not stated, but he was placed in prison sometime near the end of the first year of Jesus' ministry, and probably remained in prison for most of a year.

John was not in solitary confinement, for his disciples had some freedom to come and go, but it must have been extremely difficult for this active man of the desert to be restricted to a dungeon cell. The scripture says that Herod "laid hold on John, and bound him" (Matthew 14:3), which most certainly means he was in chains. And, as we have noted, he was no doubt tortured, since that was a common treatment of prisoners in that day.

JST Matthew 4:11 adds a matter of great interest relative to John's imprisonment, and attests to Jesus' great compassion and high regard for John. "Jesus knew that John was cast into prison, and he sent angels, and . . . they came and ministered unto him." In no other text or source do we find information suggesting that John was visited by angels during his imprisonment, but this thought has a warm and comforting aspect to it.

Sometime during John's ministry he had a personal relationship with King Herod. It is not clear from the scriptures when this was, but it is probable that they met face to face while John was a free man, and that John counseled the king and the king obeyed. This relationship may also have continued even while John was a prisoner in the king's castle at Machaerus. The precise times and circumstances are not known to us, but the scriptures certify that Herod had a certain high regard and awe for John and at times was willing to follow his counsel. This relationship is especially important to us in a discussion of John's martyrdom.

Not long after the death of John, Jesus and his disciples came through Galilee, where Herod Antipas was. Jesus performed many miracles and his fame spread abroad. Interestingly, Herod had never seen Jesus, but when he heard of this person doing these unusual things, he supposed it to be John risen from the dead. Mark's account of this is as follows, which also includes a record of events that had led to John's death (Mark 6:14–19):

> And king Herod heard of him [Jesus]; (for his name was spread abroad:) and he said, That John the Baptist was risen from the dead, and therefore mighty works do shew forth themselves in him.
>
> Others said, That it is Elias. And others said, That it is a prophet, or as one of the prophets.
>
> But when Herod heard thereof, he said, It is John, whom I beheaded: he is risen from the dead.
>
> For Herod himself had sent forth, and laid hold upon John, and bound him in prison for Herodias' sake, his brother Philip's wife: for he had married her.

For John had said unto Herod, It is not lawful for thee to have thy brother's wife.

Therefore Herodias had a quarrel against him, and would have killed him; but she could not:

At this point JST Mark 6:21 speaks of the former relationship between Herod and John: "For Herod feared John, knowing that he was a just man, and a holy man, and one who feared God and observed to worship him; and when he heard him he did many things for him, and heard him gladly."

Just what Herod had done for John we do not know, but it is clear that Herod regarded John as a holy man, and the two of them had had some contact. Perhaps, because of the context in which the subject is presented, Herod had protected John from the Pharisees and the Jewish rulers, and even now had protected him from the angry designs of Herodias. The Catholic Confraternity Bible reads for this verse: "For Herod feared John . . . and protected him." Luther's German text uses the word *verwahrte*, meaning that Herod "preserved" or "protected" John.

One thing more about John and Herod. There were those of Herod's household who were believers. In Matthew 14:1–2 and Luke 9:7, 9, we read that when Herod heard of the fame of Jesus—and supposing him to be John the Baptist risen from the dead—he was perplexed and made inquiry concerning it. He most likely inquired of his servants. Why would Herod inquire of his servants? What were they supposed to know about Jesus or John? Luke (8:3) tells us that one of the followers of Jesus was "Joanna the wife of Chuza Herod's steward." Later, in Acts 13:1, we learn that "there were in the church . . . certain prophets and teachers," among whom was Manaen, who "had been brought up with Herod the tetrarch." Herod must have known of these people in his own household; therefore, when desperate and haunted by the thought that John was risen from the dead, he inquired among those who were close to him and who he thought could give him the information he desired.

We cannot help but wonder if John laid the groundwork for the faith of these two persons of Herod's household. Herod and John must have had several face-to-face contacts, and Herod's servants may have been present on some of these occasions and heard John's testimony. Years later Paul referred to saints in Caesar's palace. It seems probable this was due to Paul's testimony and example while he was a prisoner in Rome. (Philippians 1:12–13; 4:22.) It is possible that John the Baptist was able to have a similar effect in Herod's palace.

Martyrdom

But now to return to the account of John's death. The respect and awe that Herod had for John were soon overruled by his carnal desires. Mark's account continues:

> And when a convenient day was come, that Herod on his birthday made a supper to his lords, high captains, and chief estates of Galilee;
> And when the daughter of the said Herodias came in, and danced, and pleased Herod and them that sat with him, the king said unto the damsel, Ask of me whatsoever thou wilt, and I will give it thee.
> And he sware unto her, Whatsoever thou shalt ask of me, I will give it thee, unto the half of my kingdom.
> And she went forth, and said unto her mother, What shall I ask? And she said, The head of John the Baptist.
> And she came in straightway with haste unto the king, and asked, saying, I will that thou give me by and by in a charger the head of John the Baptist.
> And the king was exceeding sorry; yet for his oath's sake, and for their sakes which sat with him, he would not reject her.
> And immediately the king sent an executioner, and commanded his head to be brought: and he went and beheaded him in the prison,
> And brought his head in a charger, and gave it to the damsel: and the damsel gave it to her mother.
> And when his disciples heard of it, they came and took up his corpse, and laid it in a tomb. (Mark 6:21–29.)

Herod's judgment was servant to his passion. To save face before those who were at the supper, to keep his oath, and maybe even to enjoy a possible new "adventure" with the dancing girl, Herod was maneuvered by his wife into issuing the death sentence for John the Baptist. Whatever kind of a dance it was that Salome performed, it was so well done that it caused the king to recklessly promise her anything she wished, even to "half of [his] kingdom." Some scholars think that the girl probably danced in the nude. This is possible, since she was brought up in pagan Rome, and the game she and her mother were playing was very serious. Herodias masterminded the whole affair, and it is not likely she would overlook any opportunity she thought would be impressive.

It is interesting that Herod, the king, should be outmaneuvered by his wife and by a dancing girl. His appetite and lust for the girl's bodily charms snared him into a compromising situation for which he afterward was very sorry. The whole caper was brought about in the first place because of his libidinous desire for Herodias, whom he had spirited away from Philip, and whom it was not lawful for him to have. It was bodily lust and passion that had caused him to forsake his wife, the daughter of Aretas, for Herodias, and now it was more of the same that made him vulnerable to the scheming of Herodias in her plan to make him destroy the very man he had previously protected. Herodias, above all others, knew what kind of a man Herod was. She knew his weakness for the flesh.

Since Herodias wished to kill John but could not because Herod protected him, she set about to devise a method not only to get John killed, but to get Herod to do it. Herod had shown himself to be a man of much passion, with fleeting moments of good intention but with little self-control and even less manly discipline. Herodias herself had beguiled him in their days at Rome, and now she again played upon his weaknesses. But this time she would use a younger woman: Salome would be the bait.

As noted above, the KJV says that "when a convenient day was come" Herodias planned the attack on John. The new English Bible is more vivid when it states, "Herodias found her opportunity." Thus it is that when Herodias was frustrated in her initial desire to kill John because Herod protected him, she sought for and found an "opportunity" to manipulate Herod into compliance with her wishes. Herodias's unladylike behavior in this event more than justifies all that John the Baptist had said about her.

In Herod, Herodias, and John, we see a trio similar to an earlier one in Israel's history: King Ahab, his wife, Jezebel, and the prophet Elijah. In that earlier day, Jezebel schemed and out-classed her morally weak husband-king and caused the death of some of the Lord's prophets. In Jezebel's day as in Herodias's, the man of God rebuked their wickedness and in turn incurred their burning hatred. What was the final outcome for Herod? As noted before, Herod's army was eventually defeated by the army of Aretas; later Herod fell out of favor with the Emperor Caligula, and in A.D. 39 he was deposed and banished to Gaul.

Although it is Stephen (Acts 7:59) who is generally so desig-nated, in reality John was the first Christian martyr of the meridian of time.

Burial

The time was probably the winter of A.D. 32; the son of Elisabeth and Zacharias, in his thirty-third year, was dead at the hands of Herod Antipas. More than thirty years earlier, Antipas's father, Herod the Great, had caused the death of Zacharias, the father of John. Of John's ministry we know much. Of his family, wife and children, we know nothing. Yet we are confident that he was a family man, for such was of major importance in Israel, and the sons of Aaron have yet an important role in the fulness of time. John deserves a righteous posterity.

John's disciples obtained his body, which they buried in a tomb, and then sought out Jesus in Galilee and told him what had happened (Mark 6:29–30; Matthew 14:12). It is noteworthy that at this dreary hour in their lives John's disciples went to Jesus. This would be exactly what John would want them to do. Perhaps the shock of John's violent death had accomplished what John himself had not been able to do: to persuade them to prefer Jesus to himself. John's witness and testimony was now an even greater reality to them than it had been while he lived. When they came to Jesus he would comfort them and draw them closer to himself.

From Mark's account we learn that the Twelve were on missions at the time of John's death, but returned soon thereafter (Mark 6:7, 12, 30). Matthew tells us that when Jesus in Galilee heard that John was beheaded, he departed "by ship into a desert place apart" with his disciples (Matthew 14:13). Many followed them, and it was at this time that Jesus miraculously fed the five thousand (Matthew 14:13–21). It is perhaps significant also that by going out of Galilee and into the desert east of the Sea of Galilee—which is the only way they could go by ship—Jesus left Herod Antipas's domain and entered the tetrarchy of Herod Philip. This may have been a safety measure.

Resurrection

Thus ended the mortal ministry of one of God's noblest men. His earthly mission was completed; he had kept himself unspotted from the world and had testified against the evils of his day. He made straight the highway of his God, announced the presence of the Messiah, baptized the very Son of God, laid the groundwork for the overthrow of the kingdom of the Jews, and prepared a people. Last of all, he suffered a martyr's violent death. Soon, in about a year and a half, the Messiah himself would be slain and his body placed in a tomb. But the Messiah had power over the grave. He would break the bands of death and come forth with his resurrected, glorified body, no more to be maimed or bruised. And the resurrection of the Messiah would bring to pass ultimately the resurrection of all mankind, including John the Baptist.

As recorded in a divine communication to Joseph Smith, John came forth from the tomb at a time following Jesus' own resurrection. He is referred to as being "with Christ in his resurrection" (D&C 133:55).

The Restoration of All Things

John died a martyr, as have many of the Lord's servants. Nearly eighteen hundred years later he appeared to Joseph Smith and Oliver Cowdery as a resurrected being, laid his hands on their heads, and ordained them to the Aaronic Priesthood. He would have to be a resurrected being to do that, since spirits cannot lay hands on mortals (D&C 129).

Joseph Smith's account of his ordination by John the Baptist in 1829 is as follows:

> While we were . . . praying and calling upon the Lord, a messenger from heaven descended in a cloud of light, and having laid his hands upon us, he ordained us, saying:
>
> *Upon you my fellow servants, in the name of Messiah, I confer the Priesthood of Aaron, which holds the keys of the ministering of angels, and of the gospel of repentance, and of baptism by immersion for the remission of sins; and this shall never be taken again from the earth until the sons of Levi do offer again an offering unto the Lord in righteousness.*
> . . .
>
> . . . [He] said that his name was John, the same that is called John the Baptist in the New Testament, and that he acted under the direction of Peter, James and John. . . . It was on the fifteenth day of May, 1829, that we were ordained under the hand of this messenger. (JS-H 1:68–72.)

John is one of the great heroes of scripture, and one with whom the youth of Aaronic Priesthood age can relate. To usher in the dispensation of the fulness of times (a dispensation incorporating all former dispensations, and embodying the restoration of all things), it was necessary that the Aaronic Priesthood be restored. Every time a young man blesses or distributes the sacrament of the Lord's Supper, or performs a baptism for the remission of sins, he can relate his service to the restoration of the Aaronic Priesthood, and can literally trace his priesthood authority back to the very day John the Baptist ordained the Prophet Joseph Smith and Oliver Cowdery.

On Temple Square in Salt Lake City there stands a bronze and granite monument with larger-than-life-sized figures of John the Baptist ordaining Joseph Smith and Oliver Cowdery. A similar monument has been placed near the Susquehanna River in Pennsylvania. These monuments, dedicated in 1958 and 1960 respectively, were financed by voluntary donations from 65,000 Aaronic Priesthood holders in the Church.

Upon seeing these structures, thousands of visitors annually will learn, or be reminded of, the important spiritual event that occurred on May 15, 1829, through the ministration of John the Baptist preparatory to the Messiah's second coming. These monuments represent a relationship of former dispensations to the fulness of times, and attest to the special place of John the Baptist in the history and doctrine of The Church of Jesus Christ of Latter-day Saints.

PART IV

The Long-Awaited Messiah's Ministry

Jesus Christ was born on earth as the Only Begotten of the Father in the flesh. The personage of spirit that inhabited that precious body was none other than the Lord Jehovah of the Old Testament. He came to earth by appointment of the Father and was preassigned to a specific mission. Ancient prophets had known him, and all of them had declared that he would come to earth. The long-awaited time had now arrived.

Being the unique combination of inheritance that he was, his earth life, though similar in many ways to that of his fellow mortals, was different in some very necessary ways. He was to atone for the fall of Adam and the sins of mankind. He must also conquer death and bring to pass a universal resurrection of the dead.

Jesus functioned with an awareness of his divine purpose. He knew who he was. Everything he said and did was calculated to further the plan of the Father and to accomplish the mission that had brought him to the world. In meekness he preached, performed miracles when expedient, and let his presence and spiritual power be known among his people. The Lord established his Church among his most trusted followers, with a definite organization, a priesthood direct from heavenly messengers, a set of ordinances, and specific doctrine.

Jesus' personal purity and clarity of doctrine were a cultural shock to many of the Jewish leaders, who were saturated with priestcraft. He was popular with the common people; but when he exposed the hypocrisy of those in positions of leadership it resulted in their intense hatred of him. The pride of worldliness gave the priests an unresting desire to have him publicly humiliated, discredited, and finally put to death.

The intrigue and machinations of the Jewish leaders against Jesus continued to increase. Every conceivable trap was set to catch him in his words, until at length they staged a trial with illegal procedures and false witnesses. They stimulated mob action, and influenced public opinion to the extent that they were able to force the timid Roman governor to pronounce the sentence of death upon him.

Jesus endured all the hardships and pains of his ministry, and shed his own blood in Gethsemane in the great spiritual struggle of sin, law, mercy, and justice. He permitted his own execution by Roman soldiers and completed every part of his assigned task.

After organizing a mission in the world of departed spirits, Jesus conquered death and came forth from the dead with his identical physical body. He then ascended to the Father. And in due time he will come again to reign on the earth.

CHAPTER 9

Fundamental Concepts
of Jesus' Ministry

This chapter is a brief statement of basic facts, influences, and relationships that were operative in Jesus' earthly life. Though some of these have been mentioned earlier, they are here presented in condensed form to promote a quick perspective at the beginning of this largest part of the book—the part on Jesus' ministry.

The books of Matthew, Mark, Luke, and John are our main sources of information about Jesus' mortal life, and because they are quite different they are complementary to one another rather than repetitious. Each was written with a different emphasis and to a different audience, and each presents something unique.

The four records are testimonies of Jesus Christ rather than biographies, and hence are scanty in their daily coverage of Jesus' life and activities. Large blocks of time are unaccounted for. The records tell who Jesus was, the type of things he said and the type of things he did, and give an account of his atonement and resurrection and his ascension into heaven.

Jesus came to earth by being born of Mary and was the literal biological Son of God the Father in the flesh. He was a God among men on the earth and had power over death. He was Jehovah the God of Israel come to the earth in a tabernacle of flesh.

People first heard about Jesus, primarily from John the Baptist, and next became acquainted with his teachings. Later they met Jesus personally and some became disciples. Still later some of the disciples became Apostles. Men were not called "off the streets" into the Quorum of the Twelve; they had a training and testing period both before and after their calling into the Twelve.

Jesus spent about a year in the early part of his ministry teaching the public, but after the Twelve were called it appears that the main emphasis was training them. He sent the Twelve and the Seventy on mission tours to give them experience while he was still on earth to counsel them. Performing miracles made Jesus very popular. Miracles are absolutely necessary because the blessings of the gospel are not of this world. Without miracles the gospel would be only a network of ideas, which, even though correct, could not raise a person above the level of fallen man. Testimony, forgiveness of sin, sanctification, redemption, and salvation would not be possible without miracles. Miracles are natural to the gospel, but are unnatural to the mortal world.

Jesus sometimes taught with parables when speaking to those who opposed him and were unrepentant. His popularity made him a target of envy from the Jewish rulers. The purpose of parables was to veil the higher truths of the gospel from them. This was not simply a merciful act to shield them from greater condemnation, but was an act of justice because of their unrighteousness. Since they did not desire nor value the greater light, Jesus withheld it from them, but they could not be saved in their self-imposed ignorance.

The Jewish rulers were highly incensed and offended at Jesus' boldness and sought diligently for two years to find some legal pretense or excuse to put him to death. He was constantly harassed, his doctrine challenged, and his character impugned by them. Jesus was equal to every occasion and often publicly exposed their selfishness and hypocrisy.

Jesus established a kingdom (church) on the earth, with a

forerunner, with officers and priesthood authority, and gave the Twelve all the keys, so that they could conduct the business of the kingdom after he was gone. The Twelve were ordained, instructed, sent on missions; and Peter, James, and John later received the fulness of priesthood keys on the Mount of Transfiguration.

Jesus gained the victory over all things, including death. This is shown in the fact that he raised at least three persons from the dead, restoring them to mortality. Last of all he atoned for the fall of Adam and also the sins of mankind, died, opened a mission in the world of spirits, and came forth from the grave with an immortal body, making immortality for all persons a reality and exaltation available through obedience. He then ascended to heaven to be with the Father.

Definition of Terms Applied to Jesus Christ

Several hundred names, titles, or descriptions for the Lord Jesus Christ are given in the scriptures. These can be observed in the Dictionary in the LDS edition of the Bible, pages 633–35. All of the name-titles are descriptive terms of Jesus' mission, and each one emphasizes some particular dimension that is different from the others. It is appropriate that a few of these be defined to clarify the sense in which they are used in this present work.

Christ. The Greek form of the Hebrew word *Messiah,* meaning "The Anointed One."

Emmanuel. From a Hebrew term meaning "God with us." Sometimes spelled Immanuel (see D&C 128:22). It refers to Jesus' status as a God in the premortal life (see "Jehovah") and also as a God in mortality. Thus when he came to earth in a body of flesh and blood he was in reality "God with us" (Matthew 1:23).

Firstborn. Has reference to Jesus (Jehovah) being the firstborn of the spirit children of the Father (D&C 93:21; Romans 8:29; Colossians 1:15).

Jehovah. A modern translation of the Hebrew consonants JHWH, being the sacred name of the God of Israel. Latter-day revelation identifies Jehovah as Jesus Christ (D&C 110:3; 3 Nephi 15:5). In The Church of Jesus Christ of Latter-day Saints standard usage applies this term to Jesus Christ beginning in, but not limited to, his premortal estate, as distinct from Elohim, who is the Father. In the King James Version (KJV) Old Testament, *Jehovah* is presented as Lord in capitals and small capitals, whereas Elohim is translated God.

Jesus. From the Greek form of the Hebrew *Joshua,* meaning a "savior." As pertaining to Jesus Christ it means he who would save from sins (see Matthew 1:21). The use of *Jesus* in Acts 7:45 and Hebrews 4:8 has reference to the Joshua of the Old Testament, not to Jesus Christ.

Messiah. From the Hebrew word for "The Anointed One." See "Christ."

Only Begotten Son. Has reference to Jesus Christ being the only person born into mortality on this earth of whose mortal body God our Father in Heaven is the biological father.

Redeemer. The concept of gaining possession of by a repurchase or redemption. Must convey the idea of a ransom achieved by deliberate or specific payment. Christ became our Redeemer by ransoming us from death and hell by his blood (1 Corinthians 6:19–20; 7:23; 1 Peter 1:18–20; 2 Peter 2:1; Acts 20:28; Ephesians 1:7).

CHAPTER 10

Mary and Joseph

The story of Mary and Joseph is beautifully told in the New Testament, but to appreciate it we must know something of their lives and recognize some special cultural and historical circumstances.

It is fundamental to know that Mary was the earthly mother of Jesus, and that Joseph was Mary's husband. Consider the implications of Mary and Joseph as the earthly parents and guardians of Jesus. Jesus Christ was the firstborn of the Father in the spirit, his Only Begotten in the flesh, and the central theme of the scriptures. Prophets, beginning with Adam, testified of him and his mission. He was Jehovah in the premortal spirit existence, the creator of the world, and was chosen by our Heavenly Father to be the Savior of mankind.

In his capacity as Savior he represented the Father in all things pertaining to the salvation of man. He was the creator of worlds, and he personally visited ancient patriarchs and prophets to make gospel covenants with them. He was known and worshipped by Adam, Enoch, Noah, Abraham, Moses, Isaiah, Nephi, Alma, and many others. He was mighty and powerful, all-wise and all-knowing, kind and merciful. He was and is the "Holy One of Israel," the God of the whole world.

Just as Jesus was selected for his redeeming mission in the

premortal world, his prophets were also preappointed for their earthly missions, according to their faithfulness (Abraham 3:22–23; Alma 13:2–10). It was in the premortal life that faithful sons and daughters of God received their first lessons in righteousness and became followers of Jesus. Some were foreordained to be prophets; others no doubt were appointed to be the fathers, mothers, and wives of prophets.

There is no impropriety, then, in believing that Mary and Joseph were selected by the Father in those ancient councils to be the earthly guardians of Jesus. Mary was given the unique privilege and responsibility of bringing the great Jehovah into the world, thereby ensuring that he would obtain a body of flesh and bones, experience mortality, and continue his mission for the redemption of mankind.

The significance of this mortal birth was more critical than many realize. It was not an experimental thing, nor an event that was optional in the plan of salvation. The coming of a part-divine, part-mortal Jesus into the world, son of Mary and the Only Begotten of the Father, was an absolute necessity. The human family could be saved in no other way. Only the Lord himself, by coming into mortality, partaking of the nature of man, living a sinless life, atoning with his blood for the sins of men, dying, and rising from the dead with his physical body— only he could bring about redemption (see Alma 34:8–16; Mosiah 7:27). Eternal justice would admit no other way. Without this particular atonement by this particular Redeemer, done in this particular way, all people, after death, would become "devils, angels to a devil, to be shut out from the presence of our God, and to remain with the father of lies, in misery, like unto himself" (2 Nephi 9:9).

The earliest scriptural allusion to Mary is found in the writings of Moses. The Father, speaking to the serpent in the Garden of Eden after the transgression of Adam and Eve, says: "And I will put enmity between thee and the woman, between thy seed and her seed; and he shall bruise thy head, and thou shalt bruise his heel" (Moses 4:21; compare Genesis 3:15). Jesus Christ is the only one born into mortality who is the seed of a woman but has no mortal father. Hence the woman referred to in this passage is Mary.

A direct reference to the Savior's earthly mother was made by Isaiah about 700 B.C.: "Behold, a virgin shall conceive, and bear a son, and shall call his name Immanuel" (Isaiah 7:14). The name Immanuel in Hebrew means "God with us," which is exactly what Mary made possible in giving birth to Jesus. The great Jehovah came to earth and dwelt among men, having a body fathered by God the Father and born of Mary. In this way, God (Jehovah) was with men on this earth. The New Testament identifies this as a prophecy referring to Mary and the birth of Jesus (Matthew 1:22–23).

The Nephites communicated in even plainer language. About six hundred years before the birth of Jesus, Nephi said:

> I beheld the city of Nazareth; and in the city of Nazareth I beheld a virgin, and she was exceedingly fair and white.
>
> And it came to pass that I saw the heavens open; and an angel came down and stood before me. . . .
>
> And he said unto me: Behold, the virgin whom thou seest is the mother of the Son of God, after the manner of the flesh. . . .
>
> And I looked and beheld the virgin again, bearing a child in her arms.
>
> And the angel said unto me: Behold the Lamb of God, yea, even the Son of the Eternal Father! (1 Nephi 11:13–14, 18, 20–21.)

Later, about 124 years before the birth of the Savior, King Benjamin told his people that an angel had visited him and explained that the Redeemer should "be called Jesus Christ, the Son of God, the Father of heaven and earth, the Creator of all things from the beginning; and his mother shall be called Mary" (Mosiah 3:8).

Still later, about eighty years before the Lord's birth, Alma taught the people: "And behold, he shall be born of Mary, at Jerusalem which is the land of our forefathers, she being a virgin, a precious and chosen vessel, who shall be overshadowed and conceive by the power of the Holy Ghost, and bring forth a son, yea, even the Son of God" (Alma 7:10).

Such specific details about Mary could not have been known so long beforehand unless she had been appointed to that calling in the premortal life.

There is another factor inherent in the selection of the Lord's mortal parentage. He was to be born of the family of David, and be the heir to the throne of David. Hence he would literally and legally be the King of the Jews by their own law. Isaiah touches upon this matter: "For unto us a child is born, unto us a son is given; and the government shall be upon his shoulder: and his name shall be called Wonderful, Counsellor, The mighty God, The everlasting Father, The Prince of Peace. Of the increase of his government and peace there shall be no end, upon the throne of David, and upon his kingdom, to order it, and to establish it with judgment and with justice from henceforth even for ever." (Isaiah 9:6–7; see also Isaiah 11:1; D&C 113:1–2.)

Since Jesus was not begotten by mortal man, his descent from David would, by necessity, be through his mother. Thus, when Mary came to earth she was born into that royal lineage so that she could transmit it to her son Jesus. That Mary was of Davidic descent is plainly set forth in the scriptures. Jesus was frequently addressed as "Son of David." He did not disclaim that title.

Paul made it clear that Jesus was of royal blood in his earthly lineage. To the Roman Saints he wrote: "Jesus Christ our Lord . . . was made of the seed of David according to the flesh" (Romans 1:3). And to Timothy he said: "Remember that Jesus Christ of the seed of David was raised from the dead" (2 Timothy 2:8; see also Acts 13:22–23; 2:30).

Mary's husband, Joseph, also was "of the house and lineage of David" (Luke 2:4; see also Luke 1:27; Matthew 1:16, 20; Luke 3:23–31). So Jesus, though not a blood descendant of Joseph, inherited legal status as a son of David through him.

At that time the Jews were ruled by Rome, and the rights of the royal Davidic family were not recognized. Herod, king of the Jews by Roman appointment, was not even an Israelite, and certainly not of David's line.

Elder James E. Talmage explained: "Had Judah been a free and independent nation, ruled by her rightful sovereign, Joseph the carpenter would have been her crowned king; and his lawful successor to the throne would have been Jesus of Nazareth, the King of the Jews" (*Jesus the Christ* [Salt Lake City: Deseret Book Co., 1948], p. 87).

Of course, like all of us, Mary lost the conscious memory of her premortal existence and appointment when she was born into mortality. But when the time drew near for the birth of the Only Begotten, Mary was born at the right time, in the right place, and in the precise lineage whereby she could fulfill her mission.

In Luke we find an account of the words of the angel Gabriel to Mary as follows: "Hail, thou that art highly favoured, the Lord is with thee: blessed art thou among women. . . . for thou hast found favour with God. And, behold, thou shalt conceive in thy womb, and bring forth a son, and shalt call his name Jesus. He shall be great, and shall be called the Son of the Highest: and the Lord God shall give unto him the throne of his father David: and he shall reign over the house of Jacob for ever; and of his kingdom there shall be no end." (Luke 1:28–33.)

Later, when visiting her cousin Elisabeth (who was soon to become the mother of John the Baptist), Mary said: "My soul doth magnify the Lord, and my spirit hath rejoiced in God my Saviour. For he hath regarded the low estate of his handmaiden: for, behold, from henceforth all generations shall call me blessed. For he that is mighty hath done to me great things; and holy is his name. . . . He hath holpen his servant Israel, in remembrance of his mercy; as he spake to our fathers, to Abraham, and to his seed for ever." (Luke 1:46–49, 54–55.)

Mary's words reveal her character and also her knowledge of Israel's history. Mention of "low estate" probably has reference to the humble circumstances of her life. Although she and Joseph were heirs to the throne of Israel, they were not privileged to exercise that honor, and Joseph apparently was not a man of wealth or political status.

Although Mary did not retain her memory of her high calling, we wonder how much the Spirit had whispered in her early years. Of great spiritual capacity and naturally inclined toward righteousness and meditation, she reflected her knowledge of the Old Testament and God's covenant and promises made to Israel. She was no doubt serious-minded, as befitting one called of God as she was. No doubt Mary was the product of years of obedience to the laws of the Lord, her mind and character molded by the Holy Ghost working in her since early childhood.

As Elder Bruce R. McConkie of the Council of the Twelve has observed: "As there is only one Christ, so there is only one Mary. And as the Father chose the most noble and righteous of all his spirit sons to come into mortality as his Only Begotten in the flesh, so we may confidently conclude that he selected the most worthy and spiritually talented of all his spirit daughters to be the mortal mother of his Eternal Son." (DNTC, 1:85.)

Apocryphal writings of the early Christian era present a significant and recurring theme about a substantial period of spiritual preparation in Mary's life in the years before she conceived Jesus. They speak of her being tutored by angels and having other spiritual manifestations (*The Lost Books of the Bible* [New York: The World Publishing Company, 1926], chapters 1 and 4–9; see also "The Gospel of Bartholomew," part 2, *The Apocryphal New Testament*, M. R. James, translator [Oxford: The Clarendon Press, 1969], pp. 170–72). These manifestations were also said to have occurred prior to the visit of the angel Gabriel.

Many details of these writings assuredly are not accurate; even so, the idea is probably correct that Mary received spiritual preparation and education for some time prior to the angel's announcement to her.

Though Jesus was the literal Son of God, as a young child he needed to be taught and cared for much like other children. This would be necessary because "over his mind had fallen the veil of forgetfulness common to all who are born to earth, by which the remembrance of primeval existence is shut off" (James E. Talmage, *Jesus the Christ*, p. 111). Luke speaks of Jesus increasing in wisdom as a youth (Luke 2:52), and the Doctrine and Covenants indicates that in the flesh he received "not of the fulness at the first, but received grace for grace" (D&C 93:12).

President J. Reuben Clark, Jr., expressed his views about the veil of forgetfulness being drawn over Jesus' mind at birth, and subsequently being lifted a little at a time. The following excerpts are from his book *Behold the Lamb of God* (Salt Lake City: Deseret Book Co., 1991).

First, pertaining to the journey from Nazareth to Jerusalem to attend the Passover when Jesus was twelve years of age:

> As we think of them moving slowly down into the valley with their donkeys laden with necessary supplies, picking their way

among the boulders that strewed the path, we cannot escape wondering what were the thoughts of Jesus. That he was exceeding wise, the experience in the temple shows. But was this wisdom earthborn from his studies, or did he have also a spiritual memory that brought to him a recollection of all that had before happened, and a vision to show what was thereafter to happen along this road to Jerusalem, a road richer in incidents of God's dealing with his children, than any other road on the face of the earth? (Pp. 138–39.)

There can be no doubt that Jesus had been deeply stirred by what he had seen and heard and done on this his first participation in the temple sacrifices and ceremonies of the Passover. We have, . . . from time to time, raised the question as to how much Jesus was conscious of the past of which he was the directing power, and with what fulness did he foresee the future. The events we shall now recount leave little reasonable doubt that he remembered, in part at least, the past and foresaw at least some of the future. It can hardly be questioned that while his mortality put him under limitations (when they were not consciously thrown off), yet that mortality and its limitations did not dominate his divinity.

That Jesus deliberately planned to stay behind when the others went, can admit of little question. (P. 155.)

From Mary's statement "thy father and I have sought thee sorrowing," we may glimpse that in the intimacies of the family circle at Nazareth, Jesus gave to Joseph the love and respect of a son, and called him father. But Jesus knew that Mary knew and that Joseph knew better than this, and so came the saying, "wist ye not that I must be about *my* Father's business?" (P. 161.)

But there was more in the saying than was known to Joseph and Mary. There was the consciousness in Jesus not alone of who he was but of his mission here on earth. He knew that centuries before God had declared to Moses: "For behold, this is my work and my glory—to bring to pass the immortality and eternal life of man" (Moses 1:39). This was his "Father's business," and he must be about it. (P. 162.)

As to the Lord's "spiritual memory" in his later years, President Clark explained:

As to memory of the past, we do know that during his later Judean ministry, while speaking to the Jews in the treasury to the temple, he declared: "I do nothing of myself; but as my Father hath taught me, I speak these things. . . . I speak that which I have seen with my Father." And out on the Mount of Olives, after they had left the Passover chamber, on the night before the crucifixion, Jesus said to his Apostles: "For all things that I have heard of my Father I have made known unto you." Thus in his later ministry, his mind was filled with knowledge gained in his pre-existence. (P. 139.)

If indeed Jesus had at least glimpses of his premortal activity, even while a boy, this could only make him a very precocious child and thus intensify the responsibility of Joseph and Mary as his earthly guardians.

When we consider the strong influence that a mother has on the personality and attitude of a young child in the home, we sense the responsibility that our Heavenly Father gave Mary by entrusting her with the rearing of his chosen and Beloved Son. This would require the adequate training of Mary, both as a premortal spirit and as a young woman in mortality. Notwithstanding her pre-earth assignment, Mary would not have been worthy to bear the Son of God and give him a body of flesh and blood unless she was clean and pure in mortal life.

And what of Joseph? What kind of person would the Father select as the husband of Mary and the guardian and earthly model for Jesus? The scriptures are not entirely silent, although direct references are few. Because the father is to teach correct principles by precept and example and be a counselor, we must conclude that our Heavenly Father made careful selection in his choice of Joseph. That Joseph was spiritually sensitive and of a kindly disposition is reflected in the scriptural record. He was susceptible to divine guidance through the ministrations of angels and by dreams (see Matthew 1:20; 2:13, 19, 22); he wished not to bring embarrassment upon Mary nor to "make her a publick example" (Matthew 1:19). In addition, we would expect to find in Joseph the moral, intellectual, and social qualities befitting his important assignment.

Mary and Joseph were careful to observe all the Lord's commandments. The law of Moses required many performances and ordinances, including the rule that male children were to be circumcised when eight days of age as a token of the covenant the Lord made with Abraham. Furthermore, forty days after the birth of a son (eighty days in the case of a daughter), the mother was to offer a special sacrifice—a lamb or two turtledoves or pigeons (Leviticus 12:1–8).

The law also stipulated that firstborn male children were sanctified to the Lord and were to be presented to him, not in sacrifice, but to his service (see Exodus 13:1–2, 11–15). Another stipulation was that every man was to go frequently to the place of the temple to bring sacrifices and offerings and to worship the Lord (Deuteronomy 12:5–7, 11–14).

The New Testament indicates that Joseph and Mary attended to all of these things. They had Jesus circumcised at the age of eight days, "And when the days of her purification according to the law of Moses were accomplished, they brought him to Jerusalem, to present him to the Lord" (Luke 2:22). That Mary offered turtledoves instead of the lamb is indicative of her meager finances and "low estate." And we read further: "Now [Jesus'] parents went to Jerusalem every year at the feast of the passover" (Luke 2:41). Thus we gain an impression of the obedient and spiritual disposition of Jesus' earthly parents and guardians.

The "just and devout" Simeon met Joseph and Mary in the temple. This man knew by the power of the Holy Ghost that the child Jesus was also the Christ, and he said to Mary: "Behold, this child is set for the fall and rising again of many in Israel; and for a sign which shall be spoken against: yea, a spear shall pierce through him to the wounding of thine own soul also; that the thoughts of many hearts may be revealed" (JST Luke 2:34–35). Mary must often have reflected upon the meaning of these words, both before and after she witnessed their fulfillment by seeing Jesus nailed to the cross and a spear actually pierce his side. But it was not all to be experienced in one day or by one event. Even though she was a special spirit, the Father did not shield her from the pains or natural consequences of mortality. Mary knew the hardships, disappointments, and struggles that are characteristic of mortal life.

In many ways Joseph and Mary lived in hard times. Judah was in bondage to Rome, and the Herods were harsh and cruel monarchs. The Jews were in apostasy and were burdened by rigid formalism and spiritual wickedness. Jewish religious leaders of that time are characterized as "the more wicked part of the world. . . . because of priestcrafts and iniquities" (2 Nephi 10:3, 5).

It was in these circumstances that the tender, pure, and chosen Mary, protected and attended by the spiritually receptive, capable, and kindly Joseph, brought forth her firstborn son and laid him in a manger. The unpretentious circumstances of this little family blessed with the special holiness of the child Jesus were in strong contrast to the spiritually barren and parched condition of a people led by proud and insistent Pharisees, sumptuous Sadducees, exclusive rabbis, and learned scribes conquered by a pagan empire. Isaiah knew of this contrast and had predicted that the Messiah would grow up "as a tender plant, and as a root out of a dry ground" (Isaiah 53:2).

No certain knowledge has come to us of the home life and childhood of Jesus, but there are many indications. We have already observed that Joseph was a carpenter, and we know that Jesus followed the same occupation (see Mark 6:3). In his teachings Jesus spoke so much about stones and rocks and so seldom about wood that we are led to the realization that in the land of Palestine, with few large trees and many rocks, a carpenter worked as much with stone as he did with wood. The atmosphere of the home was one of obedience to the Lord as commanded in the divine law. It was at home that Jesus would receive his first lessons about the history of Israel and of past deliverances of his people by the hand of the Lord; here he also undoubtedly learned of the hopes and expectations for the future, as written in the scriptures. The preparations of his parents each week to observe the Sabbath, their attendance at the synagogue, their observance of feast days, and their preparations and conversations each year as they made ready to go up to Jerusalem for the Passover would be impressive object lessons to the young Jesus.

We don't know how many other children there were in the family, but the New Testament names four boys and mentions some sisters. The Greek manuscripts are helpful here. Matthew speaks of "all" (Greek: *pantai*) his sisters (Matthew 13:56), suggesting more than two. The Greek term *hai adelphia* (the sisters) also is used in the manuscripts, signifying a plurality—that is, three or more sisters. If the record had intended to convey that there were only two sisters, it is probable that the word *amphoterai*, meaning "both," would have been used instead of *pantai*. Thus the household of Joseph and Mary apparently numbered at least five boys (including Jesus) and at least three girls—eight children—in addition to the parents.

Two lines of thought have developed as to the identity of these other children. Some hold that they were children of Joseph by a former marriage and not the children of Mary at all. In this case Jesus would be younger than they, and of no close blood relation. This is a popular concept in the Christian world today, and illustrations of the "holy family" therefore generally picture Joseph as much older than Mary.

Another view is that these were actually the children of Joseph and Mary and therefore were half-brothers and sisters to Jesus, he being the eldest. Both of these views have their advocates and there are hints in the scriptures that can be interpreted to favor either point of view. However, Jesus is termed Mary's "firstborn" son, which is indicative that she later gave birth to other children (see Luke 2:7). A more compelling reason for believing that these are Mary's children is that Joseph's firstborn son from a first wife would have been the heir to the throne of David instead of Jesus.

Mary may have lived a number of years as a widow. The last mention of Joseph occurs at Passover time in Jerusalem when Jesus was twelve years of age. At the wedding feast at Cana, when Jesus was thirty, specific mention is made that Mary and Jesus were present, but no mention is made of Joseph (see John 2:1–10). Finally, at the time of the Crucifixion Mary is said to have stood at the cross *with other women*, but again no mention is made of Joseph. At this time Jesus gave his mother over to the care of his beloved disciple, John (see John 19:25–27). The record of these events suggests that Mary was widowed sometime after Jesus was twelve years old and before he began his ministry (see also Matthew 12:46).

An apocryphal source tells, overdramatically, of Joseph's death and of Mary and Jesus discussing the matter (cited in

Montague R. James, trans., *The Apocryphal New Testament* [Oxford: Clarendon Press, 1969], pp. 85–86). While the concept may be correct, the record itself seems suspicious.

There is a poignancy in the prospect of Mary's being widowed with a family of children, all younger than Jesus. If this assumption is correct, it may be that Jesus was confronted with the responsibility in early life of providing for a widowed mother and several younger brothers and sisters. This makes most meaningful the scriptural statements that say the Lord is especially mindful of the widow and is a father to the fatherless (see Psalm 68:5; 146:9; compare James 1:27).

As Latter-day Saints we do not worship Mary, but we do regard her very highly. She is among the most worthy and noble of women—the most privileged of all mothers. And while Mary may not be typical, she is an example to all mothers.

If we listen we can still hear the echo of the angel's words: "Hail, thou that art highly favoured, . . . blessed art thou among women" (Luke 1:28). And likewise we hear Mary's own exclamation: "My soul doth magnify the Lord, and my spirit hath rejoiced in God my Saviour. For he hath regarded the low estate of his handmaiden . . . from henceforth all generations shall call me blessed." (Luke 1:46–48.)

CHAPTER 11

We Have Found the Messiah

Andrew had talked with Jesus, and he was so excited about it that the first thing he did was find Simon Peter, his brother, and tell him: "We have found the Messias." The chronicler adds, "which is, being interpreted, the Christ." (John 1:41.)

Although the passage does not detail the background nor tell what these men had talked about previous to this moment, there is enough of a clue in the way that sentence is worded to show us that finding the Messiah was important to them and must have been something they had talked about on earlier occasions. Furthermore, every devout Jew looked forward to the coming of the prophesied Messiah.

To get the full impact of what it meant to them to "find the Messiah," we need to look at the extended passage. In order to catch the force of these words, note the frequency of such terms as "seek," "behold," "findeth," "come and see," and "we have found." The account in the JST is a little richer than that in any other Bible. The setting is that John the Baptist had taught a special delegation of the Jewish leaders that the Messiah was already on the earth, among them, but they had not recognized him.

Again, the next day after, John stood, and two of his disciples,
And looking upon Jesus as he walked, he said, Behold the
Lamb of God!
And the two disciples heard him speak, and they followed
Jesus.
Then Jesus turned, and saw them following him, and said
unto them, What seek ye? They say unto him, Rabbi, (which is to
say, being interpreted, Master,) where dwellest thou?
He said unto them, Come and see. And they came and saw
where he dwelt, and abode with him that day: for it was about the
tenth hour.
One of the two who heard John, and followed Jesus, was
Andrew, Simon Peter's brother.
He first findeth his own brother Simon and saith unto him,
We have found the Messias, which is, being interpreted, the
Christ.
And he brought him to Jesus. And when Jesus beheld him, he
said, Thou art Simon, the son of Jona, thou shalt be called Cephas,
which is by interpretation, a seer or a stone. And they were fisher-
men. And they straightway left all, and followed Jesus.
The day following, Jesus would go forth into Galilee, and
findeth Philip, and saith unto him, Follow me.
Now Philip was at Bethsaida, the city of Andrew and Peter.
Philip findeth Nathanael, and saith unto him, We have found
him, of whom Moses in the law, and the prophets, did write, Jesus
of Nazareth, the son of Joseph. (JST John 1:35–45.)

There is here an underlying awareness, almost taken for
granted, that these brethren were cognizant of the things Moses
and the prophets had written about the Messiah, and that they
placed a high value on those words of the prophets and considered it of the greatest importance to find that Messiah who was
so highly spoken of in the scriptures. Notice the joy, the sense of
fulfillment, the excitement when a person is able to say, "We
have found the Messiah."
The discovery by these brethren, Andrew, Simon, Philip,
and Nathanael, reminds us of the words of the Lord to Jeremiah: "Then shall ye call upon me, and ye shall go and pray
unto me, and I will hearken unto you. And ye shall seek me,
and find me, when ye shall search for me with all your heart.
And I will be found of you, saith the Lord." (Jeremiah 29:12–14.)

This same idea has perhaps become more familiar to many of us through the words and music of Felix Mendelssohn's oratorio *Elijah*, in which it is beautifully expressed in this way: "If with all your heart ye truly seek me, ye shall ever surely find me, thus saith your God."

In the writings of Moses to a future scattered Israel, we find this promise: "But if from thence thou shalt seek the Lord thy God, thou shalt find him, if thou seek him with all thy heart and with all thy soul" (Deuteronomy 4:29). And father Abraham, after a personal manifestation and blessing from the Lord, reflected on his marvelous experience and wrote of it as follows: "Now, after the Lord had withdrawn from speaking to me, and withdrawn his face from me, I said in my heart: Thy servant has sought thee earnestly; now I have found thee; . . . and I will do well to hearken unto thy voice." (Abraham 2:12–13.)

Finding the Messiah in Every Generation

Let it be remembered and noted that this Messiah, this Jesus whom the fishermen of Galilee had found in *their* day and in *their* country, was the same Messiah, the same God, whom Moses, Abraham, Elijah, Isaiah, Jeremiah, Nephi, Jacob, Alma, and all the prophets had sought and found in their respective eras. His name was Jehovah. Jesus the Messiah in the New Testament is the same being known as Jehovah in the Old Testament.

The heart of a righteous man or woman hungers for more and more contact with the Savior, and to find him is manna to the soul. To be in his favor is even more refreshing than drinking cool water in a thirsty land; or finding a covering from the sun in time of heat. Knowledge and testimony of Christ are food for the hungry spirit, just as meat and potatoes are food for the hungry body.

Knowing the proper price to put on all its blessings, heaven has so arranged things that one has to seek and to search in order to really *find* the Messiah. He has to be discovered, as it were, by each person individually. Information *about* the Savior can be found quite easily, but there is a significant difference between knowing the Lord and only knowing about him. We may learn *about* the Savior by reading or listening, but in order to *know* him and understand much about him we must obey his commandments and be given a witness from the Holy Ghost. Jesus Christ can be *known* only by revelation. The Lord himself has promised to unveil his face and be known by his servants, but he has said that it must be in his "own time," and in his "own way," and according to his "own will."

We would do well to notice in the following passage such words as *seek, find, ask, behold, see,* and *single.*

> Draw near unto me and I will draw near unto you; seek me diligently and ye shall find me; ask, and ye shall receive; knock, and it shall be opened unto you.
>
> Whatsoever ye ask the Father in my name it shall be given unto you, that is expedient for you;
>
> And if ye ask anything that is not expedient for you, it shall turn unto your condemnation.
>
> Behold, that which you hear is as the voice of one crying in the wilderness—in the wilderness, because you cannot see him— my voice, because my voice is Spirit; my Spirit is truth; truth abideth and hath no end; and if it be in you it shall abound.
>
> And if your eye be single to my glory, your whole bodies shall be filled with light, and there shall be no darkness in you; and that body which is filled with light comprehendeth all things.
>
> Therefore, sanctify yourselves that your minds become single to God, and the days will come that you shall see him; for he will unveil his face unto you, and it shall be in his own time, and in his own way, and according to his own will. (D&C 88:63–68.)

We may think that because we live so long after the mortal life of the Savior a personal visit by vision or divine manifestation is considerably different than seeing Jesus on the roads and by-ways of Galilee, or the streets of Jerusalem. But it is not entirely different—the same crucial factor applies in both circumstances. If we had lived at that time and in that place, and had seen him in the mortal flesh, we would not have known that he was the Messiah, or that he was anything more than a man, unless the Holy Spirit whispered it to our own spirit. Many saw him but knew not who he was. John the Baptist knew him and declared plainly that he was the Messiah, the Son of God—but he also explained: "There standeth one among you, whom *ye* know not" (John 1:26, emphasis added). It was only by the testimony of the Spirit that anyone could recognize the difference between the Messiah and any other man. It is one of the functions of the Holy Ghost to bear witness of the Father and the Son (Moses 5:9). The scriptures testify of Christ, and the Holy Ghost bears record that those scriptures are true.

The earlier passage from the first chapter of John showed that two of the disciples of John the Baptist subsequently became Apostles of the Lord Jesus. These two are Andrew and John (who was later known as John the Beloved or John the Revelator, the son of Zebedee). However, other passages suggest that most if not all of the Twelve were individually and personally tutored by John the Baptist, and that it was from him that they learned their earliest lessons about the Messiah who had already come to earth and who even lived in their neighborhood.

At the time of choosing a new member of the Twelve to replace Judas, Peter said the choice would be made from among the believers who had "companied with" the Apostles all the time, "beginning from the baptism of John, unto that same day that he [Jesus] was taken up from us." This sounds significantly as if most of the Twelve had been followers of John the Baptist, and thus that from him they had learned that Jesus of Nazareth was the Messiah. John's mission was as a forerunner to prepare the way for the Savior and to prepare a people to receive him. What more effective way than for John to actively tutor and start on their way those who later became Jesus' chief witnesses? He taught them the right way to find the Messiah, and introduced many of them first to the doctrines of the Lord and then to the Lord in person.

Finding the Infant Messiah

Let us review from the scriptures exactly what it is that a person finds when and if he finds the Messiah. The shepherds near Bethlehem, being prompted by the angels of heaven, found the Messiah as a little babe, "wrapped in swaddling clothes, lying in a manger" (Luke 2:12). He looked like other babies in outward appearance, but because the shepherds knew precisely who he was they worshipped him and could hardly wait to tell others of his birth.

About forty days later, when Joseph and Mary brought the infant Jesus to the temple to fulfill the rites of purification according to the law of Moses, they met a righteous and devout man whose name was Simeon. To him it had been revealed by the Holy Ghost that before his death he should see the Messiah. He recognized the baby Jesus as that Messiah, the "Hope of Israel," took him in his arms, and praised and thanked God. This man found a unique kind of joy because by the Holy Spirit he had seen and knew for himself that in seeing this little baby he had found the Messiah (Luke 2:25–35).

At that same time Anna, a righteous woman of great age, who after only seven years of marriage had been left a widow more than eighty-four years, came into the room, saw the child and knew who he was, and gave thanks that she had seen the Messiah (Luke 2:36–38).

The wise men, being led by his star—not just *a* star, or *the* star, but as the scripture says, *his* star, a special star—found Jesus in a house, as a young child, for it was a year or two since his birth. He no doubt looked like other children his age, but the wise men, being spiritually endowed and having knowledge, knew he was wonderfully different and they brought him gifts and worshipped him (Matthew 2:1–12; JST Matthew 3:1–12). The KJV account has the wise men come seeking him who was born to be king, but from the JST we see an additional dimension and learn that they were seeking not only a *king* who would *rule* but also the *Messiah* who would *save*. He who looks for and finds the Messiah is wiser than he who looks for and finds only a king. And even today, wise men still seek the Savior.

The Messiah as a Youth

When Jesus was twelve years of age his parents took him to the temple in Jerusalem, according to the requirement of the law of Moses, for the Passover observance (Luke 2:41–42). When the formalities were over, Joseph and Mary were returning to Galilee and had journeyed about a day from Jerusalem when they discovered that Jesus was not with them. I have often reflected on the fear, the sorrow, the near-panic emotions that must have surged through Joseph and Mary to have lost track of their son in such a large and crowded city as Jerusalem at the time of Passover.

Such an experience would be almost overwhelming for any of us with our natural children—Mary and Joseph would have all the pain we would have, but more in addition, for they had lost the very Son of God. That is worse than losing 116 pages of manuscript, or almost anything else that could have happened to them. After three days of searching they found him. What did they really *find* when they found him? A normal twelve-year-old boy? "They found him in the temple, sitting in the midst of the doctors, both hearing them and asking them questions" (Luke 2:46).

It is something to write about any time a twelve-year-old boy will sit for three days and listen to a discussion of the scriptures and even ask questions. However, that is the lesser part of the story. The JST reads: "They found him in the temple, sitting in the midst of the doctors, and they [the doctors] were hearing him, and asking him questions" (JST Luke 2:46).

With this clarification, the next verse takes on more meaning: "And all that heard him were astonished at his understanding and answers."

What did the learned doctors discover when they "found" the Messiah in the temple courts? They found a youth who looked like other boys but was possessed of wisdom and knowledge and more understanding of the spiritual things of life and of the message of the scriptures than they collectively had been able to acquire through years of study and experience.

How does it happen that Jesus came by such wisdom at so early an age? When he was born a veil was placed over his mind and his memory the same as it has been with us, but he had the power of the Spirit, the Holy Ghost. In JST John 2:24 we read that Jesus "knew all things, and needed not that any should testify of man; for he knew what was in man." Speaking of the Savior, John the Baptist testified: "He whom God hath sent, speaketh the words of God; for God giveth him not the Spirit by measure, for he dwelleth in him, even the fulness" (JST John 3:34).

The JST offers another passage that permits us a glimpse of the unusual ability and personality of the Messiah as a youth and as a young man. (In KJV these verses would be inserted at the end of Matthew chapter 2.) "And it came to pass that Jesus grew up with his brethren, and waxed strong, and waited upon the Lord for the time of his ministry to come. And he served under his father, and he spake not as other men, neither could he be taught; for he needed not that any man should teach him. And after many years, the hour of his ministry drew nigh."

We often hear it said that we know but very little about the Savior's early life, but we can see from these passages that we do have some guidelines concerning what type of youth he was.

The Messiah as a Mature Man

What did people think they had found when they found the mature Jesus the Messiah? As we have already noted, some identified him as the one of whom Moses and the prophets had written. Others, when they saw him and heard him, thought he was one of the ancient prophets come back to earth again— perhaps Elijah, or Jeremiah, or one of the other prophets (see Matthew 16:14). Herod, upon hearing of his miracles and wonderful works but having never seen him, thought he was John the Baptist risen from the dead (Matthew 14:2).

Jesus is shown to be of a bold, assertive, and strong personality, but there is not a single case in the records of Matthew, Mark, Luke, or John that represents him as impatient, critical, or unkind to people who were repentant, teachable, and willing to change their lives. He forgave transgressions and mingled with publicans and sinners on condition of their repentance. He cast out devils, mobilized the lame, raised the dead, fed the hungry, opened the eyes of the blind, gave hearing to the deaf, and restored the sick to health, if they but had the faith that he could do it. But he was a terror to the workers of iniquity and those who were self-righteous, deceptive, or hypocritical. In dealing with the repentant, he was the kind, the gentle, the firm, the promised Messiah. To the proud, the haughty, and the arrogant, he was absolutely indomitable and irrepressible, and a threat to their craftiness.

As a teacher and interfacer with people, Jesus was without peer. He was in charge of every situation. He seems never to have been worried or confused or afraid, or lacking in any of his dealings with mankind.

The Jewish Rulers Find the Messiah

What did the Jewish rulers find when they encountered the Messiah? They found him to be a threat to their hypocritical, self-righteous way of life. They were amazed at his strength of character and endless wisdom. He had not gone through their training and curriculum, nor their rabbinical schools, and yet he knew so much about the scriptures and about the world of men and things. In what appears to be almost a mixture of surprise and dismay over Jesus' success as a teacher, they marvelled and cried out, "How knoweth this man letters, having never learned? Jesus answered them and said, My doctrine is not mine, but his that sent me" (John 7:15–16). John records: "And there was much murmuring among the people concerning him: for some said, He is a good man; others said, Nay; but he deceiveth the people" (John 7:12).

Three days before his crucifixion Jesus spent the entire day in a vivid confrontation with the Jewish rulers. They found that in defense of truth he was superb. He was righteousness coupled with true facts—an unbeatable combination. They learned the truth of Job's expression, "How forcible are right words" (Job 6:25). Cited below is only a portion of what the record tells us took place on that day—the Tuesday before his death. Jesus had one day previously cast the money changers out of the temple. When he came into Jerusalem and to the temple the next morning, the chief priests and the elders came to him as he was teaching and asked:

By what authority doest thou these things? and who gave thee this authority?

And Jesus answered and said unto them, I also will ask you one thing, which if ye tell me, I in like wise will tell you by what authority I do these things.

The baptism of John, whence was it? from heaven, or of men? And they reasoned with themselves, saying If we shall say, From heaven; he will say unto us, Why did ye not then believe him?

But if we shall say, Of men: we fear the people; for all hold John as a prophet.

And they answered Jesus, and said, We cannot tell. And he said unto them, Neither tell I you by what authority I do these things. (Matthew 21:23–27.)

Jesus then taught them by parables in which he pointed out several flaws in their characters, such as greed, perfidy, and spiritual blindness, which were everyday things with them. Then the Pharisees went away and held a meeting to see how they "might entangle him in his talk" (Matthew 22:15). The record continues: "And they sent out unto him their disciples with the Herodians, saying, Master, we know that thou art true, and teachest the way of God in truth, neither carest thou for any man; for thou regardest not the person of men. Tell us therefore, What thinkest thou? Is it lawful to give tribute unto Caesar, or not?"

This was a trap. No matter which way Jesus answered, they could set on him about it and seek to discredit him. "But Jesus perceived their wickedness, and said, Why tempt ye me, ye hypocrites? Shew me the tribute money. And they brought unto him a penny. And he saith unto them, Whose is this image and superscription? They say unto him, Caesar's. Then saith he unto them, Render therefore unto Caesar the things which are Caesar's; and unto God the things that are God's. When they had heard these words, they marvelled, and left him, and went their way." (Matthew 22:16–22.)

Knowing their plot, Jesus took a middle course in his response. They wanted an either-or reply. He out-maneuvered them. If he had told them not to pay tribute to Caesar (representative of the Roman Empire) these people would have been overjoyed to report him as treasonous, disloyal to Rome, a troublemaker. Maybe they could have had him arrested. However, if he had said they should pay tribute to Caesar, these same slippery fellows would have spread the word among the people that Jesus was no Messiah to the Jews for he was selling them into bondage to the Romans. His answer—to render to Caesar that which was Caesar's, and to God that which was God's—completely defused their explosive plan, and they left him. They found that he was a master in righteous rebuke and basic logic.

On the same day the Sadducees came to Jesus, hoping to publicly embarrass and discredit him. They knew he had silenced the Pharisees, but they considered themselves more capable. The Sadducees came with a "hard question" to ask him about marriage and about the resurrection. Since the Sadducees believed there was no resurrection from the dead and no afterlife, it is clear that this question was not asked in good faith with a desire to seek the truth but was another trap.

> The same day came to him the Sadducees, which say that there is no resurrection, and asked him,
>
> Saying, Master, Moses said, If a man die, having no children, his brother shall marry his wife, and raise up seed unto his brother.
>
> Now there were with us seven brethren; and the first, when he had married a wife, deceased, and, having no issue, left his wife unto his brother:
>
> Likewise the second also, and the third, unto the seventh.
>
> And last of all the woman died also.
>
> Therefore in the resurrection whose wife shall she be of the seven? for they all had her.
>
> Jesus answered and said unto them, Ye do err, not knowing the scriptures, nor the power of God.
>
> For in the resurrection they neither marry, nor are given in marriage, but are as the angels of God in heaven.
>
> But as touching the resurrection of the dead, have ye not read that which was spoken unto you by God, saying,
>
> I am the God of Abraham, and the God of Isaac, and the God of Jacob? God is not the God of the dead, but of the living.
>
> And when the multitude heard this, they were astonished at his doctrine. (Matthew 21:23–33.)

Because of the words, "for in the resurrection they neither marry nor are given in marriage," this passage is often used by others in an attempt to refute the LDS doctrine of eternal marriage. A *casual* reader could see the statement as a denial of an eternal marriage doctrine; but I believe that a *careful* reading will show this to be one of the strongest examples in the Bible of Jesus' openly teaching the doctrine of eternal marriage, and that his hearers knew it.

I had an experience that will illustrate my point. As a seminary teacher I found that friendly, playful high school students would sometimes put empty whisky bottles, empty cigarette cartons, empty coffee cans, and the like on the front porch of my house during the night. Sometimes they put cigarettes under the windshield wipers on my car. Why did those students do those particular things? Was this not a reaction to my teaching about the Word of Wisdom in seminary class? They did not put milk cartons or soft-drink bottles—only liquor and tobacco containers. Once, as an experiment, I said in class that some people feel that the eating of chocolate is contrary to the Word of Wisdom. So what was placed under the windshield wipers the same night? Of course—a chocolate candy bar. The students reacted to what was taught. (I was not astute enough at the time, but I have often thought since then that I should have quoted to them "The love of money is the root of all evil.")

Now look back to Jesus and the Sadducees. Since the Sadducees did not believe in the resurrection or in any form of afterlife beyond the grave, and since it was a hostile audience and an unfriendly confrontation, it is easy to see that these clever men were trying to give the Messiah a hard question about marriage and resurrection that they supposed he could not answer. And why would they have used the subject of marriage in the resurrected state unless it was widely known that he had been teaching such a doctrine? They were reacting to what he had said. His answer, simply put, was that this particular woman and her seven husbands had not been married by the power and authority of God, and hence there was no problem in answering this case, since none of her marriages would be eternal. They did not ask Jesus for a general statement concerning all mankind; they asked for a ruling on this woman and her seven husbands. Jesus answered their precise question—none of them would be married in eternity, because they had not been married by the power of God. I say that this passage, when read in its context, is one of the strongest evidences that Jesus taught the concept of eternal marriage and also that there is a resurrection from the dead. People around Jerusalem knew it, but the Sadducees didn't like it. It is obvious that for anyone today to deny the doctrine of eternal marriage is to be in the camp of the Sadducees.

The chapter ends with a further encounter between Jesus and the Pharisees.[1] After he had properly rebuked them for their deliberate neglect and lack of spiritual understanding, "no man was able to answer him a word, neither durst any man from that day forth ask him any more questions" (Matthew 22:46).

Finding the Messiah Today

In closing this discussion, it is appropriate to ask: What do men and women in the twentieth century find when they discover the true Messiah?

Finding the Messiah is the greatest of all discoveries. If we were to cite the most important thing about Jesus the Messiah, what would it be? If we were to go home today to our family and say, "I have found the Messiah!" what would we say about him? What is the most important thing about him that we could tell another person? Would it be his height, his weight, the color of his hair, the style of his clothing, the tone of his voice? Everything about Jesus is important, and any true detail or concept would be worth knowing, but what would be the single most important thing to find out about him?

We take a clue from the scriptures. It is summarized thus: "For God so loved the world, that he gave his only begotten Son, that whosoever believeth in him should not perish, but have everlasting life" (John 3:16).

---

1. This subject is continued in chapter 16, "A Greater Portrayal of Jesus Christ."

While that one verse expresses the central concept, it takes considerable study and spiritual experience just to know what it means. I have discovered that the greatest message about Jesus Christ is that he has conquered death—both spiritual and physical death. He is literally the light and the life of the world (D&C 10:70). Because of the fall of Adam and our own sins, death holds all mankind captive. But as Paul declared, Christ "led captivity captive" (Ephesians 4:8); in other words, the great message of Jesus is that he has captured the captor—he alone has conquered death.

We are given a plain recitation of the redeeming role of the Savior in the following scriptures.

From Paul:

> For as in Adam all die, even so in Christ shall all be made alive (1 Corinthians 15:22).

From Jacob:

> Wherefore, it must needs be an infinite atonement—save it should be an infinite atonement this corruption could not put on incorruption. Wherefore, the first judgment which came upon man [these shalt surely die] must needs have remained to an endless duration. And if so, this flesh must have laid down to rot and to crumble to its mother earth, to rise no more.
>
> O the wisdom of God, his mercy and grace! For behold, if the flesh should rise no more our spirits must become subject to that angel who fell from before the presence of the Eternal God, and became the devil, to rise no more.
>
> And our spirits must have become like unto him, and we become devils, angels to a devil, to be shut out from the presence of our God, and to remain with the father of lies, in misery, like unto himself. (2 Nephi 9:7–9.)

And from Nephi:

> And my soul delighteth in proving unto my people that save Christ should come all men must perish (2 Nephi 11:6).

Jesus made a payment with his blood in order that mercy could satisfy justice. No other person, no human being, could redeem us; the redemption could only be made by a God, as explained by Amulek:

> For it is expedient that there should be a great and last sacrifice; yea, not a sacrifice of man, neither of beast, neither of any manner of fowl; for it shall not be a human sacrifice; but it must be an infinite and eternal sacrifice.
>
> Now there is not any man that can sacrifice his own blood which will atone for the sins of another. . . .
>
> . . . Therefore there can be nothing which is short of an infinite atonement which will suffice for the sins of the world.
>
> Therefore, it is expedient that there should be a great and last sacrifice. . . .
>
> . . . And that great and last sacrifice will be the Son of God, yea, infinite and eternal. (Alma 34:10–14.)

What does this mean to us? It means our association with the Messiah is not optional, nor casual. It is critical.

By the fall of Adam, all mankind must suffer two deaths—a spiritual separation from God, and a physical death. We have all suffered the first—the separation. We will yet, with no exceptions, suffer the physical death. We are thus dominated by death because of the fall of Adam. It is absolutely necessary to our faith that we understand that Jesus, in order to be the Messiah, had to be divine, that he had to be the literal, biological Son of God in the flesh; thus he was not dominated by death and sin as is the case with all the rest of mankind. Had Jesus Christ not been the Only Begotten in the flesh, he could not have been able or worthy to pay the debt of the fall of Adam and of our own individual sins. The infinite atonement required the life and the death and the sacrifice of a God, not of a man. Jesus taught this doctrine to the Jews as follows: "For as the Father hath life in himself; so hath he given to the Son to have life in himself; and hath given him authority to execute judgment also, because he is the Son of man" (John 5:26–27).

And also: "Therefore doth my Father love me, because I lay down my life, that I might take it again. No man taketh it from me, but I lay it down of myself. I have power to lay it down, and I have power to take it again. This commandment have I received of my Father." (John 10:17–18.)

Helaman referred to this when he said that Jesus Christ "hath power given unto him from the Father to redeem" mankind (Helaman 5:11).

The plan of salvation is real. Adam and Eve were living persons in time and in space. The Fall is absolutely historical, and if we had the details we could place on a calendar the time when Adam and Eve fell. Likewise, if we had the details, we could mark on a map the precise location where Adam and Eve ate the "forbidden" fruit.

In the very same manner, the atonement of Jesus Christ is vital and necessary in time and in space. If we had the facts, we could place on a calendar the date of his birth, the date of his suffering in the Garden of Gethsemane, the date of his death, and the date of his resurrection. In like manner we could mark on a map the places of his birth, his suffering, his death, and his resurrection. All these are active events in time, space, and geography. This is the Messiah I have found, and it is the greatest message in the world. It is the message of John 3:16 in its expanded form.

When that moment comes that any of us stands with perfection of body and spirit, resurrected, cleansed, and with eternal life in the presence of God the Father and his Son the Messiah, we will know then with full meaning what we perceive today only in part when we say, "I have found the Messiah!"

CHAPTER 12

Calling of the Twelve and the Seventy

To be properly called and ordained an Apostle of Jesus Christ is one of the greatest privileges and responsibilities that can come to a man. The Lord calls whom he will to represent him. An Apostle is a chosen vessel, a special witness for Jesus Christ, but because he is still a man he sometimes has to struggle with the circumstances of his own mortality. These strugglings sometimes show through in the scriptural account. The purpose of this chapter is to examine the greatness of the calling and the honor which the Lord placed upon twelve men; also, as much as possible, to gain an insight into the character and strength of the more prominent ones among them.

The word *apostle* comes from the Greek *stellos,* meaning "to send," and *apo,* meaning "away from." Thus *apostle* means "to send away from," or "one who is sent" as an ambassador or personal representative.

An Apostle of Jesus Christ is a special witness for Christ and is sent forth by him. Since the most important things about Christ are his divinity, his resurrection, and his redeeming power, his Apostles are special witnesses for these things about him. (Acts 1:8, 20–22, 3:13–15; 4:33; D&C 107:23.)

Four listings in the New Testament give the names of the Twelve as follows:

Matthew 10:2–4	*Mark 3:16–19*
1. Simon Peter and	1. Simon Peter and
2. Andrew his brother	2. James, and
3. James, son of Zebedee, and	3. John, and
4. John his brother	4. Andrew, and
5. Philip, and	5. Philip, and
6. Bartholomew	6. Bartholomew, and
7. Thomas, and	7. Matthew, and
8. Matthew, the publican	8. Thomas, and
9. James, son of Alphaeus, and	9. James, the son of Alphaeus, and
10. Lebbaeus (Thaddaeus)	10. Thaddaeus, and
11. Simon the Canaanite, and	11. Simon the Canaanite, and
12. Judas Iscariot, who betrayed him	12. Judas Iscariot, which betrayed him

Luke 6:14–16	*Acts 1:13*
1. Simon Peter and	1. Peter
2. Andrew	2. James
3. James, and	3. John
4. John	4. Andrew
5. Philip, and	5. Philip
6. Bartholomew	6. Thomas
7. Matthew, and	7. Bartholomew
8. Thomas	8. Matthew
9. James, son of Alphaeus, and	9. James, son of Alphaeus
10. Simon (called Zelotes)	10. Simon Zelotes
11. Judas the brother of James, and	11. Judas, brother of James
12. Judas Iscariot (the traitor)	

In addition to the above, most of the Twelve are named individually in the record of John in connection with some specific event, even though John does not give a group listing.

Certain things are noticeable from a comparison of the foregoing lists, and also from the writings of John. For example:

a. Peter is always mentioned first.
b. Although the first four names are not always in the same order, they are always numbered in the first four.

c. Philip is always listed fifth.
d. The list given in the books of Matthew and Luke more or less place the names in pairs: Peter and Andrew, James and John, and so forth.
e. James, the son of Alphaeus, is always listed ninth.
f. Judas Iscariot is always listed last.

There are three sets of brothers among the Twelve: Peter and Andrew; James and John; James, the less, and Judas (not Iscariot).

Some of the men were given alternate names:

a. Simon Peter is also known as Cephas—a stone (John 1:42). He is also called Simon Bar-jona, meaning, "Simon the son of Jona" (Matthew 16:17; John 21:15). *Jona* is equivalent to our *John*, and *bar* means "son of"; hence in the most literal sense the chief Apostle was named Peter son of John, or Peter Johnson.
b. James and John, the sons of Zebedee, are also known as the "Sons of Thunder" (Mark 3:17), which is probably due to their vigor in proclaiming the gospel. (Luke 9:54)
c. Thomas is called "Didymus," which means "twin" (John 11:16; 21:2). Who his twin is, we do not know.
d. Matthew is also known as Levi, the son of Alphaeus. (Mark 2:14; Matthew 9:9)
e. James, the son of Alphaeus, is also called "the less," probably to differentiate him from James the brother of John. (Mark 15:40)
f. Judas, the brother of James, is clearly differentiated from Judas Iscariot (John 14:22) and may be the same person who was also known as Thaddaeus.
g. Simon is called "the Canaanite" (Matthew 10:4; Mark 3:18) and also the Zealot (Luke 6:15). Instead of *Canaanite*, modern translations such as the New English Bible use *Cananaean*, which has a political overtone rather than a racial designation. This is in harmony with his title as a Zealot.
h. Bartholomew may be the same person as Nathanael. Although the record of John does not contain a listing of the Twelve, "Nathanael" is mentioned only by John (John

21:2), but John does not speak of Bartholomew. It is therefore concluded that Nathanael and Bartholomew are the same person. Bartholomew is not only a name but is also a designation that means "son of Tholomew." He was possibly "Nathanael, the son of Tholomew."

i. Philip is a Greek name, and perhaps it is significant that it was Philip who was approached by certain Greeks who wished to see Jesus (John 12:20–21). This does not mean he was of Greek lineage. All of the Twelve were from Galilee except Judas Iscariot, who was a Judean.

John and Andrew were disciples of John the Baptist before they met Jesus, and it was the Baptist who introduced them to Jesus (John 1:35–40). Perhaps several others of the Twelve were also followers of John the Baptist before they became disciples of Jesus. This seems to be implied by Peter's remarks at the time of the choosing of a man to fill the vacancy in the Twelve occasioned by Judas' death. Said Peter: "Wherefore of these men which have companied with us all the time that the Lord Jesus went in and out among us, beginning from the baptism of John, unto the same day that he [Jesus] was taken up from us, must one be ordained to be a witness with us of his resurrection (Acts 1:21–22). There can be little question that it was from John the Baptist that most if not all of the Twelve received their first lessons in the gospel.

In his book *Jesus the Christ* (pages 218–26) Elder James E. Talmage discusses the Twelve individually and gives informative insights. In addition to his observations, the following is offered concerning individual members of the Twelve.

Peter

The record of several events displays the strength of Peter's character. He was mortal, but he demonstrated qualities that made him a leader. Some examples follow:

Walking on the sea. When the brethren, far out from shore on the Sea of Galilee, saw Jesus walking toward them on the water, they thought it was a spirit and were afraid. When he counseled them "Be of good cheer; it is I," Peter said, "Lord if it be thou, bid me come unto thee on the water." When Jesus invited him to "come," Peter walked on the water for a distance. Then, becoming afraid of the wind and the waves, he began to sink and cried out "Lord, save me!" (Matthew 14:23–32.) It is perhaps characteristic that of those in the ship, only Peter asked for the privilege of walking on the water.

Peter rebukes the Master. When Jesus began to teach the disciples that the Son of Man must suffer and be killed, Peter began to rebuke him, saying, "Be it far from thee, Lord: this shall not be unto thee." But Jesus rebuked Peter in return: "Get thee behind me, Satan; thou art an offence unto me." (Matthew 16:21–23.) No doubt Peter meant well, and it seems rather severe treatment for the Lord to say such harsh words to Peter, but evidently Jesus knew that it was necessary to thus speak to the "man of rock" in order to persuade him from his position.

Washing of feet. In still another instance, Jesus found it necessary to persuade Peter. As Jesus was washing the feet of the Twelve, Peter said to him, "Thou shalt never wash my feet." Jesus replied, "If I wash thee not, thou hast no part with me." So effective was this rejoinder of Jesus' that Peter completely reversed his position and said, "Lord, not my feet only, but also my hands and my head." This was more than was actually necessary, since the Lord was performing at this time the sacred and meaningful ordinance of washing of feet. Therefore Jesus once again had to correct him, this time explaining that all that was necessary was for Jesus to wash Peter's feet. (See John 13:4–10.) It is reasonable to conclude that Peter's refusal to have Jesus wash his feet was prompted by his high regard for the Master, and he felt himself unworthy to have the Son of God perform such a menial task for him. However, when he perceived how important the matter was, he was entirely willing to do all that the Savior desired, and even more.

Peter and John

Peter and John shared many experiences in the ministry. It was these two whom Jesus sent into Jerusalem to prepare the

Passover (Luke 22:7–13), and it was they who went together to
the temple, where they healed the lame beggar at the gate
Beautiful (Acts 3:1–11). It was Peter and John who were cast
into prison overnight together, and who testified to the high
priests and elders of the Jews about the resurrection of Christ
(Acts 4:1–23). And it was Peter and John who went down to
Samaria to bestow the Holy Ghost upon those whom Philip had
baptized (Acts 8:14–17).

Although Peter is thought of as impetuous and quick to act,
John is not so vividly characterized in the scriptures. John frequently veils his own identity by referring to himself as "that
other disciple" (John 20:2–8), or as "the disciple whom Jesus
loved" (John 13:23; 19:26; 20:2). For this reason he is often called
"John the Beloved" in religious literature.

There are yet two instances of record in which Peter and
John are linked, and which are instructive as to their personali-
ties and character:

Peter and John at the tomb of Jesus. When Mary Magdalene
told Peter and John that Jesus' body was not in the tomb, they
both ran to it. John outran Peter and arrived first, but did not
enter—he stooped down and looked into the place where the
body had been. When Peter arrived he went immediately in-
side, followed afterward by John (John 20:1–10).

It is possible that John was much younger than Peter and
therefore was able to run faster. Peter's nature again seems
manifest wherein he entered the sepulchre immediately,
whereas John stopped at the entrance and went in after Peter. It
may also be that John was showing deference to Peter as the se-
nior member of the Twelve, yet it seems that he did not hesitate
to outrun Peter.

Jesus (resurrected) appears by the seaside. Seven of the disciples
had fished all night but caught nothing. In the morning Jesus
stood on the shore and instructed them to cast the net on the
right side of the ship. The disciples did not know it was Jesus
who spoke to them. When they did as they were told, the net became full of fish. At this juncture it was John, first of all, who
perceived that it was Jesus who stood on the shore, and he so informed Peter. When Peter learned it was Jesus, he jumped out of
the ship, apparently to get to the shore as soon as possible. The

others seemed content to row to shore (about three hundred feet). Peter himself then drew the net to the land (John 21:1–12).

John's spirituality is evidenced by his being the first to perceive the identity of Jesus, but Peter's dominant characteristic is seen in his scramble to get to shore to see Jesus.

There is much to be admired about Peter, and it becomes evident why the Lord changed his name from Simon to Peter—a man of rock—and selected him as the chief Apostle.

John

John is mentioned by name in prophecy nearly six hundred years B.C. (1 Nephi 14:18–27). Nephi knew that one of the Twelve would be a writer, a visionary man, and would be named John. His writings were to be in the record of the Twelve Apostles. He is the only one of the Twelve that is mentioned in the Book of Mormon by name. The Book of Mormon also explains that John's earth life would be prolonged, and he would not taste of death (3 Nephi 28:1–9). (Ether 4:16 contains an additional mention of John.)

Revelations in the Doctrine and Covenants also refer to John and his writings (D&C 7:1–8; 88:139–41; 93:6–16). Another reference has John cursing the waters in the last days (D&C 61:14), but little is known of this subject.

Matthew

Matthew has been the subject of much discussion by biblical scholars. Many do not feel that Matthew Levi, the Jewish apostle, could have written "The Gospel According to Saint Matthew," or as we have identified it, The Testimony of St. Matthew. However, there are several characteristics about the book of Matthew that seem to reflect the character and training of Matthew the Apostle and would help establish his authorship.

He was a publican, a tax collector, and therefore would be skilled in writing and record-keeping. His record has the greatest number of long discourses by the Savior. He was possibly the secretary among the Twelve. There are more references to money, tax collectors, and particularly large sums of money in the book of Matthew than in the other records. The parable of the talents would be especially attractive to him. He alone mentions the circumstance of Jesus paying tribute to the tax collectors of Capernaum (Matthew 17:24–27).

The Time When the Twelve Were Called

There appears to be confusion and even contradiction in the records as to when the Twelve were called. Luke places the calling earlier than does Matthew. In Luke it is recorded that the Savior went "into the mountain" and prayed all night. The next day he called to him his disciples and of them chose twelve whom he named Apostles (Luke 6:12–13). Jesus then came down from the mountain with the Twelve, and preached to a multitude on the plain (Luke 6:17). The content of this sermon is similar in some ways to the so-called Sermon on the Mount of Matthew 5–7.

In Matthew's record the Twelve are not mentioned until chapter 10, when they are being sent on missions. This is some time after the instruction of the Sermon on the Mount. The difference between these two accounts may be more apparent than real. Perhaps Luke's report is the call, while Matthew's report is their missionary departure. Luke 9:1–2 also reports sending forth of the Twelve on a mission tour, suggesting that there was a space of time between their call and their mission tour.

A reasonable reconstruction of the events as outlined in these records is that Jesus called and ordained the Twelve on a mountain; then gave them instructions (commonly called the Sermon on the Mount); then came down from the mount and taught a multitude on the plain (commonly called the Sermon on the Plain). A few weeks later Jesus arranged the Twelve into six pairs and sent them forth on missions. Matthew's record in chapter 10 is clearly of the mission tour.

The original call of the Twelve occurred about a year into Jesus' ministry. The mission tours were apparently quite short, but did not begin until several weeks after their apostolic call.

The records are so sketchy that it is impossible to pinpoint the precise time, but the sequence of events is discernible. Often the record seems to give the impression that men were called "off the street," with little or no preparation, into the apostleship. Surely the sacredness of the calling requires that they had a period of training and testing as disciples before being called to the Twelve. For their own good, the Twelve, called to full-time service, would profit from additional preparation with the Savior before being sent on missions. The pattern given in 3 Nephi, wherein the Lord called the Twelve, then instructed them with a sermon similar to Matthew 5–7, would seem to be a clue to the way it was done in Palestine (3 Nephi 11–15). Likewise the modus operandi used in our present dispensation, in which those to be called to the original Twelve were tested and given experience before the call, gives us an understanding for the sequence of events as Jesus selected the Twelve, ordained them, and sent them forth.

The Seventy

Not as much is known about the calling of the Seventy in New Testament times. No individuals are identified as belonging to that group, but it is known that Jesus called and sent them forth on missions with a calling similar but subordinate to that of the Twelve. Luke's record is the only account we have of them, and its wording "other seventy" suggests that perhaps Jesus sent forth at least two groups of Seventy (Luke 10:1). They returned from their missions bursting with enthusiasm over their experiences (Luke 10:17).

The Seventy appear to have been appointed as "forerunners" of Jesus, for Luke specifies that the Seventy went forth "two and two before his face into every city and place, whither he himself would come" (Luke 10:1).

Since Luke was not one of the original Twelve, and since he alone mentions the Seventy, one wonders whether later he was one of them. JST labels him a "messenger of Jesus Christ" (JST Luke 1:1). We note that the modern Seventy are "to be especial witnesses . . . in all the world" (D&C 107:25).

CHAPTER 13

Jesus Instructs the Twelve

About a year after Jesus' baptism, and soon after he had called and ordained the Twelve, Jesus gave extended instruction to his disciples about their ministerial duties and also their personal conduct. The most complete account of this is recorded in Matthew chapters 5–7. Shorter, similar portions appear in Luke and Mark, but no such setting is mentioned in John. These instructions from the Lord constitute one of the most important discourses recorded in the entire Bible.

The Setting

The popular title given to this discourse is the Sermon on the Mount, because it was delivered on a mount in Galilee. Jesus is usually displayed by artists as standing on the top of a hill of considerable size, his arms outstretched, with multitudes of people situated on the hill. The image is thus created that the audience was large and the Savior stood and preached a public discourse to them.

A close look at the scriptures gives a somewhat different perspective. Matthew 4:23–25 states that as a result of his miracles Jesus became very popular and "great multitudes of people" followed him. Matthew 5:1–2 says that "seeing the multitudes, he went up into a mountain," and his disciples came to him, "and [he] taught them." As used here the word *them* can only reasonably refer to the disciples, not to the multitudes. Furthermore, JST Matthew 5:1 gives us the additional information that when "he was set down" his disciples came and he taught them. These passages give us two important facts that cannot be overlooked if one wishes to understand the Savior's teachings on this occasion. First, his audience was those who were already disciples, not the multitude; and second, he was sitting down. This suggests a smaller audience.

The concept of sitting to speak is well established in the Bible. The practice in the synagogue was that one would stand to read the scripture and then sit down to discuss it. Today the custom is different—we suppose a person is through when he leaves the pulpit and sits, but in Bible times it was not so. The custom of standing out of respect for the scripture seems to have begun at least by the time of Ezra (around 520 B.C.) when he read to the congregation and "all the people stood up" (Nehemiah 8:1–5). Further, when Jesus visited the synagogue in Nazareth (Luke 4:16–22) he "stood up for to read" aloud from the words of Isaiah. After the reading "he closed the book . . . and sat down. And the eyes of all them that were in the synagogue were fastened on him. And he began to say unto them, This day is this scripture fulfilled in your ears. And all bare him witness and wondered at the gracious words which proceeded out of his mouth." (Luke 4:16, 20–22.) The fact that the congregation looked at him so intently after he sat down shows that they expected him to speak after sitting, which he did.

The record shows that Jesus "went into a ship, and sat; . . . and he spake many things unto [the multitude] in parables." In the temple too he "sat down, and taught" the people (John 8:2).

Instead of being surprised to learn that Jesus sat down to instruct the disciples in the "Sermon" on the Mount, we should be startled if he did it in any other way. We note, though, that Webster's *New International Unabridged Dictionary* defines the word *sermon* as a formal religious, public discourse. If that is the case, strictly speaking we are incorrect in calling the Savior's private instruction to a few disciples the Sermon on the Mount. Perhaps Jesus' Instructions to the Twelve would be appropriate.

One might ask, what difference does it make? Why should we care whether the event involved the Twelve only, or thousands? One reason why we should care is simply to have it right. Another reason would be the understanding of what Jesus said. If he were speaking to a select group he might say something that would not appropriately be said to the unbelieving world (Alma 12:9–11).

Jesus said on this occasion, "Ye are the salt of the earth" (Matthew 5:13). Unless the whole world is salt, he must have been addressing a special assembly. In a revelation to the Prophet Joseph Smith the Lord explained the meaning of this phrase: "When men are called unto mine everlasting gospel, and covenant with an everlasting covenant, they are accounted as the salt of the earth and the savor of men; they are called to be the savor of men; therefore, if that salt of the earth lose its savor, behold, it is thenceforth good for nothing only to be cast out and trodden under the feet of men" (D&C 101:39–40). The information in this passage suggests that those to whom Jesus spoke on the Mount were chosen disciples who had already received at least the first principles of the gospel.

We have evidence too from the many items to be found in the Prophet Joseph's inspired restoration of Matthew 5–7, coupled with what we discern from the Book of Mormon. From these sources it is clear beyond any reasonable question that the sermon recorded in Matthew 5–7 was a private meeting, and it would be a gross misapplication of the situation and of the message to think of it as a public discourse. Of course, the moral directives are applicable to all people, but the doctrinal content can be correctly understood only in its natural original setting. To take these things out of their context is to imagine a sermon that did not actually occur.

Specific Instructions to Disciples

Some of the directives in the Savior's instructions are not applicable to the world in general. For example, Jesus said:

"Take no thought for your life, what ye shall eat, or what ye shall drink; nor yet for your body, what you shall put on. . . . Take therefore no thought for the morrow: for the morrow shall take thought for the things of itself." (Matthew 6:25, 34.)

Some readers of the New Testament think they note an impractical attitude in Jesus' teachings and cite the foregoing quotation as an example. They feel that Jesus' teachings are not applicable to our modern world. When it is understood, however, that the instruction was given to certain disciples only, it is seen that this particular injunction does not apply to the masses of mankind, or even to the general membership within the Church. This interpretation is borne out by the sermon in 3 Nephi, which is similar to the one delivered in Galilee.

In the 3 Nephi account Jesus was speaking to a combined group of a multitude of Church members that included twelve special disciples. At a particular point in the sermon he turned from the multitude and addressed himself to the twelve disciples only. This passage from the Book of Mormon is as follows: "And now it came to pass that when Jesus had spoken these words he looked upon the twelve whom he had chosen, and said unto them: Remember the words which I have spoken. For behold, ye are they whom I have chosen to minister unto this people. Therefore I say unto you, take no thought for your life, what ye shall eat, or what ye shall drink. . . . Take therefore no thought for the morrow, for the morrow shall take thought for the things of itself" (3 Nephi 13:25, 34).

Having thus directed these particular words to the Nephite Twelve, Jesus "turned again to the multitude, and did open his mouth unto them again" (3 Nephi 14:1).

It is enlightening and informative that the Savior said these particular words (which are the same as those of Matthew 6:25, 34) to the twelve disciples only and not to the whole Church or to the world, and it gives us a better understanding of the biblical record on this point. Although such specific procedural instructions were for the Twelve only, the moral principles given by the Lord are applicable to all people.

There are other evidences within the discourse itself that reveal the true setting of the biblical account. One of these is found in Matthew 5:14, in which Jesus tells his audience, "ye are the light of the world." He evidently was not addressing the world or he would not have said this group was the light. His words make a distinction between his listeners and the world. Another evidence is found in a comparison of the Lord's Prayer as in the Nephite record with that in the biblical record. To the Galilean disciples he said they should pray, "Give us this day our daily bread" (Matthew 6:11), or in other words, "Give us each day our bread for the day." This request does not occur in the Nephite account. Each of us realizes that even after we are members of the Church we must still maintain employment and earn a living in some way. Therefore, to the 2,500 persons in the Nephite multitude it would have been out of focus for Jesus to teach them to pray for their daily bread in the same way that the twelve special witnesses in Galilee were taught to pray for bread. The Twelve were to forsake their fishing nets and their tax booths or other sources of normal secular income, whereas other members of the Church must maintain their own employment and livelihood. Therefore Jesus did not instruct the multitude to pray for daily sustenance in the same way that the Twelve were to do.

Some Major Concepts in the Galilean Discourse

Matthew Chapter 5. At the beginning of the discourse the King James Version lists nine statements, each beginning with the word *blessed* (Matthew 5:3–11). These have come to be known as "beatitudes," because of the word *blessed*, meaning a happy or fortunate condition. In the biblical record as it has come to us, each *"Blessed"* statement forms a new sentence, and each seems independent of the others. But an analysis of the contents shows three general categories. The first four beatitudes and the sixth deal with how a person feels within and about himself: those who are poor in spirit, who mourn, who are meek, who hunger and thirst after righteousness, and who are pure in heart. Two of the remaining beatitudes deal with one's treatment of others: the merciful, and the peacemakers. The additional two remaining beatitudes pertain to the way one reacts to mistreatment by others: they who are persecuted for righteousness' sake, and those who are falsely reviled and evilly spoken of.

These nine beatitudes seem interesting enough and adequate until they are compared with the corresponding passages in the Book of Mormon and also the Joseph Smith Translation. We will cite the JST here because it pertains particularly to the biblical record, and is in reality the biblical meeting revisited.

Whereas, as noted above, the KJV account had three distinct categories of beatitudes, the JST clearly has four. It not only retains the three already referred to but introduces another: man's relationship to God. This is properly placed at the beginning of the list and consists of those beatitudes dealing with faith in God, repentance, baptism in water, remission of sins, and reception of the Holy Ghost. In addition to these very spiritual things, it says one must accept the Lord's special representatives as his personal agents (JST Matthew 5:1–4). Further, the statement, "blessed are the poor in spirit" is enlarged by the words "who come unto me." All of these improvements have the effect of placing man's relationship to God first. Furthermore, in the JST the word *and* occurs at the beginning of each of the beatitudes, giving the impression they are in a series rather than simply a collection of separate unrelated statements.

Viewing the beatitudes in this manner enables us to see a pattern that might otherwise have escaped our attention. We might think the Ten Commandments and the Articles of Faith consist of independent statements, but there is a consistent pattern to these also. When the Pharisees asked Jesus which was the great commandment in the law, he answered that it was to love the Lord with all one's heart, soul, and mind. The second was like unto it, to love one's neighbor as oneself. (Matthew 22: 34–40.) A quick observation shows this to be precisely the arrangement of the Ten Commandments, and also of the Articles of Faith. Those items that have to do with Deity are listed first.

When we then examine the beatitudes as they have been "preserved" in the KJV we see immediately that something very important is missing. The important category of one's relationship to God—involving faith, repentance, baptism, remission of sins, and reception of the Holy Ghost—is simply not there in the KJV. The biblical beatitudes look reasonably good until compared with a complete list, and then they are seen to be lacking in the most important category. It is significant that in supplying the missing beatitudes the Prophet Joseph Smith placed them at the beginning rather than any other place, and hence preserved the pattern. The restoration of these missing beatitudes is not simply a matter of emphasis or clarity; they represent the most significant category and are an example of the "plain and precious things" Nephi said were missing from the Bible (1 Nephi 13:26–29).

Pluck Out Thy Right Eye; Cut Off Thy Right Hand (Matthew 5: 29–30). The command to pluck out one's offending right eye or to cut off one's offending right hand is hard doctrine. The JST explains that these are figurative statements concerning one's sins (JST Matthew 5:30–34). That is, if an eye or a hand causes you to commit sin, you would be better off without it. The figurative nature of these statements is expanded in JST Mark 9:40–44 with the eye and the hand (and a foot) representing those persons to whom we look for direction and leadership. If friends lead us astray, we had best sever our relationship with them. Hence the emphasis on the right eye and right hand, since those represent strength, whereas in the ancient culture the left hand is sinister and unclean. The explanation of this figurative command concerning parts of the body is a very practical and useful contribution of the JST.

Matthew Chapter 6. The JST introduces this chapter with a clear statement that Jesus was teaching these things to his disciples (JST Matthew 6:1). The corrections to the Lord's Prayer having to do with daily bread have already been discussed in this chapter. The plea, "Lead us not into temptation" is reworded in the JST to read: "Suffer us not to be led into temptation." This is an improved way of petitioning the Lord for protection, since surely he leads no one into temptation. This correction is consistent with a correction to Isaiah 63:17, which in the KJV asks the Lord why he has "made us to err" and has "hardened our heart." The JST for these passages does not put the blame on the Lord, but asks only why the Lord allowed his people to go astray.

Returning now to the Lord's instruction in the book of Matthew we find further evidence from the JST that this was a missionary preparation meeting containing instruction to the Twelve as to their ministry: "And, again, I say unto you, go ye into the world, and care not for the world; for the world will hate you, and will persecute you, and will turn you out of their synagogues. Nevertheless, ye shall go forth from house to house, teaching the people; and I will go before you. And your heavenly Father will provide for you, whatsoever things ye need for food, what you shall eat; and for raiment, what ye shall wear or put on." (JST Matthew 6:25–27.)

Seek Ye First the Kingdom of God (Matthew 6:33). This well-known passage receives some important clarification in the JST, showing that it is not enough just to find the kingdom; we must strengthen it, and build it up, bring it forth, and establish it more firmly. It is not enough for disciples to simply be joiners; they must be developers. (See also JST Luke 12:34.)

Matthew Chapter 7. We have carefully established the fact that this discourse by the Savior was given to disciples only and consisted largely of missionary-type instruction. Matthew chapters 5 and 6 deal primarily with personal behavior and preparation of the disciples. Chapter 7 takes on a slightly different character. Whereas the two earlier chapters were teachings to the Twelve, chapter 7 consists primarily of information which they are to give to the people. They are to go among them and teach them how to judge properly, and to have confidence in prayer. They are to teach repentance, and not give the pearls of the gospel (the mysteries) to the people who are not ready for them. Furthermore the KJV would lead the reader to think Jesus called his disciples hypocrites (Matthew 7:5); whereas the JST shows that the disciples were to go among the people, especially among the scribes, Pharisees, priests, and Levites, and tell them that they were hypocrites.

Chapter 7 as given in the JST strongly reinforces the private nature of the discourse and shows clearly that Jesus was preparing his disciples (chiefly the Twelve and perhaps those who would become the Seventy) for their ministry. In this regard the JST adds yet another interesting, even dramatic, episode to the occasion. When Jesus told his disciples the strong words he wanted them to use with the Jewish religious leaders, they reacted fearfully, and protested to him their reluctance to face the people in that manner. They expressed their feeling of inadequacy to debate with the learned priests and scribes. Jesus then told them what to say, and how to say it. He told the Twelve that the Jewish priests lacked faith in God and thus also in prayer. He said the disciples were to teach the Jewish leaders how to have faith in prayer, and to tell them that God would hear and answer their prayers. None of this exchange is even hinted at in the KJV. The JST presents a dialogue of Jesus and his disciples—an aside—almost an interruption to the discourse or at best a question/answer dimension totally unknown in any other Bible. Jesus warned his disciples not to try to teach the people the mysteries until the people had first developed faith and prayer. That concept in chapter 7 is a major contribution of the JST. It is slightly evident in the KJV, but is brilliantly demonstrated in the JST. This passage in the JST is so important to the proper understanding of what Jesus said, that it is included here for easy access:

> And Jesus said unto his disciples, Beholdest thou the Scribes, and the Pharisees, and the Priests, and the Levites? They teach in their synagogues, but do not observe the law, nor the commandments; and all have gone out of the way, and are under sin.
>
> Go thou and say unto them, Why teach ye men the law and the commandments, when ye yourselves are the children of corruption?
>
> Say unto them, Ye hypocrites, first cast out the beam out of thine own eye; and then shalt thou see clearly to cast out the mote out of thy brother's eye.
>
> Go ye into the world, saying unto all, Repent, for the kingdom of heaven has come nigh unto you.
>
> And the mysteries of the kingdom ye shall keep within yourselves; for it is not meet to give that which is holy unto the dogs; neither cast ye your pearls unto swine, lest they trample them under their feet.
>
> For the world cannot receive that which ye, yourselves, are not able to bear; wherefore ye shall not give your pearls unto them, lest they turn again and rend you.
>
> Say unto them, Ask of God; ask, and it shall be given you; seek, and ye shall find; knock, and it shall be opened unto you.
>
> For everyone that asketh, receiveth; and he that seeketh, findeth; and unto him that knocketh, it shall be opened.

And then said his disciples unto him, They will say unto us, We ourselves are righteous, and need not that any man should teach us. God, we know, heard Moses and some of the prophets; but us he will not hear.

And they will say, We have the law for our salvation, and that is sufficient for us.

Then Jesus answered, and said unto his disciples, Thus shall ye say unto them,

What man among you, having a son, and he shall be standing out, and shall say, Father, open thy house that I may come in and sup with thee, will not say, Come in, my son; for mine is thine, and thine is mine?

Or what man is there among you, who, if his son ask bread, will give him a stone?

Or if he ask a fish, will he give him a serpent?

If ye then, being evil, know how to give good gifts unto your children, how much more shall your Father who is in heaven give good things to them that ask him? (JST Matthew 7:6–20.)

Sermon on the Mount and the Sermon on the Plain

In his sixth chapter Luke records an event similar to the "Sermon on the Mount" but places it on the plain after Jesus had come down from the mountain, having just ordained the Twelve (Luke 6:10–17). There is a question whether these are two different sermons or two accounts of one sermon. It has been noted that Matthew's account is to disciples only, whereas Luke's account seems to include a multitude as well as the disciples (see Luke 6:17–20). It is possible that Jesus gave instructions on the mount to the Twelve and then came down with the Twelve and delivered portions to the multitude on the plain. The specific instruction that was given only to the disciples about not having a preoccupation with food and clothing (as in Matthew 6:25, 34, noted earlier), and the references to the "salt of the earth" and the "light of the world" are not found in Luke's account, which would be proper if the Sermon on the Plain was directed to the multitude generally and not to the Twelve specifically. Although the Twelve were present, there would be no need to repeat that which he had spoken specifically to them on the mount a few hours before.

CHAPTER 14

The Miracles of Jesus

This chapter is a study of the miracles performed by Jesus during his ministry as recorded in the books of Matthew, Mark, Luke, and John. A miracle as dealt with here is defined as a divinely performed act beyond the common order of nature that man cannot accomplish by himself.

Many events inherently miraculous in the life of Jesus are not dealt with in this chapter. This includes such things as Jesus' ability to read men's thoughts, the ministry of angels, the transfiguration, Jesus' resurrection from the dead, and his ascension.

The purposes of the accompanying charts are as follows:

Chart 1: To illustrate the range of Jesus' miraculous works.

Chart 2: To illustrate the proximity of Jesus to the action. It is not always clearly stated just how Jesus went about the healing or miraculous process. In some instances it is plainly stated that he had physical contact by the laying on of hands (Mark 6:5–6), or the touch of a finger (Mark 7:32–37), and so forth. In other cases he was near enough to touch but no direct mention is made of it (Luke 6:6–11). Another category consists of miraculous events for which Jesus was responsible but which took place at such a distance as to make physical contact impossible.

What Jesus Said About His Miracles

Jesus regarded his miracles as part of the evidence of his divine calling. For example, he said, "I cast out devils by the Spirit of God" (Matthew 12:28). Also: "I with the finger of God cast out devils" (Luke 11:20). He also reminded the disciples of the miracles of feeding the five thousand and the four thousand which he had earlier performed, saying, "Do ye not yet understand, neither remember" these things? (Matthew 16:9–10).

Jesus said he had "done among them the works which none other man did" (evidently referring to his miracles) (John 3:2; 7:31; 10:32–37; 15:24).

When the messengers from John the Baptist came to Jesus, asking if he was the one they were to "look for," he replied, "The blind see, the lame walk, the lepers are cleansed, the deaf hear, the dead are raised." (Luke 7:20–22).

Probably the most spectacular miracles of Jesus were his raising the dead. Walking on the water would also be quite attention-getting. The casting out of devils is probably the least understood, because we do not know the laws that govern the spirit realm.

Characteristics of Jesus' Miracles

Certain characteristics are seen in Jesus' miracles. His supernormal power was not used for curiosity or to gratify lust, as evidenced in his refusal to give a "sign" (Matthew 16:1–4), or to turn stones into bread when he was hungry (Matthew 4:3–4).

His miracles were always harmonious with the purpose of his whole life and character. They were generally of the kind that showed compassionate service to the afflicted, but never strange, bizarre, or clownish things.

Miracles are denied by many today as being unscientific. But that is because as mortals we do not know exactly how miracles operate. A gospel miracle is no doubt a spiritual law overriding a temporal law. Consider what the gospel of Jesus Christ would be without any miraculous content! We cannot conceive of Jesus

CHART 1

A Classification of Miracles According to Kind

Healings

Diseases	Physical Imperfections	Caused by Evil Spirits
Palsy	Blindness	Matt. 12:22 (Blind and dumb)
Issue of blood	Withered hand	Matt. 9:32–34 (Dumb)
Fever	Impotent man (John 5:1–9)	Matt. 15:22–28; Mark 9: 25–27
Leprosy	Malchus's ear	
	Dumbness	
See also	Dropsy	
Matt. 4:23	Speech impediment	
Matt. 14:14	(string of his tongue	
Mark 6:5	loosed) Mark 7:32–37	
Luke 9:11		
John 6:2		
Mark 1:32–34		
Many touched hem of garment (Matt. 14:35–36; Mark 6: 55–56.)		
Matt. 15:29–31		

Miracles of Nature

Calming a storm	Walking on water
Turning water into wine	Feeding 5,000
Feeding 4,000	Money in fish's mouth
Great haul of fishes	Draught of fishes
Cursing of fig tree	

Raised from Dead

Jairus's daughter
Son of widow of Nain
Lazarus

Unclassified

Passing through crowd unseen
Forgiving sins (healing the soul, as well as the body)
Reading men's thoughts (looking into the secret recesses of another's mind) Luke 5:17–26; Mark 2:1–12; Matt. 9:2–8; Luke 6:8; Luke 11:17
Resurrection from the dead

CHART 2

A Classification of Miracles According to Jesus' Proximity to the Action

Miracles in Which Direct Physical Contact Is So Stated	Miracles in Which Direct Physical Contact Is Possible but Is not Expressly So Stated	Miracles at a Distance Precluding Jesus' Physical Contact
1. Peter's mother-in-law healed of a fever. (Matt. 8:14–15; Mark 1:30–31; Luke 4.)	1. Water into wine. (John 2:1–11.)	1. Greek woman's daughter healed. (Matt. 15:22–28; Mark 7:25–30.)
2. A leper healed. (Matt. 8:1–4.)	2. Passing unseen through a crowd. (Luke 4:28–30. See also John 8:59.)	2. Money in fish's mouth. (Matt. 17:24–27.)
3. Two blind men healed. (Matt. 9:27–31.)	3. Draught of fishes. (Luke 5:1–11.)	3. Great haul of fishes. (John 21:1–8.)
4. Deafness and speech impediment healed. (Mark 7:32–37.)	4. An unclean spirit cast out. (Mark 1:21–28; Luke 4:31–37.)	4. Calming the storm. (Matt. 8:23–27; Mark 4:35–41; Luke 8:22–25.)
5. Blindness healed. (Mark 8:22–26.)	5. Palsy healed. (Matt. 9:2–8.)	5. Healing the Nobleman's son. (John 4:46–54.)
6. A demoniac child healed. (Matt. 17:14–21; Mark 9:14–29; Luke 9:37–43.)	6. Healing at pool of Bethesda. (John 5:1–9.)	6. Healing centurion's servant of palsy. (Matt. 8:5–13; Luke 7:1–10.)
7. Woman healed of issue of blood. (Compare Matt. 9:20–22; Mark 5:25–34; Luke 8:43–48.)	7. Withered hand healed. (Luke 6:6–11.)	
8. Jairus's daughter raised. (Matt. 9:18–25; Mark 5:38–42; Luke 8:35–42.)	8. One blind and dumb healed. (Matt. 12:22–23.)	
9. Walking on the sea. (Matt. 14:25–33; Mark 6:47–51; John 6:16–21.)	9. Restoring life to widow's son at Nain. (Luke 7:11–17.)	
10. Healing of man born blind. (John 9:1–7.)	10. Casting devils out of Gadarene demoniac. (Matt. 8:28–34; Mark 5:1–20; Luke 8:6–29.)	
11. Healing of woman with infirmity of 18 years. (Luke 13:10–13.)	11. Casting out a devil. (Luke 11:14.)	
12. Blind man healed. (Matt. 9:27–31; 20:29–34.)	12. Man with dropsy healed. (Luke 14:1–6.)	
13. Feeding five thousand. (Matt. 14:14–21; Mark 6:33–44; Luke 9:11–17; John 6:1–14.)	13. Lazarus raised from the dead. (John 11:43–44.)	
14. Feeding four thousand. (Matt. 15:29–38; Mark 8:1–9.)	14. Ten lepers healed. (Luke 17:11–19.)	
15. Malchus's ear healed. (Luke 22:50–51.)	15. Blind Bartimaeus healed. (Mark 10:46–52; Luke 18:35–43.)	
See also Mark 3:9–10	16. Withering curse on the fig tree. (Matt. 21:18–19; Mark 11:12–14, 20.)	
	See also Matt. 8:16; Mark 1:32–34	

as a teacher of ethics only! He claimed to work miracles. If he did not do so, then he cannot even be considered a great ethical teacher, but rather as one who misled the people. Jesus' miracles are a major part of his ministry. Without miracles the gospel has no saving power and is simply a philosophy. Without miracles there is no salvation, because man is fallen, unable to save himself, and must be rescued or redeemed by some person having greater power than mankind naturally has.

It is also evident that where faith was lacking the greater miracles could not be manifest. At Nazareth he could "do no mighty work, save that he laid his hands upon a few sick folk, and healed them. And he marvelled because of their unbelief." (Mark 6:5–6.)

Jesus said that he was able to perform greater miracles among the Nephites than among the Jews because the Nephites had greater faith than the Jews (3 Nephi 19:35–36).

Jesus' Methods of Treating Illness

1. *Jesus did not employ medicines.* The scriptures do not record any instances of Jesus using medicines, not even juices of herbs or grasses.

2. *The use of materials.* Jesus made use of spittle in healing (Mark 7:33; 8:23); and also of clay made with spittle (John 9:6); and probably oil. It is nowhere stated that Jesus used oil in healing, but the disciples did (Mark 6:13; James 5:14–15), under his direction. He told the man born blind to wash in the pool (John 9:7) in addition to his eyes having been anointed with clay, and until he did so the miracle did not happen.

3. *Touching and laying on of hands.* Jesus touched a leper (Matthew 8:3), the hand of Peter's mother-in-law (Matthew 8:15), the eyes of blind men (Matthew 9:29; 20:34), the tongue of the deaf and dumb man (Mark 7:33), and the servant's ear (Luke 22:51). He put his fingers in the ears of the deaf man (Mark 7:33).

Also, at times Jesus was physically touched by the person being healed (Mark 3:10; 6:56; Luke 6:19; Matthew 9:20; Mark 14:36).

The laying on of hands was sometimes emphatically stated (Mark 6:5–6; Matthew 9:18; Luke 4:40).

Jesus often touched the eyes, ears, or tongues of an afflicted person in the process of healing, when the problem seems to have been organic. But when the impediment was caused by an evil spirit, touching the afflicted part does not seem to have been done (Matthew 9:32–34; Mark 7:32–37).

4. *Healed by the word*. It is occasionally stated that Jesus cured by the "word," and although he often was near enough to touch the afflicted person, it is not always expressly stated that he touched (see Chart 2).

Some healings were so far distant from Jesus' person that no physical contact was possible (see Chart 2). These were done by his word only.

5. *Permanency*. There is no record of Jesus' experiencing a failure, nor any instance of a healing being temporary. All cures were immediate, complete, and permanent.

Speaking Directly to the Elements

Scripture says that Jesus directly commanded the elements, or the person involved, rather than asking the Father to perform the act. Jesus likewise spoke directly to the evil spirits, commanding them to "come out" (Mark 1:25). He said that with faith one may "say unto this mountain, Remove hence . . . and it shall remove" (Matthew 17:20). He "rebuked the wind and said unto the sea, Peace be still" (Mark 4:39).

In the minds of some rationalists there is a question whether Jesus actually spoke to the elements or whether the words were really intended for the ear of the disciples. They feel that words are meaningless to inanimate objects, and that if they were intended for the disciples it was a deception to pretend to command the elements.

In latter-day revelation, however, matter and element are spoken of as though they have intelligence, as in Doctrine and Covenants 88:25–26. The Nephite prophets considered it proper to speak directly to the elements. This principle is itemized with specific references later in this chapter, under the heading: "Confirmatory Accounts and Evidences in the Book of Mormon."

A Key for Understanding the Purpose of Each Miracle

The Prophet Joseph Smith explained: "I have a key by which I understand the scriptures. I enquire, what was the question which drew out the answer. . . . To ascertain its meaning we must dig up the root and ascertain what it was that drew the saying out of Jesus." (TPJS, 276–77.) Although this was said in relation to parables, its application would be useful in understanding the miracles also. Since there are several different kinds of miracles, it follows that there would be more than one purpose involved at different times. For example:

1. To prove the Savior's divine mission and power so that the Jews would believe in him, and so that those who believed would be strengthened (John 2:11; 3:21; 4:53; 11:47–48; 14:10–11; Matthew 9:5; 11:2–6).

2. To exercise his compassion and kindness, especially in healing the sick (Matthew 9:35; Luke 7:13–15).

3. To cause men to realize their own spiritual weakness and to raise their thoughts above the natural events of mortal life (Mark 2:1–11; Matthew 4:19; 21:18–21).

4. To prevent men in their ignorance or wickedness from frustrating the purposes of God (Luke 4:28–30; John 8:59). This may have a connection with Jesus' frequent comment that his "time had not yet come." That is, they could not kill him or silence him before his work was done and the time to die had arrived.

How Many Miracles?

It is impossible to say how many miracles were performed by Jesus, since the writers did not list each miracle separately, often simply stating that on occasion Jesus cured "all manner of sickness," and so forth (Matthew 4:23–24; 12:15; Mark 1:32–34). One thing is certain: Jesus performed a great many visible miracles, and the people knew it.

Contributions of the Joseph Smith Translation

The JST confirms the supernatural events known as miracles. While not contributing any new miraculous events to the ministry of Jesus, it supplements and confirms the KJV record. Its corrections emphasize and substantiate every miraculous event the KJV records. Most of the changes regarding the miracles performed by Jesus serve to clarify ambiguous passages but do not alter the sense nor the fact of the miracles themselves. The JST particularly emphasizes that evil spirits are real and afflict mankind, and may be cast out by the power of God.

Confirmatory Accounts in the Book of Mormon

During Jesus' mission in mortality. Nephi saw in vision (approximately 600 B.C.) that Jesus would heal "multitudes of people who were sick, and who were afflicted with all manner of diseases, and with devils and unclean spirits." This healing would be done "by the power of the Lamb of God." (1 Nephi 11:31.) King Benjamin was told by an angel (about 124 B.C.) that Jesus would work "mighty miracles, such as healing the sick, raising the dead, causing the lame to walk, the blind to receive their sight, and the deaf to hear, and curing all manner of diseases. And he shall cast out devils, or the evil spirits which dwell in the hearts of the children of men." (Mosiah 3:5–6.) Jacob referred to Jesus' "mighty miracles" among the Jews. (2 Nephi 10:4.) Abinadi spoke of the "many mighty miracles" Jesus would do while in mortality. (Mosiah 15:6.) Moroni wrote of the "many mighty miracles" of Jesus. (Mormon 9:18.)

During Jesus' postmortal mission to the Nephites. Jesus asked the Nephites to bring their sick and afflicted for him to heal. Listed are the lame, blind, halt, maimed, leprous, withered, deaf, dumb, and "afflicted in any manner." When they were brought forth Jesus healed every one of them. He stated that his desire was motivated by *his* compassion and *their* faith. (3 Nephi 17:7–9.) "So great faith have I never seen among all the Jews; wherefore I could not show unto them so great miracles, because of their unbelief." (3 Nephi 19:35; compare Mark 6:5–6.)

Accounts of miraculous events similar to but having no direct connection with those in the New Testament. A storm at sea calmed after Nephi prayed. (1 Nephi 18:21; compare Luke 8:22–25.) Food miraculously provided for a multitude. (3 Nephi 20:6–7; compare Matthew 15:32–38.) One raised from the dead. (3 Nephi 7:19; 19:4; compare Luke 7:11–17.) Devils and unclean spirits cast out. (3 Nephi 7:19; compare Mark 1:23–27.)

Speaking directly to the elements. Moses spoke to the waters of the Red Sea. (1 Nephi 4:2; see also 1 Nephi 17:26, 29; Helaman 8:11.) If Nephi were to command the water to become earth, it could be done. (1 Nephi 17:50.) "We truly can command in the name of Jesus and the very trees obey us, or the mountains, or the waves of the sea." (Jacob 4:6.) "If ye shall say unto this temple . . . [or] unto this mountain. . . ." (Helaman 10:8, 9.) The elements respond to the command of God. At his voice all things (except man) immediately obey. (Helaman 12:7–22.) "The brother of Jared said unto the mountain Zerin, Remove—and it was removed." (Ether 12:30.)

An Analysis of the Miracles

In the following analysis of the miracles in the books of Matthew, Mark, Luke, and John, the miracles are arranged chronologically as far as available information permits, and the information is discussed in the following order:
Reference and name of miracle
Background information
A description of the occasion
A statement as to the purpose of the miracle
A discussion of the results or consequences
Special considerations, when appropriate

Water into Wine
John 2:1–11; 4:46

Background: Persons involved were Jesus, his mother, the disciples (probably about four), servants, the bridegroom, ruler of the feast. The place was Cana of Galilee.

Occasion: On the third day of the week a wedding feast was held in Cana, to which Jesus and his disciples were called. When the wine supply was exhausted, Jesus' mother informed him of the situation. She also instructed the servants to do whatsoever Jesus asked.

Purpose: Book authors offer many and varied explanations as to Jesus' purpose in this miracle. Some see a symbolic connection to Jesus' ministry and atonement. The most likely reason is that the hosts had not provided enough refreshment and Jesus had compassion on them. One thing is certain: Jesus' attendance at the wedding and his miracle performed there show his approval of marriage and families.

Discussion:

1. There is no direct identification as to the wedding couple.
2. If the marriage was for a near relative of Jesus (sister, perhaps) it would account for Mary's concern over the shortage of wine and also why she sought Jesus' help.
3. This is generally considered Jesus' first miracle (John 2:11) but may be simply his first in Galilee at the beginning of his ministry.
4. Six water pots, containing two or three firkins apiece, "filled to the brim," would contain from 120 to 180 gallons.
5. This miracle is different than others involving food because it involves a qualitative change, whereas feeding the five thousand involved only a quantitative change.

Special considerations:

1. The record implies that the wine was of alcoholic and fermented content, having qualities associated with age. Yet it is evident that the miracle occurred immediately, involving much less time than the natural process of fermentation. This invites the thought that by some similar near-instantaneous occurrence or power the earth also might show properties and contain ingredients suggesting greater antiquity than the actual length of time involved since creation.
2. The JST adds something to the setting but in no way alters the miracle itself. "On the third day" is identified as the "third day of the week" (John 1:1). Generally, in biblical

commentaries "the third day" is interpreted to mean the third day after the call of Philip and Nathanael spoken of in John 1, whereas it really means the wedding was performed on the third day, or Tuesday.

a. Verse 4: "Woman, what have I to do with thee? Mine hour is not yet come" is changed in the JST to read: "Woman, what wilt thou have me to do for thee? That will I do, for mine hour is not yet come." It is kinder than the KJV and agrees with the Greek, which reads as if to say, "Never mind, don't be worried."

b. Verse 11: ". . . and his disciples believed on him" is changed to say: ". . . and the faith of his disciples was strengthened in him."

Healing the Nobleman's Son of Fever
John 4:46–54

Background: Persons involved were Jesus, the boy, the boy's father (nobleman), servants of the nobleman. The place is Cana and Capernaum.

Occasion: Jesus came again to Cana after having been in Judea. A nobleman, evidently having heard of Jesus' healing and/or miraculous powers, asked him to heal his son, who was sick at Capernaum. Jesus commented on the desire of people to see signs and wonders. The man persisted in his desire to have Jesus heal his son. Jesus told the man that his son would live. The nobleman believed the words of Jesus, and while journeying to Capernaum was met by his servants, who told him his son was well. They checked the time when the son began to mend and found it was the same hour that Jesus had made the promise, which by this time was the day previous.

Purpose:

1. Jesus healed out of compassion for the man and his son.
2. The exact meaning of John 4:48 ("Except ye see signs and wonders, ye will not believe") is not clear, but some suggest it to mean that Jesus healed the son in the way he did as a "sign and a wonder," so that the people would believe. A more likely interpretation is that Jesus was lamenting the fact that the people sought signs and wonders.

Discussion:

1. The nobleman probably lived in Capernaum; it is implied but not so stated in the record. The age of the son is not given. That he was a boy still under his father's immediate care is implied but not expressly stated. "Nobleman" means "royal official," probably of Herod's court.

2. The promise of Jesus that the son would live was given at about 1:00 P.M. The loss of fever must have been quite sudden for the servants to have taken note of it so seriously, not having known at the time about Jesus' conversation with the nobleman.

3. This is an example of Jesus' healing a person from a distance, having no direct physical contact with the individual. It could not have been a psychological effect that caused the son to get well.

Passing Unseen Through a Crowd
Luke 4:28–30; see also John 8:59

Background: Persons involved were Jesus, a crowd, and people of the synagogue. The place was Nazareth; and also a similar event at the temple at Jerusalem.

Occasion: At Nazareth Jesus read and expounded the scriptures in the synagogue. When they wanted him to show his "works" (miracles) as in other places, he pointed out how few in the past had been ministered to by a prophet. He said that a prophet was not accepted in his own country. They were filled with anger and attempted to throw him over the "brow of the hill" near the city.

Purpose: To preserve Jesus from an untimely death or injury, because "his time was not yet come"; and for his self-protection.

Discussion: It was sometimes necessary for Jesus to escape from or avoid a situation that would have threatened his safety and that of his disciples, or that would have produced other undesirable results. In this category could be also any interruption the Lord may make to divert, or avert, an inevitable clash or situation that would interfere with the purposes of his ministry. (Consider the event in Alma 19:22.)

A Great Haul of Fishes
Luke 5:1–11

Background: Persons involved were Jesus, Peter, James, John, others in the boat. The place was the Sea of Galilee.

Occasion: Jesus took Simon Peter (and at least one other) and Simon's boat into the sea, and told him to cast his net. Simon reported that he had fished all night without success; but doing as requested, he casted, and got so many fish that the net broke. Simon beckoned his partners in the other ship to help. They filled both ships with fish, until they began to sink. Peter was much moved and fell at Jesus' feet.

Purpose: Used as a teaching device. An object lesson to convince Peter and other fishermen of their mission. As a follow-up to the miracle itself, Jesus said to Peter and others: "Follow me, and I will make you fishers of men," thus illustrating the purpose of the miracle. It might also have a corollary meaning as expressed in John 15:5, "Without me ye can do nothing." Not even fish well.

Discussion:
1. The miracle had its desired effect, for upon reaching the shore Peter, Andrew, James, and John left their fishing nets for the gospel net and became fishers of men. They were to "catch" others as Jesus "caught" them.
2. This miracle shows Jesus to be Lord of the sea as well as the land. That a school of fish should be present, precisely at the time and the place required, is the substance of the miracle. The inhabitants of the sea are just as subject to Christ as are other creatures in heaven and earth.

Special considerations: The JST makes no real change in the account, but in verse 2, "washing their nets" is changed to read, "wetting their nets." In verse 8, "when Simon Peter saw it" is changed to be more clear, "When Simon Peter saw the multitude of fishes." This clarifies the antecedent of the pronoun "it," which could otherwise be assumed to have reference to the sinking of the boat, but in either case the *net* effect of the miracle would be the same (even without the pun). The JST definitely emphasizes the impact of the miracle on Peter.

An Unclean Spirit Cast Out
Mark 1:21–28; Luke 4:31–37

Background: Persons involved were Jesus, a man with an unclean spirit, people of the synagogue. The place was Capernaum.

Occasion: At Capernaum Jesus entered the synagogue where the people were astonished at his doctrine. Among those in the synagogue was a man with an unclean spirit. The spirit spurned Jesus' teachings but proclaimed Jesus to be the Holy One of God. Jesus rebuked the spirit and commanded it to leave the man. The spirit threw the man "in the midst" and went out, leaving the man uninjured.

Purpose:

1. Jesus would not tolerate testimony of his Messiahship from an evil spirit. Certainly the devils are not commissioned to bear witness of him. To silence the shouting demon, Jesus evicted it from the physical body in which it gained utterance. Hence the words, "Hold thy peace, and come out of him."
2. Jesus' compassion for the suffering man would also be a factor.

Discussion: It is possible that the possessed man had stood and interrupted Jesus' discourse in the synagogue. This could be the background and the reason for the words, "What have we to do with thee?" as a rebuke or rejection of Jesus by the evil spirit in the man.

Peter's Wife's Mother Healed of Fever
Matthew 8:14–15; Mark 1:29–31; Luke 4:38–39

Background: Persons involved were Jesus, Peter's wife's mother, James, John, Peter, Andrew. The place was Capernaum.

Occasion: Jesus entered Peter's house and was asked to heal Peter's mother-in-law, who lay sick with a fever.

Purpose: No doubt the healing was a result of Jesus' compassion, Peter's faith, the woman's faith, and Jesus' being asked to heal her.

Discussion:
1. Capernaum was noted for its fevers, due to the marshy land surrounding it.
2. The healing of Peter's mother-in-law may have taken place on the same Sabbath day between casting out the evil spirit (see miracle just previous) and the miracles of healing spoken of as being "in the evening" (Matthew 8:16).
3. The report of this miracle also shows that Peter was a married man.

A Leper Healed
Matthew 8:1–4; Mark 1:40–45; Luke 5:12–15

Background: Persons involved were Jesus and a man with leprosy. The place was Galilee.

Occasion: Jesus was thronged by multitudes, among which was a leper, asking to be cleansed. Jesus healed him and requested that he tell no one but the priest.

Purpose: He had compassion for the afflicted one and healed him in response to a request.

Discussion:
1. "Tell no man." Jesus did not wish to be known primarily for his miracles, hence the frequent injunction "Tell no man." Yet frequently the person told it abroad, as in this case, "insomuch that Jesus could no more openly enter into the city"; hence he withdrew into solitary and wilderness places.
2. When Jesus was not desirous of remaining in an area, he sometimes told those whom he had healed to tell others. (Luke 8:38–39.)

Palsy Healed
Matthew 9:2–8; Mark 2:1–12; Luke 5:17–26

Background: Persons involved were Jesus, a man with palsy, a multitude. The place was Capernaum.

Occasion: Many people, including Pharisees, scribes, and doctors of the law from throughout Galilee and Judea, were gathered around Jesus in a house. Being unable to get in through the door by reason of the multitude, a palsied man, carried by four, was let down through the ceiling. Jesus forgave the man of his sins, which caused an inner murmuring among the scribes and Pharisees, some of whom told themselves Jesus was guilty of blasphemy. Jesus perceived their thoughts and replied that it was easier to say that sins were forgiven than to cause the man to walk. He then commanded the man to rise and walk. The man obeyed and all were amazed.

Purpose: Jesus showed compassion. He also used this miracle as a teaching device, showing that he could forgive sins as well as cure physical sickness.

Discussion:

1. The relation between the amount of faith required for healing the body as compared with that required to obtain a forgiveness of sins is presented here. It arises again in James 5:14–16. Jesus could have told the palsied man that his sins were forgiven, and no observer would have been able to prove or disprove whether it actually was so. But when he commanded a sick man to rise and walk, the validity of his power was immediately able to be tested. Hence in a hostile situation it is easier to say that sins are forgiven. But so that those present would know that he had power to do both, Jesus used the healing of the body as evidence of his power to forgive sins.

2. This episode is a turning point in the life of Jesus, it being the first time he had been accused of blasphemy. It marked a determination in the minds of the Pharisees and rabbis to regard Jesus as a dangerous threat to them and their priestcraft.

Special considerations: The JST contains several changes, resulting mainly in clarification.

Matthew 9:2: "seeing their faith" is changed to "knowing their faith." Also: "go thy way and sin no more" is added to Jesus' comment that the palsied man's sins were forgiven.

Verse 5: "For whether is easier to say . . . or . . . ," is changed to read: "For is it not easier to say . . . than . . ."

Verse 6: "I said this" is added before "that ye may know."

Verse 8: "And he arose," reads "And he immediately arose."

Mark 2:1: "Some days" is changed to "many days." "Abroad" is added after "noised."

Verse 2: "them" is changed to "the multitude."

Verse 3: Reads ". . . borne of four persons."

Verse 9: "Whether is it easier to say . . . or . . ." is changed to say, "Is it not easier to say . . . than . . ." (4:7).

Verse 12: "We never saw it on this fashion" reads, "We never saw the power of God after this manner" (4:9).

Luke 5:18–22 contains slight variations in reading but no real change of meaning.

Verse 23: "Whether is easier to say . . . or . . . " is changed to "Does it require more power to forgive sins than to make the sick rise up and walk?"

Verse 24: To emphasize why the Lord performed the miracles, the JST adds to "But that ye may know that the Son of Man hath power on earth to forgive sins," the words "I said it."

Healing at the Pool of Bethesda
John 5:1–16

Background: Persons involved were Jesus and a man at the pool. The place was the pool of Bethesda.

Occasion: Jesus was in Jerusalem for the Passover. He went to the pool of Bethesda on the Sabbath and healed a man who had been infirm for thirty-eight years. The Jews sought to kill Jesus because he healed on the Sabbath.

Purpose: Compassion for the suffering.

Discussion:

1. There is some question at which feast this took place. It was probably Passover.

2. There is a suggestion that this man's affliction was the result of sin, for when Jesus met him later, he said: "Behold thou art made whole: sin no more, lest a worse thing come unto thee" (verse 14). However, this does not absolutely mean his illness was due to sin, and may only have had reference to loss of salvation being a greater tragedy than loss of health. Jesus said in another place: "Fear not them which kill the body, but are not able to

kill the soul; but rather fear him which is able to destroy both soul and body in hell" (Matthew 10:28).

3. Jesus asked the man: "Wilt thou be made whole?" (verse 6). This seems an odd question, since anyone stricken would want to be healed, and his presence at the healing pool attests to his desire to be healed. Perhaps the man was thoroughly discouraged. It is stated that he had been at the pool for a "long time" and had not been healed. And to one having an infirmity of thirty-eight years' duration, discouragement certainly would be possible. Jesus may have been reinforcing the man's desire and focusing it on the Lord.

Healing a Withered Hand
Matthew 12:9–13; Mark 3:1–5; Luke 6:6–10

Background: Persons involved were Jesus, man with withered right hand, scribes and Pharisees. The place was at a synagogue in Galilee.

Occasion: On the Sabbath Jesus entered a synagogue in which there was a man who had a withered hand. The Pharisees and scribes watched him to see if he would heal on the Sabbath, so they might accuse him. Knowing their thoughts, he asked them if they would not do as much for a sheep. By his logic they were embarrassed and took counsel with the Herodians "how they might destroy" Jesus. He healed the man.

Purpose: Compassion, as always, was a prominent factor, but Jesus also turned the event into a teaching lesson to the scribes and Pharisees. The emphasis is not so much on the healing itself as on whether it was permissible on the Sabbath.

Discussion:

1. This event well illustrates how the Jewish rulers would lie in wait to catch Jesus, and also how completely he could defend his actions and refute theirs.

2. The question about whether it was lawful "to do good on the Sabbath to save life or to kill," did not originate with Jesus. The rabbis had long discussed this, and it was current policy in Jewry that it was lawful to do good, and to save life on the Sabbath. Jesus pointed out, by using the

comparison with a sheep, that they themselves had done less commendable work on the Sabbath.

3. There is a certain impact in Jesus' question: "Is it lawful to do good on the Sabbath days, . . . to save life or to kill?" Was the latter phrase "to kill" an allusion to the murderous intents of the Pharisees toward him even on the Sabbath? They had hated him—even on the Sabbath. Perhaps a note of sarcasm from Jesus to these "simon-pure" Pharisees?

4. It is evident from the fact that the Pharisees fully expected him to heal this man that on Sabbath days Jesus often healed those who were afflicted.

5. Only Luke indicates it was the right hand; but then, of course, he was a physician by training (Luke 6:6).

6. In the culture of the day the left hand was sinister, and unclean. The left hand was used for unclean tasks. A man with a withered right hand, unusable, was an outcast from society because he could not shake hands, or caress, or do anything except with the unclean left hand. When Jesus healed the right hand he restored the man to society.

The Centurion's Servant Healed of Palsy
Matthew 8:5–13; Luke 7:2–10

Background: Persons involved were Jesus, centurion, centurion's servant (in Luke, also elders of the Jews and friends of the centurion). The place was Capernaum.

Occasion: Jesus entered the village of Capernaum. A centurion, friendly to the Jews, sent some elders of the Jews to Jesus asking that he come and heal his servant. Jesus started toward the centurion's place but was met by friends of the centurion carrying his message that he felt unworthy for Jesus to come under his roof—but if Jesus would only speak the word, the healing would occur. Jesus, impressed with his faith and humility, said that it would be done. The servant "was healed in the selfsame hour."

Purpose: Jesus' compassion, as always, but of equal import was the great faith and humility of the centurion.

Discussion:
1. The centurion was of non-Jewish lineage; however, he was especially friendly to the Jews, "for he loveth our nation, and he hath built us a synagogue."
2. Matthew states that the centurion came personally to Jesus. Luke says he sent the elders of the Jews to contact Jesus.
3. Jesus referred to the adoption of Gentiles into the house of Israel when he was impressed with the faith of the centurion and said, "Many shall come from the east and west, and shall sit down with Abraham, Isaac, and Jacob, in the kingdom of heaven" (Matthew 8:11).

The Widow's Son Raised from the Dead
Luke 7:11–17

Background: Persons involved were Jesus, a widow, and her dead son. The place was Nain.

Occasion: The day after healing the centurion's servant at Capernaum, Jesus went to the city of Nain. At the gates of the city he met people carrying a dead person, the only son of a widow. Having compassion on the mother, he told her not to weep. He touched the bier, and commanded the young man to arise. The dead man sat up and began to speak. Jesus presented him to his mother alive. There came a "fear" on all who were present.

Purpose: Compassion for the mother (verse 13), and evidence of Jesus' power over death.

Discussion: No hint as to the age of the dead son was given except that he was a "young man." The record specifies that he was an only son, but does not specify that he was an only child.

Special considerations: Jesus had compassion on the mother. One wonders whether he foresaw his own mother, his own death, and her sorrow. A prophecy had been uttered that when the spear pierced him it would be the wounding of her own soul (Luke 2:35). Jesus may have been additionally moved on this occasion because of regard for his mother.

One Blind and Dumb Healed
Matthew 12:22–23

Background: Persons involved were Jesus and a demoniac. The place was Galilee.

Occasion: Apparently soon after the healing of the man with the withered hand, one possessed with a devil was brought to Jesus. The man was both blind and dumb. The people were greatly amazed at this healing.

Purpose: Compassion is the best motive available, since very little information is given on this miracle.

Discussion:

1. As a result of this miracle, the Pharisees accused Jesus of being in league with Beelzebub, the prince of the devils. Jesus reasoned with them why this could not be so (verses 24–26). Satan does not cast out his own followers from the bodies they have falsely inhabited.

2. Jesus also pointed out to the Jews that there were those among them (evidently followers of Christ) who cast out devils also, and he asked: Were they too given power by the devil? (verses 27–28).

Special considerations: The JST makes no real change in the miracle but offers subsequent and related changes.

Verse 23: "Is not this the son of David?" reads "Is this the Son of David?" (verse 19.)

Verse 24: "But when the Pharisees heard it" is changed to "But the Pharisees heard that he had cast out the devil" (verse 20), thus clarifying the antecedent of "it," which might otherwise be mistaken to refer to the saying of the people, "Is not this the son of David?"

Verse 22: "Cast them out" is clarified to read "cast out devils" (verse 22).

Verse 28: "For they also cast out devils by the Spirit of God, for unto them is power given over devils, that they may cast them out," is added (verse 23). There must have been some members of the Church, being Jewish, who had cast out devils by the priesthood they had been given. Jesus uses this as a defense of his own ability to cast out devils.

Calming a Terrible Storm
Matthew 8:23–27; Mark 4:35–41; Luke 8:22–25

Background: Persons involved were Jesus, his disciples, those in other small boats. The place was the Sea of Galilee.

Occasion: While Jesus and the disciples were crossing the Sea of Galilee from Capernaum toward the east, toward Gergesa, a storm arose. Jesus was asleep. The disciples were afraid and awoke him. He chided them for lack of faith, and rebuked the wind and the waves. The storm stilled and the sea became calm. The disciples were greatly amazed.

Purpose: This miracle was evidence of Jesus' compassion, and it also teaches the disciples to have faith in him under every circumstance.

Discussion:

1. This "nature miracle" illustrates Jesus' power over the elements.
2. It was in the late evening that the miracle occurred, perhaps on the same day the parables of the mustard seed, sower, tares, and so on, were given (Mark 4:33–35).
3. Among those who do not believe that miracles are real, an event such as this is considered as being essentially true in detail, except for the *cause* of the storm being stilled. It is felt by some rationalists that everything happened about as it is reported but not because Jesus willed it so; a mistaken causal relationship between Jesus' word and the calm. See discussion earlier, under "Speaking Directly to the Elements."

Special considerations: The JST has the following corrections:

Mark 4:37: "the waves beat into the ship" is changed to "the waves beat *over* into the ship."

Luke 8:23: ". . . And they were filled with water, and were in jeopardy" is changed to read: "and they were filled with fear and were in danger."

That the disciples would be filled with "fear" instead of "water" appears to be a more reasonable declaration. The JST change also shifts the emphasis and meaning of the passage. As recorded in the KJV, it might be concluded that it was the boat that was being filled with water; but the JST clearly directs attention to the disciples. The narrative goes on to report that Jesus reprimanded them for their unbelief, saying, "Where is your faith?" which is a logical indictment as a consequence of their fear but would not have been evoked by the boat's being filled with water. The textual change made by the Prophet in this passage (Luke 8:23) is therefore much more consistent with the whole story, especially of Jesus' comments, than is the KJV wording. JST Matthew contains no changes for this story.

A Demoniac Healed of Evil Spirits
Matthew 8:28–34; Mark 5:1–20; Luke 8:26–37

Background: Persons involved were Jesus and a man (Matthew says two men; Mark and Luke say one man). See note under *Special considerations*. The place was Gadara, near the southeastern coast of the Sea of Galilee.

Occasion: After stilling the tempest at sea, Jesus landed with the disciples at Gergesa or Gadara. Immediately he was met by a man "out of the tombs" possessed with devils, who hailed him as the Son of God. The spirits requested that he not send them out into the "deep," but rather into a nearby herd of swine. He permitted this, and the swine rushed down the hill and were drowned in the sea.

Purpose: The compelling force was compassion for the afflicted man, or men. Perhaps there were two, but if one were more sorely afflicted than the other the story might center around him.

Discussion:

1. The word *deep* (Luke 8:31), rather than having reference to the sea, may mean "empty," as if the devils said: "Do not cast us out into the empty—or out of a body into the nothing." Apparently, being deprived of a body of flesh of their own, they preferred an animal's body to no body.

2. The healed man became a "missionary" throughout all the area. Jesus told him to tell others "how great things the Lord hath done for thee" (Mark 5:18–20). Generally, Jesus instructed those whom he healed to "tell no man," but in this instance, as he did not intend to remain in the area, having been asked by the people to leave, he let the

healed man bear the testimony. (Mark 5:19–20; Luke 8:38–39.)

3. It may be wondered why there were so many swine available, given the prohibition in Israel against the eating of swine's flesh. But there were many non-Israelitish people, particularly Greeks, living in that section of the country. Gadara was an important Gentile town. Decapolis was mainly, but not exclusively, Gentile. It was probably Gentiles who owned the pigs.

Special considerations: Some interesting changes are made by the JST, primarily clarifying antecedents and emphasizing that a miracle did take place.

It changes Matthew 8:28 to read *"a man,"* rather than "two" (verse 29), and consistent with this, "they" in verse 29 is changed to "he" (verse 30). This harmonizes with Mark and Luke.

Mark 5:9: "And he asked him, What is thy name?" reads: "And he commanded him saying, Declare thy name" (verse 6).

Verse 14: "it" is changed to say "all that was done unto the swine." "The people" is also added in the sentence (verse 11).

Verse 16: "And they that saw it," becomes "And they that saw the miracle." Also: "told them" is enlarged to say, "told them that came out . . . and how the devil was cast out" (verse 13).

Verse 18: "prayed him" is supplemented with "spoke to Jesus, and" (verse 15).

Verses 30 to 33 in Luke 8 are rearranged in the following order: 30, 32, 31, 33. They contain minor variations of wording.

Verse 34: "them" is clarified to read: "the *swine*," ascertaining the antecedent; also "it" is changed to read *"the people"* (verse 35).

Verse 36: "They also which saw it" reads, "They also who saw the miracle" (verse 37).

Raising of Jairus's Daughter from the Dead
Matthew 9:18–26; Mark 5:22–43; Luke 8:41–56

Background: Persons involved were Jesus, Jairus's twelve-year-old daughter, Jairus and his wife, Peter, James, John, a multitude, a messenger from Jarius's house. The place was Capernaum.

Occasion: Jairus, a ruler of the synagogue, whose twelve-year-old daughter lay dying, asked Jesus to lay hands on her that she would live. While they were on the way, a messenger came saying the girl had died. Jesus told Jairus to have faith. Upon reaching the house, Jesus told the people there that she "sleeps." They laughed him to scorn. Taking only Peter, James, John, and the parents into the room with him, Jesus took the girl by the hand and commanded her to rise. She arose, and Jesus requested that she be given something to eat.

Purpose: Jesus had compassion for the parents and also for the girl. The miracle was evidence of the power of Jesus Christ over death.

Discussion:

1. Matthew says the girl was about twelve years of age. Mark says a "little daughter," Luke says an "only daughter."
2. Jesus said the girl was asleep. Rationalists assume from this that Jesus did not raise her from the dead, but only from a coma. However, Jesus made the "diagnosis" before he saw the girl, and hence he possessed miraculous powers either way.
3. No hint is given as to the cause of her sickness or death.

Special considerations:

1. Note Jesus' directive to give the daughter something to eat. Jesus is frequently associated with events that involve eating.

2. The JST contains no significant changes, only a few slight variations of wording. Matthew 9:24 changes the condition of the girl from "dead" to "dying," consistent with Mark and Luke.

The Woman Healed of an Issue of Blood
Matthew 9:20–22; Mark 5:25–34; Luke 8:43–48

Background: Persons involved were Jesus, a woman, a multitude, the disciples. The place was Capernaum.

Occasion: While Jesus, the disciples, Jairus, and a multitude were on the way to Jairus's house, a woman with an affliction sought to touch the hem of Jesus' garment, believing that by so doing she would be healed. Jesus felt "virtue" leave him and enter her, and he asked, "Who touched me?" The woman at length made herself known.

Purpose: The compelling force was compassion in response to faith.

Discussion:

1. The scripture doesn't say that the woman touched only his garment. Luke's account says "Who touched me?" (Luke 8:45–47). She wanted to touch at least his garment.
2. The issue of blood had lasted twelve years.
3. She had sought a cure from the physicians at great cost, but her condition had worsened (Mark 5:26).
4. Care must be taken not to attribute healing powers to the clothes worn by Jesus. She had faith to be healed (Matthew 9:22). It is a mistake to suppose that special healing powers are attached to so-called relics or items once owned by either real or presumed prophets and holy men.
5. "Who touched me?" Jesus asked, not because he was ignorant of the woman's identity but because he wished to publicize the true nature of what had taken place. Had he let the woman go unnoticed, it is likely that she would have spread it abroad that Jesus' clothing had special powers of healing. To keep the record straight, he made a public display of the matter, avowing the facts of the case: (1) that he felt the healing power leave his person, (2) it was done because of her faith. It was necessary that she and also the bystanders be correctly informed.

Special considerations:

1. Joseph Smith had a similar experience. While blessing children he felt spiritual strength go out of him. (TPJS, 280–81.)

2. The word *virtue* comes from a Greek word meaning strength or power. Webster's *New International Dictionary* gives ten meanings for virtue, of which the identification with chastity is only one, and is listed seventh. All the other meanings have reference to power, courage, strength, truth, force, excellence, energy, right, morality, wisdom, and authority. The

word carries with it the connotation of activity: an active force, an active power, and so on.

Two Blind Men Healed
Matthew 9:27–31

Background: Persons involved were Jesus and two blind men. The place was Capernaum.

Occasion: When Jesus left Jairus's house, two blind men followed, asking to be healed. When he entered a house he asked if they believed he could give them sight. They answered, "Yea, Lord." He touched their eyes and said it would be according to their faith. Their eyes were opened. Jesus told them to tell no one, but they spread it throughout all that country.

Purpose: Jesus had compassion in response to their belief and faith. Perhaps the reason he rather ignored them until they followed him into the house was to prove them, which he did by their actions and by confession from their lips.

Discussion:

1. Although Jesus sometimes touched the afflicted part of the person (Matthew 9:29; 20:30–34; Mark 7:32–37; 8:22–26; John 9:6–7), it was not an essential part of every one of his healings. Possibly Jesus did it for blind or deaf persons to enable them to develop increased faith in him, since they were physically denied the full impact of seeing his countenance or hearing his words.

2. It is nowhere recorded that Jesus opened the eyes of the blind by word only, although such would be within his power.

3. Why had Jesus asked if they believed he could heal them? Asking questions about circumstantial detail was not simply a method of Jesus' obtaining information. More often than not, it seems to have been a device he used to clarify the situation in the mind of the person he asked. In this manner Jesus "instructed" the woman he healed from an issue of blood, and also the two blind men.

Special considerations: The JST makes no substantial change in the account but adds two clarifications.

Verse 27 adds the word *"Jesus"* (verse 33).

Verse 30 adds "Keep my commandments, and see ye tell no man in this place" (verse 36). By this addition Jesus placed an obligation on the two men to obey him.

Dumb Man Healed
Matthew 9:32–34

Background: Persons involved were Jesus and a person possessed of an evil spirit. The place was Capernaum.

Occasion: On the same day, after Jesus had healed two blind men, a person dumb and possessed with a devil was brought to him. Jesus cast out the devil, the dumb man spoke, the people marvelled, and the Pharisees renewed their complaint that Jesus worked by the power of the devil (verse 34; see Mark 3:22).

Purpose: As almost always, compassion seems to be the determining factor in this healing.

Discussion: The dumbness was probably caused by the evil spirit rather than by an organic defect of the man's speaking apparatus. This may account for the fact that this time Jesus did not touch or anoint the afflicted man's mouth, as he did in other healings.

Feeding the Five Thousand
Matthew 14:14–21; Mark 6:33–44; Luke 9:11–17; John 6:1–14

Background: Persons involved were Jesus, "about five thousand men, besides women and children," disciples (John says also "a lad"). The place was near Bethsaida in Galilee.

Occasion: Seeing the multitude who had been with him most of the day Jesus had compassion. Rather than send them away for food as the disciples suggested, he provided food himself for them. Five thousand were fed from five loaves and two fishes. Twelve baskets of fragments were taken up afterwards.

Purpose: Christ had compassion for a hungry multitude. He had earlier healed the sick among them and taught them. "The day was far spent" and apparently they had eaten little or nothing, and had no food to eat. Jesus manifested Godlike and fatherly care.

Discussion:

1. This miracle offers difficulty to the rationalists because it seemingly violates natural law and physical economy. Many nonmiraculous explanations are given by unbelievers, including one that Jesus gave the multitude a lecture on generosity and they came forth with food they had secretly concealed because of their selfishness.

2. Another explanation by skeptics is that Jesus was near a cave in which was an adequate supply of food; that this was handed out to him, and from him to the disciples.

3. Just when the food became increased is not stated; whether it was in the hands of Jesus (which is unlikely), or in the hands of the disciples (most likely, in order that there be enough to distribute), or in the hands of the multitude.

4. This miracle has certain similarities to and differences from a later event of feeding four thousand. See later notes on that event.

5. A somewhat similar miracle occurred during Jesus' ministry among the Nephites. (3 Nephi 20:3–7.)

6. For Jesus to be able to multiply food in this manner is a demonstration of his power over nature and the laws of nature as we understand them.

Special considerations: The JST makes no substantial change in the account but offers several clarifications:

Mark 6:33: "Outwent" is changed to "outran."

Verse 35: "desert place" is changed to "solitary place" (verse 36); same change to Luke 9:12.

Luke 9:13 adds "we can provide no more food for all this multitude."

Verse 14, first sentence, adds "in number."

Luke 9:11–17 contains a few other very slight variants.

John 6:12: "When they were filled," is enlarged to say: "When they had eaten and were satisfied."

Jesus Walks on the Sea
Matthew 14:24–33; Mark 6:47–52; John 6:16–21

Background: Persons involved were Jesus and the disciples. The place was the Sea of Galilee.

Occasion: Following the miracle of feeding the five thousand, Jesus sent the disciples to Bethsaida, westward on the sea, while he stayed behind to dismiss the multitude. A storm arose at sea, and the wind was "contrary" to their desired direction. They were forced to row, but made little headway. During the fourth watch of the night, Jesus walked on the sea toward them. Thinking they were seeing a spirit, the disciples were afraid. Jesus said, "It is I." Peter also walked for a distance on the sea; then, terrified, began to sink when his faith failed. Jesus saved him; the storm calmed; and, convinced that Jesus was the Son of God, the disciples worshipped him.

Purpose: The purpose seems to have been to keep a scheduled rendezvous with the disciples, and to come to their aid in the boisterous sea; also to demonstrate again to them that he had power over the elements and the natural forces of the earth. It also demonstrates that such power could be given to men, but only through faith, since Peter walked on the water until he feared.

Discussion:

1. The fourth watch of the night is between 3:00 and 6:00 A.M.
2. The disciples had been on the sea for eight to ten hours, from the previous evening, and had rowed twenty-five to thirty furlongs (three and a half miles).
3. Although not emphasized in the account, it is strongly implied that Jesus also calmed the storm (Matthew 14:32; Mark 6:51).
4. It may also be implied that a further miracle is involved since "immediately the ship was at the land" (John 6:21).

Special considerations: The JST makes virtually no change in the miracle but clarifies one point.

Mark 6:48: ". . . and about the fourth watch of the night he cometh unto them, walking upon the sea, and would have passed by them," is changed to say ". . . as if he would have passed by them" (verse 50).

This change in the JST is certainly more consistent, and eliminates a contradiction. Mark and Matthew say that Jesus was walking on the water so as to join the disciples, seeing that they were in difficulty with the rough sea. Yet, Mark adds that Jesus "would have passed by them." The thought of the JST is that he wished to appear *as though* he would pass by so as to test them. His intention was to come to the disciples, but they were to receive some training and conditioning in the process.

Healing the Woman's Daughter Who Had an Evil Spirit
Matthew 15:22–28; Mark 7:25–30

Background: Persons involved were Jesus, a Greek woman, the woman's daughter, the disciples. The place was the region of Tyre and Sidon.

Occasion: Jesus was in the "coasts of Tyre and Sidon," probably to escape persecution and to find a season of rest. A Greek woman whose daughter was possessed with a devil asked Jesus to cast it out. At first Jesus did not answer, and the disciples asked him to send her away. She persisted and said, "Lord, help me." He said it was not proper to take the food of the children's table to give to strangers. She asked only for crumbs. Impressed by her faith, Jesus told her that it would be according to her will. The devil left her daughter that very hour.

Purpose: Jesus showed compassion; he rewarded the faith and diligence of the mother. See note from JST under *Special considerations*.

Since Jesus probably had withdrawn into the area to escape the active persecution of the scribes and Pharisees and possibly also to allow a period of education for the Twelve, it is likely that he used this event as a teaching situation for them, to illustrate that, dependent upon a person's faith, the gospel was for people of any nation. This idea is strengthened with the fact that Matthew (who probably was present) mentions the attitude of the disciples; whereas Mark (who probably was not present) does not. This was a lesson to the Twelve: The gospel was to be preached first to Israel, then to the Gentiles.

Discussion: The real question is whether Jesus is Savior of Israel *only* or also of the Gentiles. From the fact that he healed the daughter it is evident that although salvation was first offered to Israel, non-Israelites can also become heirs by faith. The Lord has a plan, a timetable for offering the gospel to the various nations.

Special considerations: The JST makes no change in the miraculous event, but does add something to the circumstance relative to Jesus' compassion and why he performed the miracle at all.

Mark 7:24: ". . . and entered into an house, and would have no man know it: but he could not be hid," is clarified thus: ". . . and entered into a house, and would that no man should come unto him. But he could not deny them; for he had compassion upon all men." (Verses 22, 23.) The explanation here is that it was Jesus' compassion that brought him out of seclusion, whereas the KJV tends toward an interpretation that he was physically unable to hide himself from the people.

Mark 7:27: "Let the children first be filled," is changed to say "Let the children of the kingdom first be filled" (verse 26).

A Deaf Man with Speech Impediment Healed
Mark 7:32–37

Background: Persons involved were Jesus and an afflicted man. The place was in Decapolis.

Occasion: Having left the borders of Sidon and Tyre, Jesus went into Decapolis. A deaf man with a speech impediment was brought to him. Jesus took him aside, put his fingers into the man's ears, spit, and touched his tongue. The man was immediately able to hear and to speak easily. Jesus commanded the people not to tell of this healing, but they published it much, and said "he hath done all things well."

Purpose: Jesus had compassion for the afflicted man.

Discussion:

1. Those who brought the afflicted one to Jesus asked Jesus to "put his hand" upon him. Evidently, Jesus used the laying on of hands commonly, although our records do not emphasize the fact. In fact in this case he seemed to employ a different manner of "laying on of hands."

2. From the fact that Jesus touched the afflicted parts, we may conjecture that this man's affliction was caused by a structural and organic imperfection. Compare this with a healing recorded in Matthew 9:32–34, wherein dumbness was caused by an evil spirit and Jesus did not touch the man's mouth, apparently because the affliction was not structural.

Feeding the Four Thousand
Matthew 15:29–38; Mark 8:1–9

Background: Persons involved were Jesus; four thousand men, besides women and children; and the disciples. The place was Decapolis.

Occasion: Jesus went "up into a mountain, and sat down." Multitudes brought their lame, sick, and afflicted, and he healed them. The people had been with him for three days. With seven loaves and a few fishes, Jesus fed the multitude consisting of four thousand men plus an unstated number of women and children. Seven baskets of leftovers remained.

Purpose: Jesus felt compassion on the multitude after three days in the solitary place with him. Also, the event may have a symbolic meaning of Christ's salvation for non-Israelites, since these people were most probably not Israelites. It would therefore be a teaching device for the Twelve and the people as well as an act of kindness.

Discussion:

1. Comparison of this event with the earlier one of the five thousand plus shows many similarities and some differences. They are without doubt two separate occasions. See Matthew 16:9–10; Mark 8:19–20.
2. Some similarities are: Same general area; similar miraculous increase of a small supply of food.
3. Some differences are: four thousand as opposed to five thousand plus women and children in both cases; the people remained three days, whereas accounts of the other event do not specify; larger supply of food to begin with—seven loaves and a few fish as contrasted with five loaves and two fish; seven baskets remaining instead of

twelve; these people were probably non-Jewish, whereas the five thousand were probably mostly Jewish, as hinted in Matthew 15:31.

4. The disciples seemed strangely perplexed with what to do with this multitude. This is strange, since they had seen Jesus feed more than five thousand a few months before. But maybe they did not expect Jesus to feed non-Israelites.

Special considerations: The JST makes no change in the miraculous account but contains a few variant readings:

Matthew 15:30: "those that were" is changed to "some."

Mark 8:7: ". . . and he blessed, and commanded to set them also before the people," is changed to read ". . . and he blessed them, and commanded to set them also before the people, that they should eat."

Verse 8: "meat" is changed to "bread" (verse 7).

Blindness Healed
Mark 8:22–26

Background: Persons involved were Jesus and a blind man. The place was Bethsaida.

Occasion: While Jesus was at Bethsaida, a blind man was brought to be healed. They asked Jesus to "touch him." He led the blind man out of town, spit on his eyes, put his hands on him, and asked if he could see anything. The man replied, "I see men as trees, walking." Jesus put his hands again on the man's eyes and made him look up. He then saw "every man clearly." Jesus told him to tell no one in the town.

Purpose: Jesus had compassion for the afflicted man.

Discussion:

1. This seems to illustrate a progressive-type healing that is not depicted in the other miracles. Could this have been due to the lack of faith on the part of the man himself? or due to the nature of the defect?

2. Jesus touched this man and also "spit on his eyes."

3. Jesus, as in an earlier event (see Mark 7:32–33), took the man aside, apart from others, before healing him. Evidently,

Jesus had some special reason for this, as it was not always his custom. It may have had some connection with the character of the townspeople.

An Evil Spirit Cast Out of a Person
Matthew 17:14–21; Mark 9:14–29; Luke 9:37–43

Background: Persons involved were Jesus, a father, the man's child, disciples, the multitude also to some extent. The place was probably near Mount Hermon, several miles north of the Sea of Galilee, or a nearby height.

Occasion: Coming down from the Mount of Transfiguration, Jesus found the scribes questioning his disciples. A man, kneeling, asked Jesus to heal his only son, who was possessed of a devil. The man told Jesus that the disciples had tried and failed to cure the son. Jesus questioned the father and obtained a statement of anguished belief. Jesus then healed the son. In reply to the disciples' query as to why they could not cast the spirit out, Jesus explained the necessity of prayer and fasting to obtain spiritual power in such cases.

Purpose: Jesus had compassion for the afflicted and for the father. Also, it served as a teaching device for the Twelve regarding faith, prayer, and fasting.

Discussion:

1. Matthew and Mark imply that this event took place the same day as the transfiguration, but Luke (9:37) points out that Jesus came down from the mount the day after the transfiguration, which means he spent the night on the mount.

2. Mark 9:15 reports that the people were greatly amazed when Jesus came and they ran to him and saluted him. Was it that the glory he had enjoyed on the mount was still shining to some degree? Such was the case with Moses (Exodus 34:28–35) and Abinadi (Mosiah 13:5).

3. The action of the afflicted person so much resembles epilepsy that it is often so attributed today, rather than to an evil spirit. Most modern translations of the Bible read incorrectly "an epileptic."

Special considerations: Matthew 17:21 (the statement about prayer and fasting) is not found in the Revised Standard Version or other modern translations. This is a great loss.

The JST makes clear that a devil was the cause of the dumbness.

Mark 9:17: ". . . which hath a dumb spirit," is complemented with "that is a devil" (verse 15).

Verse 18: "And wheresoever he taketh him," is altered to read "And when he seizeth him" (verse 15).

Verse 20: ". . . and when he saw him" becomes "and when *the man* saw him" (verse 17).

Verse 21: "Of a child" is changed to "when a child."

There are a few other word changes of little consequence. The effect of the major changes in Mark is to suggest that the possessed person was then a man, and no longer a child whereas the KJV seems to leave the impression that he is still a youngster.

Money Found in the Fish's Mouth
Matthew 17:24–27

Background: Persons involved were Jesus, a tax collector, and Peter. The place was Capernaum.

Occasion: While Jesus was in the house, the tax collector asked Peter outside if Jesus paid tribute. Peter said yes. When Peter came into the house, Jesus questioned him about it, and then told him to go to the sea, cast in a hook, and that he would find enough tax money for Jesus and Peter in the mouth of the first fish that he caught.

Purpose: This was given as a teaching lesson to Peter "lest we should offend them." That is, we'll pay the tax rather than cause an unnecessary commotion at this time.

Discussion:

1. It was not a civil but an ecclesiastical tax. Originally instituted by Moses, it was an atonement for sins. As Jesus had no sin, he was exempt.
2. The piece of money had to be a "stater," which had the value of four drachmae, and therefore would be enough to pay the tax for two persons.

3. Matthew does not say that Peter actually went to the sea and found the fish, but it is implied.
4. Many rational interpretations have been given by those who do not believe, such as:
   a. This was an ordinary event (fish have swallowed money before), and later it was cloaked with mysterious trappings (legend, and so on.).
   b. The fish could be sold for the amount needed to pay the tax. To open its mouth had reference to taking out the hook.
5. Apparently Peter and Jesus were not together when the tax collector questioned Peter. Yet Jesus seemed to know all about the conversation. Another example of Jesus' miraculous powers.
6. The discussion between Jesus and Peter about who should pay the tax would serve to reimpress Peter with the status of Jesus as the Son of God. Jesus used logical reasoning with Peter (verses 25–26).

Special considerations: The JST makes no change in the miraculous element in the record, but changes one word in relation to Jesus' confrontation with Peter. Verse 25: "Jesus prevented him" is changed to "Jesus rebuked him" (verse 24).

Casting Out of a Devil—Dumbness Cured
Luke 11:14–15

Background: Persons involved were Jesus, and a man, and some observers. The place was somewhere in Judea.

Occasion: Jesus cast out a devil, and the man formerly dumb spoke. Again Jesus was accused of being in league with the devil.

Purpose: He showed compassion for the afflicted man. It also set the situation for a statement or illustration about evil spirits being cast out and then returning.

Discussion:
1. So little information is given of this event that it is difficult to see it as different from several other healings that were the result of casting out evil spirits.

2. No doubt Luke's purpose for including the miracle was not to explain anything different about miracles but rather to show how much of an uproar it caused among his accusers (possibly Pharisees, though this is not stated).

Special considerations: The JST does not change the miraculous nature, but clarifies the event a little. Luke 11:14: "And he was casting out a devil and it was dumb," is changed to read "And he was casting a devil out of a man, and he was dumb" (verse 15).

Healing of a Man Born Blind
John 9:1–7

Background: Persons involved were Jesus, a man born blind, and the disciples. The place was the pool of Siloam in Jerusalem.

Occasion: Jesus passing by saw a man who had been blind from birth. The disciples asked if his condition was the result of this man's sin or of his parents' sin, since he had been born blind. Jesus replied that it was neither, that in this case it was that the works of God should be made manifest in him. Jesus spit on the ground, made clay, anointed with it the eyes of the blind man, and told him to wash in the pool of Siloam. The man obeyed and came away seeing. This was done on the Sabbath day.

Purpose: Jesus showed he had compassion and that "the works of God may be made manifest." It also set up the situation for a heated discussion between Jesus and the Pharisees about their spiritual blindness (verses 39–41).

Discussion:
1. The man was "of age" (verse 23), hence older than thirteen years and one day, by Jewish terminology.
2. Note that Jesus anointed the man's eyes with clay—probably to make it possible for him to have the sense of touch to strengthen his faith, since he could not see Jesus at the time.
3. This miracle, being done on the Sabbath, touched off a further conflagration about Jesus' Sabbath activities, and

also his divine calling. The healed man was "cast out" by the Jews (excommunicated from the synagogue), but his parents would not boldly affirm the cause of the miracle. Jesus went to the man afterwards and taught him.

Special considerations: The JST makes no change in the event, but adds a comment of some import relative to curing of blindness in general: Verse 32: "Since the world began was it not heard that any man opened the eyes of one that was born blind, except he be of God." This important addition changes the whole meaning of that verse. I had often thought it strange that with so many prophets holding the priesthood as there had been since Adam, no one had ever performed this service before Jesus' time. The JST gives a suitable answer to this query by adding "except he be of God" (John 9:32). Presumably, then, there were some such instances, but none have been preserved in the Old Testament.

Healing of a Woman
Luke 13:10–17

Background: Persons involved were Jesus and a woman. The place was in Perea.

Occasion: Jesus, in one of the synagogues on the Sabbath, saw a woman with an affliction she had endured for eighteen years. He called her to him, laid his hands on her, and said: "Woman, thou art loosed from thine infirmity." He was accused by a ruler of the synagogue of working on the Sabbath. Jesus made his critics ashamed by saying they watered their cattle on the Sabbath. All his disciples "rejoiced for all the glorious things which were done by him."

Purpose: Christ had compassion on the woman. He probably also wanted to expose the hypocrisy of the Jewish leaders, and also clarify the thinking about proper Sabbath observance in the mind of anyone who would hear.

Discussion: This is another example of how easily Jesus could expose the hypocrisy of the Jewish rulers.

Special considerations: The JST makes no substantial change in the account, only a few minor alterations in wording. Verse 17 says the *disciples* rejoiced over the glorious things he did.

A Man with Dropsy Healed on the Sabbath
Luke 14:1–6

Background: Persons involved were Jesus, a man, lawyers and Pharisees in Perea.

Occasion: Jesus was at the house of a chief Pharisee on the Sabbath to eat. Critics watched him. A man with dropsy came before Jesus. Jesus asked the Pharisees if it was lawful to heal on the Sabbath. They remained silent. He healed the man. Jesus asked further questions about Sabbath work. None could answer his questions.

Purpose: The miracle was used to show compassion for the afflicted, and as a teaching device to the self-righteous Pharisees about proper work on the Sabbath.

Discussion:

1. It is possible that the presence of the afflicted man had been prearranged by the Pharisees as a trap to embarrass Jesus as a Sabbath breaker.
2. Symptoms of dropsy: An accumulation of serous fluid in the cavities and tissues of the body. Caused by a stoppage in the discharge of the fluid, and/or a change in the blood. It is not so much a disease as such as it is the result of other ailments, such as heart disease, anemia, kidney trouble, headache, fever, and so on.
3. Only Luke mentions this event, and he diagnoses it. As a physician he would be interested in such things. The affliction is called "edema" today.

Raising of Lazarus from the Dead
John 11:17–46

Background: Persons involved were Jesus, Lazarus, Mary, Martha, disciples, multitude. The place was Bethany.

Occasion: While in Perea, Jesus received word that Lazarus was sick. He abode two days more where he was before going to Bethany to see Lazarus. When he arrived, Lazarus had been dead for four days. After considerable discussion with Mary and Martha, Jesus called Lazarus forth from the tomb, after having the stone rolled away and having prayed to the Father. Lazarus was loosed and came forth, bound with grave clothes.

Many Jews believed, but some others went to tell the Pharisees what had happened.

Purpose: Jesus had compassion for Lazarus, and perhaps even more so for Mary and Martha. It was also a teaching method for those around Judea, to show for a third time that Jesus had power over death.

Discussion:

1. The other restorations to life had been done in Capernaum (Mark 5:22–43) and Nain (Luke 7:11–17), and now, near the close of his ministry, he gave absolute proof of his power over death to those in Judea (see verse 4).
2. This miracle resulted in a determined effort on the part of the Pharisees and the chief priests to destroy Jesus, and also Lazarus (verses 46–57).

Special considerations: The JST makes no change in this event. There is a slight change of wording in verse 29, but it is of no consequence to the story. Of related significance is a change in verses 1, 2, and 17, which seem to say that the house in which Lazarus, Mary, and Martha lived was owned by Martha. This may help explain the situation in Luke 10:39–43, wherein Martha busied herself with household chores.

Ten Lepers Healed
Luke 17:11–19

Background: Persons involved were Jesus and ten men. The place was in either Galilee or Samaria.

Occasion: After a brief stay in Ephraim, probably for seclusion and rest, Jesus started for Jerusalem through the midst of Samaria and Galilee. Ten lepers saw him and asked for mercy. He told them to show themselves to the priests. While on their way to do so, they were cleansed. One returned, fell on his face before Jesus, and gave thanks. Jesus asked if there were not ten, and where the other nine were.

Purpose: Compassion for the afflicted.

Discussion:

1. These men were very likely Samaritans, which is characteristic of Luke's Testimony.

2. The comment of Jesus to the grateful leper, "Thy faith hath made thee whole," must have reference to his salvation, or to what his faith will do toward his eventual wholeness of salvation, for all ten were healed of leprosy. This individual statement must mean more than the mere physical healing that all ten had received.

Blind Bartimaeus Healed
Matthew 20:29–34; Mark 10:46–52; Luke 18:35–43

Background: Persons involved were Jesus and Bartimaeus (a blind beggar). Matthew mentions another blind man also. The place is near Jericho.

Occasion: Bartimaeus, the blind son of Timaeus, was sitting by the side of the road as Jesus and the multitude went by. The blind man called to Jesus. Jesus asked what he wanted, and he replied, "Lord, that I might receive my sight." Jesus touched his eyes, and he was able to see immediately. He followed along with the multitude. Those who witnessed this event praised God.

Purpose: This miracle showed Jesus' compassion and the result of the blind man's faith.

Discussion:

1. There is some question as to whether there were two blind men or one, but this is immaterial to the miraculous part of the event.
2. There were probably two men, since blind men often went about in pairs to help each other, but the more enterprising one was spokesman for the other.
3. As repeated in so many events, Jesus said: "Thy faith hath saved thee," emphasizing the true nature of the occasion.

Cursing the Fig Tree
Matthew 21:18–21; Mark 11:12–21

Background: Persons involved were Jesus and the disciples. The place was near Bethany.

Occasion: While Jesus and the Twelve were travelling from Bethany to Jerusalem, Jesus was hungry. He saw in the distance a fig tree in leaf. He went to see it; it had no figs, but leaves only.

It was not the season for figs. He said to the tree, "Let no fruit grow on thee henceforward for ever." The disciples heard him say it. As they passed by the next morning, they saw that the fig tree had withered away.

Purpose: The miracle was given as an object lesson to the disciples. The overriding principle here seems to be that we should be fruitful in our lives, and serve a practical purpose. Foliage (appearance) is not enough. However, it is expressly stated that it was *not* the season for figs. This could mean that men and women are expected to be fruitful both in season and out of season (compare Paul's exhortation in 2 Timothy 4:2). That Jesus had more purpose in mind than mere fig-picking is suggested by the JST (see *Special considerations*).

Discussion: In March or April a fig tree generally had neither leaves nor fruit. This particular tree, having leaves, had put forth a pretension to be something more than other trees, hence was a type of hypocrite. In fig trees, fruit generally appears before the leaves.

Special considerations: The JST makes several minor changes, mostly clarifications. But one item of considerable importance is in Mark as follows:

KJV 11:13: "And seeing a fig tree . . . having leaves, he came, if haply he might find any thing thereon: and when he came to it, he found nothing but leaves; for the time of figs was not yet." This is enlarged and altered thus:

JST 11:14: ". . . And seeing a fig tree afar off having leaves, he came to it with his disciples; and as they supposed, he came to it to see if he might find any thing thereon." Verse 15: "And when he came to it, there was nothing but leaves; for as yet the figs were not ripe."

These changes imply a difference of purpose as to why Jesus really came to the fig tree and why the disciples *thought* he came to the tree. This is consistent with other changes occurring throughout the JST, which tend toward greater knowledge and power for Jesus. Since it is expressly stated that it was not the time for ripe figs, it is to be expected that Jesus would at least know that, and his real purpose would be something other than the mere gathering of figs. Hence the JST places the emphasis upon the teaching content of this miracle, it being about hypocrisy.

Malchus's Ear Healed
Matthew 26:51–52; Mark 14:47;
Luke 22:50–51; John 18:10–11, 26

Background: Persons involved were Jesus, Malchus, and Peter. The place was Gethsemane.

Occasion: On the night of Jesus' arrest when men laid hands on Jesus, Peter drew his sword and cut off the right ear of Malchus, the high priest's servant. Jesus touched Malchus's ear and healed it, and told Peter to put away his sword.

Purpose: No doubt compassion for Malchus was a major aspect in this healing.

Discussion:
1. Only Luke mentions that Jesus healed the ear (22:51) although all four records speak of the damage to the ear.
2. Only Luke and John mention it was the right ear. (Luke 22:50; John 18:10.)
3. Only John mentions that the servant's name was Malchus (18:10).
4. Only John discloses that it was Peter who dealt the blow (18:10, 26).
5. This miracle is unique. There is no other account of Jesus restoring a severed member of the body.

Special considerations:
1. The JST makes no change in the event, but it adds the healing episode to the book of Mark (14:53), whereas the KJV has this only in Luke.
2. The stroke with the sword may have been intended to sever the head of the high priest's servant and not just the ear.

Great Haul of Fishes
John 21:1–8

Background: Persons involved were Jesus, Peter, Thomas, Nathanael, James, John, and two other disciples. The place was Sea of Galilee (Tiberias).

Occasion: After Jesus' resurrection, seven disciples were at the Sea of Galilee, fishing. They fished all night and caught nothing. The next morning Jesus (unrecognized by them) stood on the shore and asked if they had any meat. They answered no. Jesus told them to cast their net on the right side of the boat; and when they did this, they were not able to draw the net for the multitude of fish. John first discerned that the person on the shore was Jesus, but Peter was apparently first to reach him.

Purpose: This miracle was given as a sign to the disciples, as further evidence that he was truly risen and still cared for them. It was also a teaching lesson to the disciples that they were called to fish for men, not for fish, but "without me ye can do nothing" (John 15:5).

Discussion: Both the original call to Peter, James, and John (Luke 5:1–11) and now a renewal of that call were demonstrated by a miraculous catch of fish.

CHAPTER 15

The Parables of Jesus

That Jesus often taught with parables is well known to readers of the New Testament. Why he used parables is a topic about which there is considerable misunderstanding. Furthermore, just what a parable is and how it differs from other stories or other forms of symbolic language is often not even given consideration.

A careful reading of the books of Matthew, Mark, and Luke (John has no true parables) reveals that Jesus used parables when teaching the multitudes and the Jewish leaders but rarely for teaching the disciples. Jesus did not use parables in the beginning of his ministry, but adopted that method when opposition became strong against him. He was at least a year and a half into his ministry when he began to teach with parables (Matthew chapter 13).

Veiling Greater Truths

Jesus gave his own reasons for using parables, saying it was so that the multitudes would *not* understand: "And the disciples came, and said unto him, Why speakest thou unto them [the multitudes] in parables? He answered and said unto them,

Because it is given unto you to know the mysteries of the kingdom of heaven, but to them it is not given." (Matthew 13:10–11.)

His reason for using parables is emphasized by the JST.
After a period of debate and conflict with the Jewish religious
leaders, Jesus said: "And, again, hear another parable; for unto
you that believe not, I speak in parables; that your unrighteousness may be rewarded unto you" (JST Matthew 21:34).

Alma explained the way in which "unrighteousness may be
rewarded unto" an unbeliever.

> It is given unto many to know the mysteries of God; neverthe-
> less they are laid under a strict command that they shall not im-
> part only according to the portion of his word which he doth
> grant unto the children of men, according to the heed and dili-
> gence which they give unto him.
>
> And therefore, he that will harden his heart, the same re-
> ceiveth the lesser portion of the word; and he that will not harden
> his heart, to him is given the greater portion of the word, until it is
> given unto him to know the mysteries of God until he know them
> in full.
>
> And they that will harden their hearts, to them is given the
> lesser portion of the word until they know nothing concerning his
> mysteries; and then they are taken captive by the devil, and led by
> his will down to destruction. Now this is what is meant by the
> chains of hell. (Alma 12:9–11.)

This is the principle upon which Jesus taught with parables.
The parable was a device or a method of giving the lesser portion of the word to those whose hearts were hardened.

After Jesus had taught the multitudes with parables, and
when the disciples of Jesus were alone with him, they would
ask him to give them the meaning, which he did, but the multitude were not favored with the Lord's explanation (see
Matthew 13:18–23, 34, 36–43). However, that Jesus expected his
audience to ponder the lesson of a parable is shown from his
frequent admonition, "Who hath ears to hear, let him hear"
(Matthew 13:9).

The Bible Dictionary in the LDS edition of the Bible contains
an excellent statement about parables, of which the following is

an excerpt: "The parable conveys to the hearer religious truth exactly in proportion to his faith and intelligence; to the dull and uninspired it is a mere story, 'seeing they see not,' while to the instructed and spiritual it reveals the mysteries or secrets of the kingdom of heaven. Thus it is that the parable exhibits the condition of all true knowledge. Only he who seeks finds." (Pp. 740–41.)

Since not all persons are equally prepared to receive the truth, the parable veils or hides great truth from those who should not have it. There may be a drop of mercy in this, so that they may be spared greater condemnation. But it is more than that. There is an element of justice also. It is the principle of not casting pearls before swine. For those who do not want the greater truths that Jesus has to offer, there is no compulsion. But such cannot be saved in their wilful ignorance.

Paul referred to giving the lesser portion of the word in terms of diet, declaring that he was selective with the meat and the milk, asserting that meat was for those who were mature (see 1 Corinthians 3:1–3; Hebrews 5:11–14).

The withholding of information may also have been done for the protection of the disciples, so as to shield them from the envy of the Jewish leaders and from the consequent persecution that plainer speech might have provoked at that stage of the ministry. Had Jesus spoken plainer the wicked might have figured out what strong doctrine he was teaching and sought to kill him earlier than they did.

Figurative Expressions

The word *parable* is Greek in origin and means a "setting side-by-side" or a "comparison." The popular use of the word *parable* is very broad, and is often not correct because it is used to refer to all sorts of symbolic language, including similitudes, allegories, and even proverbs.

Jesus used many figurative expressions to communicate. But true parables are longer stories, and he used them to conceal the central meaning. Since not all symbolic language forms are true parables, it will be worth the effort to define the various figures of speech. Forms of symbolic language consist of single words, phrases, sentences, stories, or whole discourses. We will consider the most common types.

Simile and Metaphor. These represent the simplest forms of figurative speech. In both cases one thing is compared with another. With a simile this comparison is simply expressed, whereas with a metaphor there is a transfer of the characteristics from one to another. Thus, to say, "He sprang on them *like a lion,*" is to use a simile; however, to say that he would *"be a lion* in their path," is to express a metaphor. Jesus used a metaphor when he said to his disciples, "Ye are the salt of the earth" (Matthew 5:13).

Hyperbole. Hyperbole is deliberate exaggeration used for effect; hence it must be understood according to context and circumstances. To state that the mustard seed is the "least of all seeds," or that the mustard plant is the "greatest among herbs" (Matthew 13:32) is more than the botanical truth, but it establishes the desired contrast.

Similitude and Parable. A similitude is an expanded simile but is less than a full-grown parable. It is a word picture that depicts familiar scenes and relationships and is painted in some detail. The word picture of the shepherd who seeks a lost sheep and rejoices over its recovery is a similitude (Matthew 18: 12–14).

A parable is somewhat akin to a similitude, but in the strict sense a parable is longer and is presented in narrative form. A parable is a story, whereas the similitude is a graph. A similitude may begin with "What man of you" or "How think ye"; a parable usually opens with something such as "The kingdom of heaven is likened unto a man which . . . " (Matthew 13:24).

Parables and Allegories. In an allegory every point is made to represent something. With a parable this is not so. This important distinction must be remembered in attempting to interpret parables. Violence is done to both the nature and the message of a parable when it is pressed for a meaning in every detail, but such would be acceptable in an allegory. The Testimony of John has no true parables but has two allegories: The Good Shepherd (John 10) and the Vine (John 15).

A Flash of Light

The message of a parable may be compared to a flash of light, like a beacon on a hill. Some parables are more literal than others, but all of them may be pressed beyond the limits of the original intent of the author. It is unnecessary to strain or to stretch the interpretation of an item in a parable to get more out of it than was originally intended. Interpreters sometimes engage in pulverizing a passage until it has but faint resemblance to its original form. There is little to be gained through defining and refining a parable until it is reduced to dust and powder—a process that is exhausting to the reader as well as to the text. Proper interpretation will draw out the intended meaning without belaboring a passage as if squeezing the last bit from a tube of toothpaste.

In this chapter we are concerned only with the true parables uttered by Jesus and do not attempt to discuss the many other figurative statements.

Interpreting, Applying, and Classifying the Parables

Each parable had an original meaning intended by the Savior at the time he uttered it. Other meanings, appended by interpreters, are secondary to the original. But how does one get at the original meaning of a parable? The Prophet Joseph Smith had a key: "I have a key by which I understand the scriptures. I enquire, what was the question which drew out the answer, or caused Jesus to utter the parable. . . . To ascertain its meaning, we must dig up the root and ascertain what it was that drew the saying out of Jesus." (TPJS, 276–77.)

There is a difference between the interpretation and the application of a parable. The first deals with original meaning, the second with the use that is made of the parable today.

The LDS Bible Dictionary, p. 741, makes the following comparison between interpretation and application: "The only true interpretation [of a parable] is the meaning the parable conveyed, or was meant to convey, when first spoken. The application of a parable may vary in every age and circumstance. But if the original meaning is to be grasped, it is important to consider its context and setting. The thought to which it is linked, the connection in which it is placed, the persons to whom it is addressed, all give the clue to the right interpretation."

Arrangement thus depends upon the point of view of the interpreter, what he sees in the parable, and what he wishes to point out. As a consequence, most books about the parables are heavily stacked with sectarian-type information and often go beyond what the original purpose was, because most commentators have thought that Jesus used parables in order to make things clear and easy to understand, when in reality he used them to veil and conceal the great truths.

The accompanying chart shows three types of parables uttered by Jesus. This arrangement is my own and was made according to the purpose for which each parable was originally given as far as this could be determined from the New Testament.

It is interesting to note that parables of instruction were generally given to the multitudes, whereas parables of chastisement were generally given to the Pharisees, scribes, Sadducees, and lawyers. Any arrangement of the parables is subjective, and often it is evident that a parable has certain elements that would justify placing it in more than one category.

Help from Latter-day Revelation

Assistance in interpreting the parables comes from several sources of latter-day literature, particularly the Doctrine and Covenants, the JST, and *Teachings of the Prophet Joseph Smith*. Usually the JST and the Doctrine and Covenants do not change the text of the parables, but their help consists in pointing the reader's attention to the central meaning, or in establishing the time frame to which the parable applies. The one exception to this is the Wheat and the Tares (Matthew 13:30 and D&C 86:7), in that the Doctrine and Covenants version, as compared with Matthew's, reverses the order of gathering. Joseph Smith's teachings are particularly informative for showing the context in which many of the parables were uttered.

Classification of the Parables According to Type

Parables of Instruction	Parables of Chastisement	Parables About the Kingdom
Individual Response and Readiness The Sower (Soils) The Ten Virgins The Talents The Pounds The Man Taking a Far Journey The Shut Door The Sheep and the Goats **Enduring to the End** The Uncompleted Tower The King's Warfare The Unjust Judge **Willingness to Labor** The Laborers in the Vineyard **Forgiving Others** The Unmerciful Servant **Do Not Trust in Worldly Riches** The Foolish Rich Man **The Principle of Sacrifice** The Hidden Treasure The Pearl of Great Price	**Rebuke for Self-Righteousness** The Lost Sheep, Lost Coin, and Lost (Prodigal) Son **Rebuke for Selfishness** The Rich Man and Lazarus The Two Debtors The Good Samaritan **Rebuke for Indifference to and Mismanagement of the Kingdom** The Great Supper The Royal Marriage Feast The Wicked Husbandman	**Beginning of the Kingdom** The Sower (Soils) **Conditions Within the Kingdom** The Wheat and Tares (first half) **Transfer of the Kingdom from the Jews to the Gentiles** The Great Supper The Royal Marriage Feast **The Kingdom in the Last Days** The Wheat and Tares (second half) The Mustard Seed The Leaven The Pearl of Great Price The Hidden Treasure The Gospel Net

Scriptural references for each parable are listed at the conclusion of the chapter.

Following are examples of the help obtained from latter-day sources.

The Gospel Net (Matthew 13:50). The JST makes no change in the parable, but by way of explanation adds, "And the world is the children of the wicked" (verse 50), which means that the "end of the world" is not the end of the planet earth but of wickedness on the earth.

The Wicked Husbandmen (Matthew 21:33–45). Jesus told this lengthy parable to the Jewish religious leaders on Tuesday of the last week of his mortal life. It was a day of strong confrontation and debate between him and those leaders. Hearing the parable, they perceived that Jesus meant them as the wicked husbandmen. A detailed explanation of the parable was given only to the disciples and is found only in the JST. A parallel arrangement of the KJV and the JST clearly shows the contribution of the JST. The JST has everything the KJV has about this parable, and adds information at the beginning and the end.

King James Version **Matthew 21:33–45**	*Joseph Smith Translation* **Matthew 21:34–56**
33 Hear another parable: There was a certain householder, which planted a vineyard, and hedged it round about, and digged a winepress in it, and built a tower, and let it out to husbandmen, and went into a far country:	34 And again, hear another parable; for unto you that believe not, I speak in parables; that your unrighteousness may be rewarded unto you.
34 And when the time of the fruit drew near, he sent his servants to the husbandmen, that they might receive the fruits of it.	
35 And the husbandmen took his servants, and beat one, and killed another, and stoned another.	
36 Again, he sent other servants more than the first: and they did unto them likewise.	

37 But last of all he sent unto them his son, saying, They will reverence my son.

38 But when the husbandmen saw the son, they said among themselves, This is the heir; come, let us kill him, and let us seize on his inheritance.

39 And they caught him, and cast him out of the vineyard, and slew him.

40 When the lord therefore of the vineyard cometh, what will he do unto those husbandmen?

41 They say unto him, He will miserably destroy those wicked men, and will let out his vineyard unto other husbandmen, which shall render him the fruits in their seasons.

42 Jesus saith unto them, Did ye never read in the scriptures, The stone which the builders rejected, the same is become the head of the corner: this is the Lord's doing, and it is marvellous in our eyes?

43 Therefore say I unto you, The kingdom of God shall be taken from you, and given to a nation bringing forth the fruits thereof.

44 And whosoever shall fall on this stone shall be broken: but on whomsoever it shall fall, it will grind him to powder.

45 And when the chief priests and Pharisees had heard his parables, they perceived that he spake of them.

48 And they said among themselves, Shall this man think that he alone can spoil this great kingdom? And they were angry with him.

49 But when they sought to lay hands on him, they feared the multitude, because they learned that the multitude took him for a prophet.

50 And now his disciples came to him, and Jesus said unto them, Marvel ye at the words of the parable which I spake unto them?

51 Verily, I say unto you, I am the stone, and those wicked ones reject me.

52 I am the head of the corner. These Jews shall fall upon me, and shall be broken.

53 And the kingdom of God shall be taken from them, and shall be given to a nation bringing forth the fruits thereof; (meaning the Gentiles.)

54 Wherefore, on whomsoever this stone shall fall, it shall grind him to powder.

55 And when the Lord therefore of the vineyard cometh, he will destroy those miserable, wicked men, and will let again his vineyard unto other husbandmen, even in the last days, who shall render him the fruits in their seasons.

56 And then understood they the parable which he spake unto them, that the Gentiles should be destroyed also, when the Lord should descend out of heaven to reign in his vineyard, which is the earth and the inhabitants thereof.

The additional 237 words of the JST enable present-day readers to see clearly what Jesus told his disciples about the kingdom being taken away from the Jews and given to the Gentiles in the meridian of time, and also that the stone that falls upon the people is Jesus as he descends at the Second Coming, he being the chief cornerstone, and will descend from heaven in the last days to the destruction of the wicked.

The Ten Virgins (Matthew 25:1–13). The JST introduces this parable with the words, "And then, at that day, before the Son of Man comes, the kingdom of heaven shall be likened unto ten virgins." The Doctrine and Covenants gives mention of this parable on two occasions, (45:56; 63:54), both of which place the fulfillment at the time of the Lord's second coming.

The Shut Door (Luke 13:23–25). At the beginning the JST puts a focus upon this parable by inserting the following words at the end of verse 24: "for the Lord shall not always strive with man." The addition of these words give a sense of urgency to securing one's entry into the kingdom of God.

The Uncompleted Tower; The King Going to War (Luke 14: 28–33). The JST gives the meaning of these two parables as

28 Wherefore, settle this in your hearts, that ye will do the things which I shall teach, and command you.

29 For which of you intending to build a tower, sitteth not down first, and counteth the cost, whether he have money to finish his work?

30 Lest, unhappily, after he has laid the foundation and is not able to finish his work, all who behold, begin to mock him,

31 Saying, This man began to build, and was not able to finish. And this he said, signifying there should not any man follow him, unless he was able to continue; saying,

32 Or what king, going to make war against another king, sitteth not down first, and consulteth whether he be able with ten thousand, to meet him who cometh against him with twenty thousand.

33 Or else, while the other is yet a great way off, he sendeth an embassage, and desireth conditions of peace.

34 So likewise, whosoever of you forsaketh not all that he hath he cannot be my disciple.

These two parables are pretty much the same as in the KJV, but the JST makes unmistakably clear that their message is that, having started, one is required to endure to the end.

The Lost Sheep (Luke 15:4). The parable is about a man with a hundred sheep, who left the ninety-nine "in the wilderness" to go after one that was lost. The JST makes an interesting clarification that the shepherd leaves the ninety-nine somewhere in safety, then goes "into the wilderness after that which is lost."

The Rich Man and Lazarus (Luke 16:19–31). The JST makes no essential changes in the parable, but introduces it with a statement of the Lord to the Pharisees, with whom he is having a strong confrontation: "Verily I say unto you, I will liken you unto the rich man." The parable of the rich man and Lazarus is more explicit when it is read with the knowledge that it was the Pharisees who were selfish and wicked, and who would go to hell for having failed to hear Moses and the prophets during their mortal lifetime. The meaning of the parable is thus changed from general to specific. This one sentence added by the JST ties the whole conversation together as mortar ties the blocks of a building or a wall.

The Parable of the Unjust Judge (Luke 18:1–8). This parable was spoken to the disciples to teach them diligence and perseverance. It tells of a judge who has the power to help a poor widow but is not concerned for her plight. After much importuning on her part, the judge responds because he is weary with her persistent pleas. The parable was restated in the Doctrine and Covenants (101:81–85) with application to the Saints in the 1830s seeking legal redress for loss of property by mob action in Missouri. The Prophet Joseph used the parable in the same way in a letter to the afflicted Saints in Missouri (TPJS, 36). The JST offers no substantial assistance or change.

The foregoing are the parables that received the most help in interpretation from the JST and the Doctrine and Covenants. Other parables are not included because they are not thus supplemented in latter-day scripture.

Several parables received extensive attention by the Prophet Joseph as he taught the Saints. Three of these are: The Lost Sheep; The Lost Coin; The Lost (Prodigal) Son (Luke 15:1–32).

These three parables all deal with lost things that are eventually found. They were spoken by Jesus to the Pharisees and scribes. The explanation by Joseph Smith shows that he regarded the Savior's teachings on this occasion as having a note of cutting sarcasm and rebuke to the Pharisees because of their pride and their refusal to do anything to help others in need. Here are the Prophet's words:

> In reference to the prodigal son, I said it was a subject I had never dwelt upon; that it was understood by many to be one of the intricate subjects of the scriptures; and even the Elders of this Church have preached largely upon it, without having any rule of interpretation. What is the rule of interpretation? Just no interpretation at all. Understand it precisely as it reads. . . .
>
> While Jesus was teaching the people, all the publicans and sinners drew near to hear Him; "and the Pharisees and scribes murmured, saying: This man receiveth sinners, and eateth with them." This is the keyword which unlocks the parable of the prodigal son. It was given to answer the murmurings and questions of the Sadducees and Pharisees, who were querying, finding fault, and saying, "How is it that this man as great as He pretends to be, eats with publicans and sinners?" Jesus was not put to it so, but He could have found something to illustrate His subject, if He had designed it for a nation or nations; but He did not. It was for men in an individual capacity; and all straining on this point is a bubble. "This man receiveth sinners and eateth with them."
>
> And he spake this parable unto them—"What man of you, having an hundred sheep, if he lose one of them doth not leave the ninety-and-nine in the wilderness, and go after that which is lost, until he find it? And when he hath found it, he layeth it on his shoulders, rejoicing. And when he cometh home, he calleth together his friends and neighbors, saying unto them, Rejoice with me; for I have found my sheep which was lost. I say unto you, that likewise joy shall be in heaven over one sinner that repenteth, more than over ninety-and-nine just persons which need no repentance." The hundred sheep represent one hundred Sadducees and Pharisees, as though Jesus had said, "If you Sadducees and Pharisees are in the sheepfold, I have no mission for you; I am sent to look up sheep that are lost; and when I have found them, I will back them up and make joy in heaven." This represents hunting after a few individuals, or one poor publican, which the Pharisees and Sadducees despised.
>
> He also gave them the parable of the woman and her ten pieces of silver, and how she lost one, and searching diligently, found it again, which gave more joy among the friends and neighbors than the nine which were not lost; like I say unto you, there is

joy in the presence of the angels of God over one sinner that repenteth, more than over ninety-and-nine just persons that are so
righteous; they will be damned anyhow; you cannot save them
(TPJS, 276–78).

Parables about the Kingdom of God on the Earth. A proper order
to the seven parables in Matthew 13 was seen by the Prophet
Joseph Smith in an article upon the subject written for the benefit
of the elders of the Church. This most interesting and enlightening article places a direct application of the seven parables to the
gathering of Israel and the establishment of the Church in the
last days.

The Prophet's explanation draws a sharp distinction between the Parable of the Tares and those which come after it by
making it the dividing line between those parables having an
allusion to the Church in the Savior's day and those parables
having an allusion to the Church in the latter days. His division
is as follows:

Soils (sower)
Tares (first half)[1]

Tares (second half)
Mustard Seed
Leaven
Pearl of Great Price
Hidden Treasure
Gospel Net

The parables of the sower, the tares, the mustard seed,
leaven, pearl of great price, hidden treasure, and gospel net all
have to do with preaching the gospel, gathering converts into
the Church, the sacrifice that must be made to secure one's salvation beyond mere membership, and the final judgment, for
the gospel net has collected all kinds. The Prophet Joseph discussed each one of these in his article (see TPJS, 94–102). In his

---

1. The Parable of the Tares has a broad application because it bridges the gap
between the meridian of time and the last days.

explanation the Prophet sees these parables as having application to missionary work, the Book of Mormon, the Three
Witnesses, the Church in the latter days, the JST, and the
covenants the Lord has made with the Latter-day Saints. His
words on these matters are:

"The Kingdom of Heaven is like unto leaven which a woman
took and hid in three measures of meal till the whole was
leavened." It may be understood that the Church of the Latter-
day Saints has taken its rise from a little leaven that was put into
three witnesses. Behold, how much this is like the parable! It is
fast leavening the lump, and will soon leaven the whole. . . .

"Again, the Kingdom of Heaven is like unto a net that was
cast into the sea, and gathered of every kind, which when it was
full they drew to shore, and sat down, and gathered the good into
vessels, but cast the bad away." For the work of this pattern, behold the seed of Joseph, spreading forth the Gospel net upon the
face of the earth, gathering of every kind, that the good may be
saved in vessels prepared for that purpose, and the angels will
take care of the bad. So shall it be at the end of the world—the angels shall come forth and sever the wicked from among the just,
and cast them into the furnace of fire, and there shall be wailing
and gnashing of teeth.

"Jesus saith unto them, Have ye understood all these things?
They say unto Him, Yea, Lord." And we say, yea, Lord; and well
might they say, yea, Lord; for these things are so plain and so glorious, that every Saint in the last days must respond with a hearty
Amen to them.

"Then said He unto them, therefore every scribe which is instructed in the kingdom of heaven, is like unto a man that is an
householder, which bringeth forth out of his treasure things that
are new and old."

For the works of this example, see the Book of Mormon coming forth out of the treasure of the heart. Also the covenants given
to the Latter-day Saints, also the translation of the Bible—thus
bringing forth out of the heart things new and old, thus answering to three measures of meal undergoing the purifying touch by
a revelation of Jesus Christ, and the ministering of angels, who
have already commenced this work in the last days, which will
answer to the leaven which leavened the whole lump. Amen.
(TPJS, 100, 102.)

List of Parables with References

The following alphabetical listing of the parables is provided for easy reference:

Barren Fig Tree
Luke 13:6–9

Chief Seats
Luke 14:7–11

Empty House
Matthew 12:43–45;
Luke 11:24–26

Foolish Rich Man
Luke 12:13–21

Friend at Midnight
Luke 11:5–13

Good Samaritan
Luke 10:25–37

Gospel Net
Matthew 13:47–50

Great Supper
Luke 14:16–24

Hidden Treasure
Matthew 13:44

King's Warfare
Luke 14:31–33

Laborers in the Vineyard
Matthew 19:27 to 20:16

Leaven
Matthew 13:33

Lost Coin
Luke 15:8–10

Lost Sheep
Luke 15:1–7

Lost (Prodigal) Son
Luke 15:11–32

Man Taking a Far Journey
Mark 13:34–37

Mustard Seed
Matthew 13:31–32

Pearl of Great Price
Matthew 13:45–46

Pharisee and Publican
Luke 18:9–14

Pounds
Luke 19:11–27

Rich Man and Lazarus
Luke 16:19–31

Royal Marriage Feast
Matthew 22:1–14

Sheep and the Goats
Mattthew 25:31–46

Shut Door
Luke 13:23–30

Talents
Matthew 25:14–30

Ten Virgins
Matthew 25:1–13

Treasures New and Old
Matthew 13:51–52

Two Debtors
Luke 7:36–50

Two Sons
Matthew 21:28–32

Seed Growing Secretly
Mark 4:26–29

Sower (Soils)
Matthew 13:1–9, 18:23;
Mark 4:1–8, 14–20;
Luke 8:5–8, 11–15

Uncompleted Tower
Luke 14:25–30

Unjust Judge
Luke 18:1–8

Unjust Steward
Luke 16:1–13

Unmerciful Servant
Matthew 18:21–35

Unprofitable Servants
Luke 17:5–10

Wheat and Tares
Matthew 13:24–30, 36–43

Wicked Husbandmen
Matthew 21:33–46;
Mark 12:1–12;
Luke 20:9–18

Allegories:

Good Shepherd
John 10:1–16

Vine and the Branches
John 15:1–8

CHAPTER 16

A Greater Portrayal of Jesus Christ

Translating the New Testament was a learning and revelatory experience that taught the Prophet Joseph Smith many things he had not known before. We also can have a learning experience with this translation when we study for ourselves the information that has thus come to us through Joseph Smith. In the Joseph Smith Translation we discover facts about Jesus and his life that are not revealed in any other translation of the Bible. It is almost like having the Prophet at our side to tutor us. As we progress through the chapters we will identify some of this new information and occasionally will use the KJV for comparison so that the contribution of Joseph Smith will shine forth more clearly. The KJV is the version of the Bible the Prophet used in making his translation.

Jesus, the Prince Born in Bethlehem

As recorded in the KJV, wise men from the east inquired of Herod about the birth of the "King of the Jews." Consequently, Herod asked the priests and scribes "where Christ should be born." He was told that it was written, "And thou Bethlehem, in the land of Juda, art not the least among the princes of Juda: for out of thee shall come a Governor, that shall rule my people Israel." (Matthew 2:2–6.)

However, as given in the JST, the men from the East asked Herod a more searching question: "Where is *the child* that is born, *the Messiah of the Jews*?"[1] Herod was told by the scribes that the prophets had written, "And thou, Bethlehem, *which lieth* in the land of *Judea, in thee shall be born a prince, which* art not the least among the princes of *Judea*; for out of thee shall come the *Messiah, who* shall *save* my people Israel" (JST Matthew 3:6).

As presented in the JST, then, it is not Bethlehem but Jesus who is the prince; and he is not simply a governor come to rule but the *Messiah* come to *save* Israel. Surely it was Jesus (and not Bethlehem) who was the prince, for he (and not the whole village) was to inherit the throne of David and rule Israel "with judgment and with justice . . . for ever" (Isaiah 9:6–7).

Jesus as a Developing Youth

After it was known to Herod that the prince, the heir to the throne of David, was born in Bethlehem, he sought to slay Jesus; whereupon Joseph, being warned in a dream, took Mary and Jesus into Egypt. A short time later Herod died, so they returned to Israel and settled in Galilee. Jesus is spoken of at this time as a "young child" (JST Matthew 2:20–23), probably not more than three or four years of age. The KJV continues without interruption: "In those days came John the Baptist, preaching in the wilderness of Judea" (Matthew 3:1).

Since John was only six months older than Jesus, it would be a remarkable feat for John "in those days" to be preaching and baptizing in the Jordan River, he being little more than a "young child," the same as Jesus. It is evident that there has been a lapse of many years about which nothing is said in the passage from Matthew. Indeed, because of the absence of information in the

---

1. In this chapter the changes in the JST are shown in italics.

KJV, many have thought that nothing is known of Jesus' early life except for one event at age twelve when he was in the temple. However, it is just at this point, between the return to Galilee and the preaching of John, that the JST inserts the following information.

> *And it came to pass that Jesus grew up with his brethren, and waxed strong, and waited upon the Lord for the time of his ministry to come.*
> *And he served under his father, and he spake not as other men, neither could he be taught; for he needed not that any man should teach him.*
> *And after many years, the hour of his ministry drew nigh.*
> *And in those days came John the Baptist, preaching in the wilderness of Judea.* (JST Matthew 3:24–27.)

Here the JST has provided just what is needed—a transitional period, a space of time in which John and Jesus could grow to maturity. And the passage gives an interesting glimpse into the personality and the developing years of Jesus during that time.

The Boy Jesus Teaches the Doctors at the Temple

The account of Jesus at the temple at age twelve is recorded in Luke 2:41–50. In the KJV Jesus was "sitting in the midst of the doctors, both hearing them, and asking them questions" (verse 46). The succeeding verse states that "all that heard him were astonished at his understanding and answers." The record of the event is strengthened in the JST, where Jesus was not only sitting with the learned doctors, but *"they were hearing him, and asking him* questions" (JST Luke 2:46). This clarification is necessary in order to make the event newsworthy. There is nothing essentially divine in a twelve-year-old boy's listening to his elders. But to be able to teach mature scholars and astound them with his knowledge of the scriptures is an event worth reporting. The KJV barely touches the real message of this passage, whereas the JST states it plainly.

This event, told only by Luke and in the JST, is in harmony with the earlier passage we discussed about Jesus' boyhood.

Both examples speak clearly of Jesus' spirituality and unusual intellect and personality as a growing youth approaching the time of his ministry.

The Baptism of Jesus

As reported in the KJV, Jesus came from Galilee to the Jordan and requested and received baptism from John. The account tells that when Jesus came out of the water "the heavens were opened unto him, and he saw the Spirit of God descending like a dove, and lighting upon him: and lo a voice from heaven, saying, This is my beloved Son, in whom I am well pleased" (Matthew 3:16–17).

As here reported, it was Jesus only who saw the Holy Ghost and heard the Father's voice. The JST corrects this passage by declaring: "*And John saw*, and lo, the heavens were opened unto him, and he saw the Spirit of God descending like a dove and lighting upon *Jesus*. And lo, *he heard* a voice from heaven, saying, This is my beloved Son, in whom I am well pleased. *Hear ye him.*" (JST Matthew 3:45–46.)

No doubt Jesus also witnessed these things, but we learn from the JST that John himself heard the voice of the Father and saw the Spirit descend upon Jesus. This view strengthens our appreciation for John and stresses the significance of his mission. He was called to bear witness of the Messiah, and the JST shows that he received the special training and experience that enabled him to do it. This concept is all but lost in other Bibles.

Forty Days in the Wilderness

The KJV records that after his baptism Jesus was led by the Spirit into the wilderness "to be tempted of the devil. And when he had fasted forty days and forty nights, he was afterward an hungred." (Matthew 4:1–2.)

The JST gives a different view: "Then Jesus was led up of the Spirit, into the wilderness, *to be with God*. And when he had fasted forty days and forty nights, *and had communed with God,* he was afterwards an hungered, *and was left to be tempted of the devil."* (JST Matthew 4:1–2.)

Furthermore, the account given by Luke states that Jesus was "forty days tempted of the devil" (Luke 4:2). The JST corrects this by saying, *"And after forty days, the devil came unto him, to tempt him"* (JST Luke 4:2).

The KJV further states in both Matthew and Luke that "the devil taketh" Jesus to a high mountain and also to a "pinnacle of the temple." However, according to the JST, it was not the devil but *"the Spirit"* who transported Jesus to these places, after which the devil then appeared to him. (Compare KJV Matthew 4:5–8 and Luke 4:5–9 with JST Matthew 4:5–8 and Luke 4:5–9.)

Thus the JST contributes in three ways toward a better understanding of Jesus' experience in the wilderness. First, his purpose for going there was not to seek out the devil, but to commune with God; second, he was not tempted for the forty days, but *after* the forty days were over; and third, it was the Spirit of God, not the devil, who conveyed Jesus to the mountain and the pinnacle. The JST account is also more reasonable than that of the KJV, for one would not fast and seek solitude in order to be tempted of the devil, but would do so to commune with God.

Jesus at the Wedding in Cana

The book of John tells of a wedding feast at Cana of Galilee early in Jesus' ministry, to which Jesus and his disciples were invited. The mother of Jesus was also there. When the refreshments were not of sufficient quantity for the multitude of the guests, Jesus' mother came to him and explained the situation. The KJV records the event: "And when they wanted wine, the mother of Jesus saith unto him, They have no wine. Jesus saith unto her, Woman, what have I to do with thee? mine hour is not yet come." (John 2:3–4.)

It seems a little brusque for Jesus to speak to his mother in this fashion. Fortunately the JST gives us a better view: "Jesus said unto her, Woman, what *wilt thou have me to do for thee? that will I do;* for mine hour is not yet come." (JST John 2:4.)

The JST account is more consistent with other accounts of the Savior's respect for his mother, and also blends better with the next verse, which reads: "His mother saith unto the servants, Whatsoever he saith unto you, do it" (John 2:5). This last comment would have little meaning if Jesus had turned down his mother's request.

Jesus Is Lord of the Sabbath

While Jesus was in Galilee the Pharisees criticized him for letting his disciples pluck ears of corn to eat on the Sabbath as they traveled through the fields. Jesus defended their behavior by comparing it to an event in the Old Testament in which David in a time of emergency ate shewbread from the tabernacle, which was ordinarily reserved only for the priests. As reported in the KJV, Jesus said to the Pharisees, "The sabbath was made for man, and not man for the sabbath." Apparently the intent of the passage was to present a compelling argument, as seen by the concluding sentence: "Therefore the Son of man is Lord also of the sabbath." (Mark 2:27–28.) The *therefore* indicates that Jesus had presented to the critical Pharisees some decisive or irrefutable facts to explain why the Sabbath was instituted and how he became the Lord of it. In the abbreviated condition of the passage as it now exists in the KJV the argument is simply not there.

The JST remedies the situation by retaining all that the KJV has and adding several key factors to the discussion: "And he said unto them, The Sabbath was made for man, and not man for the Sabbath. *Wherefore the Sabbath was given unto man for a day of rest; and also that man should glorify God, and not that man should not eat; for the Son of Man made the Sabbath day,* therefore the Son of Man is Lord also of the Sabbath." (JST Mark 2:25–27.)

The reasoning is thus completed: the purpose of the Sabbath is explained, and the final *therefore* is consistent with the Savior's declaration that since he made the Sabbath he is the Lord of it.

New Wine in Old Bottles

In Matthew chapter 9 the disciples of John the Baptist question Jesus as to why Jesus' disciples are not required to fast. John's disciples say that they themselves fast often, as do also the Pharisees. Jesus' reply is that the day will come when his disciples will fast, but the time is not yet. He then says, as recorded in the KJV, "No man putteth a piece of new cloth unto an old garment. . . . Neither do men put new wine into old bottles." (Matthew 9:15–17.)

Since these verses follow immediately after the question about fasting, the reader is led to believe that the comment about new cloth and new wine has something to do with that question. The JST, however, separates the question about fasting from the comment about the wine and the bottles, and records a second question—this one from the Pharisees—that has nothing to do with fasting:

> *And while he was thus teaching,* there came to him the disciples of John, saying, Why do we and the Pharisees fast oft, but thy disciples fast not?
>
> And Jesus said unto them, Can the children of the bridechamber mourn, as long as the bridegroom is with them?
>
> But the days will come, when the bridegroom shall be taken from them, and then shall they fast.
>
> *Then said the Pharisees unto him, Why will ye not receive us with our baptism, seeing we keep the whole law?*
>
> *But Jesus said unto them, Ye keep not the law. If ye had kept the law, ye would have received me, for I am he who gave the law.*
>
> *I receive not you with your baptism, because it profiteth you nothing. For when that which is new is come, the old is ready to be put away.*
>
> For no man putteth a piece of new cloth on an old garment; for that which is put in to fill it up, taketh from the garment, and the rent is made worse.
>
> Neither do men put new wine into old bottles; else the bottles break, and the wine runneth out, and the bottles perish; but they put new wine into new bottles, and both are preserved. (JST Matthew 9:15–23.)

Thus the symbolism of the patch of cloth and of the bottle of wine have to do with baptism, not with fasting as implied in the

KJV. Other significant additions to this passage include the statements that Jesus is the author of the law [of Moses]; that the law was about to be fulfilled in Jesus; and that the Pharisees' baptism was now useless, because the people needed to be baptized into the new dispensation by proper authority since the old dispensation was coming to an end. Very little of the doctrinal content of the JST can be discerned from the KJV, even by the most astute scholar. The JST reconstructs the scene, allowing the reader to observe more fully what took place.

Did Jesus Personally Perform Baptisms?

In KJV John 3:22 we read that Jesus came with his disciples into the land of Judea, "and there he tarried with them, and baptized." The passage seems to say that Jesus himself performed some of the baptisms. However, a little later we find: "When therefore the Lord knew how the Pharisees had heard that Jesus made and baptized more disciples than John, (though Jesus himself baptized not, but his disciples,) he left Judea, and departed again into Galilee" (John 4:1–3).

This passage denies that Jesus performed baptisms himself, contradicting the passage in John 3. The matter is resolved by the Prophet's translation, which brings into harmony the various statements about Jesus performing baptisms: "When therefore *the Pharisees had heard* that Jesus made and baptized more disciples than John, *they sought more diligently some means that they might put him to death; for many received John as a prophet, but they believed not on Jesus. Now the Lord knew this, though he himself baptized not so many as his disciples; for he suffered them for an example, preferring one another. And* he left Judea, and departed again into Galilee." (JST John 4:1–5.)

Not only does the JST clearly state that Jesus performed baptisms (see also JST Mark 1:6 and John 1:28) but it also explains why Jesus left the area. The KJV leaves us dangling because it mentions the Pharisees but doesn't say what they have to do with the story. The JST explains that they wanted to kill Jesus because of his popularity, and therefore he left Judea and went into Galilee.

Perceiving Others' Thoughts

Those who accept the divinity of Jesus Christ have no difficulty in believing that Jesus had a perfect personality, possessed great knowledge, and could even discern the thoughts of his companions. There is much evidence for this in the scriptures, but the JST strengthens our perception of these characteristics.

KJV Matthew 16 relates an event in which Jesus discusses a matter with the disciples, and they afterward "reasoned among themselves" about it. "Which when Jesus perceived, he said unto them. . . ." (Matthew 16:7–8). An impression is given here that a little time elapsed before Jesus understood the situation. The JST, on the other hand, provides this account: *"And when they reasoned among themselves,* Jesus perceived *it; and* he said unto them. . . ." (JST Matthew 16:9).

Matthew chapter 26 tells of a similar experience in which the disciples murmured about an expenditure of money for ointment. The KJV says: "When Jesus understood it, he said unto them. . . ." (Matthew 26:10). Again the impression is given that time elapsed before Jesus comprehended the situation. A different impression is given in the JST: "When they had said thus, Jesus understood them, and he said unto them. . . ." (JST Matthew 26:7).

Another instance of Jesus' ability to discern thoughts is found in Matthew chapter 12, in which "when Jesus knew it . . ." (verse 15) is revised in the JST to read, *"But* Jesus knew *when they took counsel . . ."* (verse 13). Similarly, KJV Matthew 19:26, which reads "But Jesus beheld them . . . ," is corrected to say, "But Jesus beheld *their thoughts.* . . ." (JST Matt. 19:26.)

The nature of the Savior's personal characteristics is further clarified in several other passages that were corrected by the Prophet Joseph Smith. We learn from JST Matthew 8:9 that it was not Jesus but they who were with him who marveled when the centurion from Capernaum expressed faith in the Lord's healing powers. And in JST Mark 14:36 we are told that it was not Jesus but the disciples who were "sore amazed" while in the Garden of Gethsemane.

Seeking Solitude

Jesus is occasionally reported to have left the noise and bustle of urban areas to go to "a desert place" (KJV Mark 6: 31–32; Luke 4:42; 9:10, 12). In the JST these same places are called "solitary" places. While a desert area may indeed be "solitary," a "solitary" place need not be a desert. It was probably not the hot drifting sand, the cacti, the crawling bugs, the snakes, and the flies, with the glare of the sun on the desert that Jesus sought, but rather he wanted seclusion, rest, and quietude. The choice of *solitary* in the JST has a little different inflection than the *desert* of the KJV and emphasizes this particular dimension of Jesus' personality. A close look at the context of these passages shows that the word *rest* is often used in the same verse, and that Jesus invites the Twelve to go with him to a solitary place to rest from the demanding conditions of their ministry. This is particularly clear in JST Mark 6:32–33: "And he said unto them, Come ye yourselves apart into a *solitary* place, and rest a while; for there were many coming and going, and they had no leisure, not so much as to eat. And they departed into a *solitary* place by ship, privately."

Jesus' Compassion

During his travels, Jesus took his disciples "into the borders of Tyre and Sidon." The KJV states that while there, Jesus "entered into an house, and would have no man know it: but he could not be hid" (Mark 7:24). The impression gained from this is that Jesus sought seclusion but could not obtain it because people found him in spite of his efforts to remain hidden.

The JST introduces a spiritual dimension to this passage which enhances our understanding of Jesus' personality. It records that Jesus "entered into a house, and would *that no man should come unto him. But he could not deny them; for he had compassion upon all men.*" (JST Mark 7:22–23.)

We know Jesus could remain hidden if the only considerations were physical. But his compassion overruled his need and desire for rest.

Jesus and Little Children

While in Galilee, Jesus placed a little child before his disciples and explained that the meekness and humility of little children are necessary qualifications for entering heaven. He emphasized children's favored status by declaring "that in heaven their angels do always behold the face of my Father which is in heaven. For the Son of man is come to save that which was lost." (KJV Matthew 18:10–11.)

In the JST, Jesus enlarges upon this event: "For the Son of man is come to save that which was lost, *and to call sinners to repentance; but these little ones have no need of repentance, and I will save them*" (JST Matthew 18:11).

This single improvement is by itself immensely significant, but it is followed by yet another event having to do with children. Following this episode in Galilee, Jesus traveled with his disciples into Judea some sixty miles to the south. While he was in Judea there were "brought unto him little children, that he should put his hands on them, and pray: and the disciples rebuked them" (KJV Matthew 19:13).

Why the disciples acted as they did is not stated in the KJV, and the reader is left to wonder at their motives. Did they think Jesus was too busy? Or were they themselves annoyed by the interruption?

Fortunately, the JST adds clarifying words: "And the disciples rebuked them, *saying, There is no need, for Jesus hath said, Such shall be saved*" (JST Matthew 19:13). From the text of the JST we see that the action of the disciples in Judea was influenced by the Savior's teachings in Galilee just a day or two earlier. The JST clarifies the motives of the disciples and speaks of the Savior's atoning sacrifice for little children. The reader's enjoyment of these two events is thereby significantly increased.

To Reject Christ Is to Reject the Prophets Also

The JST also portrays Jesus as very assertive and plain-spoken in his dealings with those who would not receive him as the Messiah. One such event occurs immediately after Jesus had declared what is required of anyone who seeks to be his disciple. The regimen includes obeying Jesus' commandments, enduring to the end, and being unafraid to lay down one's life for Jesus' sake. That this was more than some were willing to commit to is seen in JST Luke 14:26, 35–36, 38, which presents the following conversation. The KJV has no trace or hint of this word exchange: *"Then certain of them came to him, saying, Good Master, we have Moses and the prophets, and whosoever shall live by them, shall he not have life? And Jesus answered, saying, Ye know not Moses, neither the prophets; for if ye had known them, ye would have believed on me; for to this intent they were written. For I am sent that ye might have life. . . . These things he said, signifying that which was written, verily must all be fulfilled."*

Jesus' directness in challenging what they thought was their own true faith in the words of the prophets, but which he said was flawed on their part is quite forceful. Such a method would quickly separate the humble from the proud among his listeners.

Jesus Rebukes the Pharisees

The Jesus that is portrayed in the JST is more assertive and plainspoken than in the KJV. Even in the KJV Jesus is bold to rebuke the Jewish rulers, but in the JST he rebukes them more often and more thoroughly. A case in point is found in Luke 16:13–23. In this situation Jesus scolds the Jews for their overabundant interest in worldly things, and the Pharisees don't like his criticism and take strong exception to his teachings. The KJV seems to jump from one subject to another at this juncture, and speaks of self-justification, the law and the prophets, adultery, and a parable about a rich man and a beggar. The KJV does not tie these various blocks of information together, nor does it relate them directly to the Pharisees.

At this point the JST renders a service to our understanding by supplying connecting links between the blocks, and also giving many additional words of condemnation that Jesus spoke to the Pharisees on this occasion.

No servant can serve two masters; for either he will hate the one, and love the other; or else he will hold to the one, and despise the other. Ye cannot serve God and mammon.

And the Pharisees also who were covetous, heard all these things; and they derided him.

And he said unto them, Ye are they who justify yourselves before men; but God knoweth your hearts; for that which is highly esteemed among men, is an abomination in the sight of God.

And they said unto him, We have the law, and the prophets; but as for this man we will not receive him to be our ruler; for he maketh himself to be a judge over us.

Then said Jesus unto them, The law and the prophets *testify of me; yea, and all the prophets who have written, even* until John, *have foretold of these days.*

Since that time, the kingdom of God is preached, and every man *who seeketh truth* presseth into it.

And it is easier for heaven and earth to pass, than for one tittle of the law to fail.

And why teach ye the law, and deny that which is written; and condemn him whom the Father hath sent to fulfill the law, that ye might all be redeemed?

O fools! for you have said in your hearts, There is no God. And you pervert the right way; and the kingdom of heaven suffereth violence of you; and you persecute the meek; and in your violence you seek to destroy the kingdom; and ye take the children of the kingdom by force. Woe unto you, ye adulterers!

And they reviled him again, being angry for the saying, that they were adulterers.

But he continued, saying, Whosoever putteth away his wife, and marrieth another, committeth adultery; and whosoever marrieth her who is put away from her husband, committeth adultery. *Verily I say unto you, I will liken you unto the rich man.* (JST Luke 16:13–23.)

As can be seen, the JST moves naturally from concept to concept, directly associates the Pharisees with the major sins, and makes the Pharisees the rich man portrayed in the parable. The parable itself is part of Jesus' condemnation of the Pharisees, for the rich man when he dies goes to hell. He did not go there just because he was rich, but because he trusted in his riches and also did not obey the prophets in his mortal life.

With the fact established that the Pharisees (at least some of them) are guilty of adultery, we are able to gain an increased appreciation for another event which is recorded in the book of John. The enhanced view that the JST gives in Luke 16 contributes to an understanding of John 8:1–11, wherein the Pharisees bring to Jesus a woman whom they say has committed adultery—caught in the very act. They remind Jesus that the law of Moses stipulates that such should be stoned. They have no concern for the woman, but they want to test Jesus against the law given through Moses. They hope, if he recommends leniency, that they can accuse and discredit him publicly.

Jesus, who knows the hearts of every person, knows the hearts of those Pharisees. He also knows that no woman commits adultery alone, and that she might well have been a victim of a trap by those adulterous men. He does not answer them directly, but writes on the ground. What he wrote we are not told. When they continue to press him for an opinion, he says: "He that is without sin among you, let him first cast a stone at her" (John 8:7), and he writes again on the ground. The Pharisees, each convicted by his own conscience, leave one by one.

We do not know what Jesus wrote, but we know that he regarded many of the Pharisees as adulterers themselves. When he said that any in that crowd who was "without sin" could cast a stone, he didn't mean just any sin, he meant anyone there who was not as guilty of adultery as she was. We may only surmise what he wrote on the ground, but it is possible he spelled out particular persons, times, places, and partners wherein those Pharisees had performed the act.

A reader of these events cannot avoid getting a clearer mental picture of this event because of the conditioning and increased image of the Pharisees provided by the JST. It also enhances our awareness of Jesus' courage and forthrightness.

"Father, Forgive Them"

Luke reports that while Jesus was on the cross he cried out, "Father, forgive them; for they know not what they do" (KJV

23:34). The JST adds to this the following clarification: "(*Meaning the soldiers who crucified him*)" (JST Luke 23:35).

The Color of Jesus' Robe

At the time of scourging, prior to the Crucifixion, the soldiers placed a robe on Jesus. The KJV has varying reports as to the color. Matthew 27:28 says it was scarlet; Mark 15:17 and John 19:2 declare that it was purple; and Luke 23:11 says, simply, that it was gorgeous. In the JST, Matthew (27:30) is corrected to say "purple," and Luke remains unchanged with "gorgeous." In the JST manuscript for John 19:2 there is an explanatory note declaring that purple is the correct color and should so be stated "in all the Testimonies."

The significance of this correction is perhaps two-fold. First, purple is the color of royalty, which befits Jesus' royal lineage as king of Israel. Second, it is impressive that the Prophet Joseph Smith would have such precise knowledge about the matter and that he felt it was important enough to be corrected and emphasized.

Angels at the Tomb of Jesus

In each of the four records of the KJV, mention is made of the appearance of an angel, or angels, at Jesus' tomb on the morning of his resurrection. Luke (24:4–6) and John (20:11–13) specify that two angels were present, whereas Matthew (28:1–7) and Mark (16:5–6) indicate there was but one.

The JST is so worded as to make Matthew (28:2–4) and Mark (16:3–4) agree with the other testimonies that there were indeed two angels at the tomb.

It may seem to be relatively insignificant whether there were two angels or one angel at the tomb, since the important event was that Jesus Christ had risen from the grave. However, it is probable that these angels were there for more reasons than to roll the stone away. They were very likely official witnesses of the greatest event that has occurred on this earth, and according to the law of the scriptures, "in the mouth of two or three witnesses shall every word be established" (2 Corinthians 13:1; see also Deuteronomy 19:15). Their presence at the tomb as witnesses may account for the Prophet's care in causing all of the accounts to agree that two angels were present at the time of Jesus' resurrection. The angels did indeed bear witness to those who came to the sepulcher that Jesus had risen from the dead, and they may yet in a time to come—such as on the Day of Judgment—testify of this important occurrence. The scriptures do not tell who the angels were, but we may be assured that their selection for such an important task was not casual.

We have here sampled some interesting and important passages from the JST concerning the personality and ministry of the Savior. There are many similar passages waiting to be discovered by the gospel student; and given the 1979 LDS edition of the Bible, the discovery is now easier than ever before.

CHAPTER 17

The Jesus that
Joseph Smith Knew

I t is the basis of this chapter that the Prophet Joseph Smith had something unique to say about the mission of the Lord Jesus Christ, especially the circumstances of his earthly ministry. The Prophet was completely familiar with everything the scriptures say about Jesus, and he had personally seen the Savior a number of times in which he both saw and talked with him. The Prophet also had many revelations through the Holy Ghost, which would give him knowledge. All of these gave him an immense reservoir of understanding. No one since Peter was as qualified to discuss the doctrine and the personality of Jesus Christ.

The excerpts from Joseph Smith's statements used in this chapter were spoken or written by him at numerous times and circumstances. He did not incorporate the materials into a formal treatise on the Savior, but he uttered them from the depths of his understanding as he discoursed on many gospel-related subjects. Many of them came forth extemporaneously and hence reveal his spontaneous feelings about the Savior's personality and nature. When Joseph Smith spoke it was not "as the scribes," with reasoned, tradition-based conclusions. He spoke from firsthand spiritual experience.

These utterances are arranged in this chapter by subject-matter categories. Of particular significance are those items in which the Prophet explained what Jesus said and why he said it, his purposes, and so forth. It is in this subject area that the Prophet gave the most unique type of information concerning Jesus. Doctrinal matters can be learned from the standard works. Yet it is a special experience to feel the certitude and familiarity of the Prophet as he opens to our view the personality and methods of the Son of God.

Except where designated otherwise, all of the quotations in this chapter are taken from the book *Teachings of the Prophet Joseph Smith*. Page numbers refer to that source.

The Fundamental Doctrine of Jesus Christ

The fundamental principles of our religion are the testimony of the Apostles and Prophets, concerning Jesus Christ, that He died, was buried, and rose again the third day, and ascended into heaven (p. 121).

Jesus Atoned for the Fall

The Son of God came into the world to redeem it from the fall (p. 12).

The Gospel Was Always Preached in the Name of Jesus Christ

In the former ages of the world, before the Saviour came in the flesh, "the saints" were baptized in the name of Jesus Christ to come, because there never was any other name whereby man could be saved; and after he came in the flesh and was crucified, then the saints were baptized in the name of Jesus Christ, crucified, risen from the dead and ascended into heaven, that they might be buried in baptism like him, and be raised in glory like him, that as there was but one Lord, one faith, one baptism, and one God and father of us all, even so there was but one door to the mansions of bliss (p. 266).

Whenever the Lord revealed Himself to men in ancient days, and commanded them to offer sacrifice to Him, . . . it was done that they might look forward in faith to the time of His coming, and rely upon the power of that atonement for a remission of their sins (pp. 60–61).

Jesus Made Promises of Salvation in Premortal Life

It is necessary that the sealing power should be in our hands to seal our children and our dead for the fulness of the dispensation of times—a dispensation to meet the promises made by Jesus Christ before the foundation of the world for the salvation of man (p. 356).

Christ Can Be Known Only by and Through the Holy Ghost

The Prophet commented on 1 Corinthians 12:3:

[The statement] "No man can say that Jesus is the Lord, but by the Holy Ghost," should be translated, "no man can know that Jesus is the Lord, but by the Holy Ghost" (p. 223).

The Testimony of Jesus

No man is a minister of Jesus Christ without being a Prophet. No man can be a minister of Jesus Christ except he has the testimony of Jesus; and this is the spirit of prophecy. (P. 160.)

Jesus' Earthly Ministry

Intelligence of Jesus as a Boy

While instructing the Brethren in Carthage Jail, the Prophet said it would be well not to tell all the truth about their enemies for the present, because the Church was small and not able to defend itself. To illustrate his point, he said:

Even Jesus, the Son of God, had to refrain from doing so, and had to restrain His feelings many times for the safety of Himself and His followers, and had to conceal the righteous purposes of His heart in relation to many things pertaining to His Father's kingdom. When still a boy He had all the intelligence necessary to enable Him to rule and govern the kingdom of the Jews, and could reason with the wisest and most profound doctors of law and divinity, and make their theories and practice to appear like folly compared with the wisdom He possessed; but He was a boy only, and lacked physical strength even to defend His own person; and was subject to cold, to hunger and to death. (P. 392.)

Character and Perfection of Jesus

I do not think there have been many good men on the earth since the days of Adam; but there was one good man and his name was Jesus (p. 303).

Jesus Christ . . . had no need of repentance, having no sin (p. 266).

Who, among all the Saints in these last days, can consider himself as good as our Lord? Who is as perfect? Who is as pure? Who is as holy as He was? Are they to be found? He never transgressed or broke a commandment or law of heaven—no deceit was in His mouth, neither was guile found in His heart. . . . Where is one like Christ? He cannot be found on earth. (P. 67.)

None ever were perfect but Jesus; and why was he perfect? Because He was the Son of God, and had the fullness of the Spirit, and greater power than any man. (Pp. 187–88.)

Difficulty of Jesus' Mortal Life

[Jesus] is also the express image and likeness of the personage of the Father, possessing all the fullness of the Father, or the same fullness with the Father; being begotten of him, and ordained from before the foundation of the world to be a <u>propitiation</u> for *appease* the sins of all those who should believe on his name, and is called the Son because of the flesh, and descended in suffering below that which man can suffer; or, in other words, suffered greater sufferings, and was exposed to more powerful contradictions than any man can be. But, notwithstanding all this, he kept the law of God, and remained without sin, showing thereby that it is in the power of man to keep the law and remain also without sin; and also, that by him a righteous judgment might come upon all flesh, and that all who walk not in the law of God may justly be condemned by the law, and have no excuse for their sins. And he being the Only Begotten of the Father, full of grace and truth, and having overcome, received a fullness of the glory of the Father. (*Lectures on Faith*, 5:2.)

The Obedience of Christ

Christ Himself fulfilled all righteousness in becoming obedient to the law which he had given to Moses on the mount, and thereby magnified it and made it honorable, instead of destroying it (p. 276).

If a man gets a fulness of the priesthood of God he has to get it in the same way that Jesus Christ obtained it, and that was by keeping all the commandments and obeying all the ordinances of the house of the Lord (p. 308).

Meekness and Lowliness of Jesus

Some of the company thought I was not a very meek Prophet; so I told them: "I am meek and lowly in heart," and will personify Jesus for a moment, to illustrate the principle, and cried out with a loud voice, "Woe unto you, ye doctors; woe unto you, ye lawyers; woe unto you, ye scribes, Pharisees, and hypocrites!" But you cannot find the place where I ever went that I found fault with their food, their drink, their house, their lodgings; no, never; and this is what is meant by the meekness and lowliness of Jesus. (P. 270.)

The Authority of Jesus

The Lord [is] a priest forever, after the order of Melchizedek, and the anointed Son of God, from before the foundation of the world (p. 265).

After explaining that John the Baptist held the keys of the Aaronic Priesthood, the Prophet said:

Christ came according to the words of John, and He was greater than John, because He held the keys of the Melchizedek Priesthood and the kingdom of God (p. 274).

The Savior said unto John, I must be baptized by you. Why so? To fulfill all righteousness. John refuses at first, but afterwards obeyed by administering the ordinance of baptism unto him, Jesus having no other legal administrator to apply to.

There is no salvation between the two lids of the Bible without a legal administrator. Jesus was then the legal administrator, and ordained His Apostles. (P. 319.)

When Jesus Christ came to any of John's disciples, He baptized them with fire and the Holy Ghost (p. 336).

Christ was the head of the Church, the chief corner stone, the spiritual rock upon which the church was built, and the gates of hell shall not prevail against it. He built up the Kingdom, chose Apostles, and ordained them to the Melchizedek Priesthood, giving them power to administer in the ordinances of the Gospel. (P. 318.)

The Priesthood is everlasting. The Savior, Moses, and Elias [Elijah], gave the keys to Peter, James and John, on the mount, when they were transfigured before him. (P. 158.)

Messiah is above the spirit and power of Elijah, for He made the world, and was that spiritual rock unto Moses in the wilderness (p. 340).

Jesus Christ is the heir of this [celestial] Kingdom—the Only Begotten of the Father according to the flesh, and holds the keys over all this world (p. 323).

Belief in Christ Is Insufficient Without Obedience

Jesus said unto His disciples, "In my Father's house are many mansions, if it were not so, I would have told you. I go to prepare a place for you, and I will come and receive you to myself, that where I am ye may be also."

Any man may believe that Jesus Christ is the Son of God, and be happy in that belief, and yet not obey his commandments, and at last be cut down for disobedience to the Lord's righteous requirements. (P. 311.)

Christ's Atonement Applies to Animals

In explaining the Revelation given to John on the Isle of Patmos, the Prophet made these comments concerning the salvation of animals through the Lamb of God:

But John saw the actual beast in heaven, showing to John that beasts did actually exist there, . . .

John saw curious looking beasts in heaven; he saw every creature that was in heaven,—all the beasts, fowls and fish in heaven,—actually there, giving glory to God. How do you prove it? (See Rev. 5:13.) "And every creature which is in heaven, and on the earth, and under the earth, and such as are in the sea, and all that are in them, heard I saying, Blessing, and honor, and glory, and power, be unto Him that sitteth upon the throne, and unto the Lamb for ever and ever."

I suppose John saw beings there of a thousand forms, that had been saved from ten thousand times ten thousand earths like this,—strange beasts of which we have no conception: all might be seen in heaven. The grand secret was to show John what there was in heaven. John learned that God glorified Himself by saving all that His hands had made, whether beasts, fowls, fishes or men; and He will glorify Himself with them. (P. 291.)

Why Jesus Sometimes Spoke in Parables

Although it is popularly thought that Jesus used parables so that everyone could understand his teachings, it will be seen that the Prophet Joseph Smith said that was not the case. Jesus used parables to veil and withhold the doctrines from the unbelieving. Nor was it an act of mercy to shield them from judgment. Jesus used parables so that the unbelieving who would not hear would remain in spiritual darkness by their own choice. (See also chapter 15 concerning "Parables.") Here are the Prophet's words on the subject:

> "And the disciples came and said unto Him, Why speakest thou unto them in parables? [I would here remark, that the 'them' made use of in this interrogation, is a personal pronoun, and refers to the multitude.] He answered and said unto them, [that is unto the disciples] because it is given unto you, to know the mysteries of the Kingdom of Heaven, but to them, [that is, unbelievers] it is not given; for whosoever hath, to him shall be given, and he shall have more abundance; but whosoever hath not, from him shall be taken away even that he hath."

We understand from this saying, that those who had been previously looking for a Messiah to come, according to the testimony of the prophets, and were then, at that time looking for a Messiah, but had not sufficient light, on account of their unbelief, to discern Him to be their Savior; and He being the true Messiah, consequently they must be disappointed, and lose even all the knowledge, or have taken away from them all the light, understanding, and faith which they had upon this subject; therefore he that will not receive the greater light, must have taken away from him all the light which he hath; and if the light which is in you become darkness, behold, how great is that darkness! "Therefore," says the Savior, "speak I unto them in parables because they, seeing, see not, and hearing, they hear not, neither do they understand; and in them is fulfilled the prophecy of Esaias, which saith, By hearing ye shall hear, and shall not understand; and seeing ye shall see, and not perceive."

Now we discover that the very reason assigned by this prophet, why they would not receive the Messiah, was, because they did not or would not understand; and seeing, they did not perceive; "for this people's heart is waxed gross, and their ears are dull of hearing, and their eyes they have closed, lest at any time they should see with their eyes, and hear with their ears, and understand with their heart, and should be converted, and I should heal them." But what saith He to His disciples? "Blessed are your eyes for they see, and your ears for they hear; for verily I say unto you, that many prophets and righteous men have desired to see those things which ye see, and have not seen them; and to hear those things which ye hear, and have not heard them."

We again make remark here—for we find that the very principle upon which the disciples were accounted blessed, was because they were permitted to see with their eyes and hear with their ears—that the condemnation which rested upon the multitude that received not His saying, was because they were not willing to see with their eyes, and hear with their ears; not because they could not, and were not privileged to see and hear, but because their hearts were full of iniquity and abominations; "as your fathers did, so do ye." The prophet, foreseeing that they would thus harden their hearts, plainly declared it; and herein is the condemnation of the world; that light hath come into the world, and men choose darkness rather than light, because their deeds are evil. This is so plainly taught by the Savior, that a wayfaring man need not mistake it. . . . Men are in the habit, when the truth is exhibited by the servants of God, of saying, All is mystery; they have spoken in parables, and, therefore, are not to be understood. It is true they have eyes to see, and see not, but none are so blind as those who will not see; and, although the Savior spoke this to such characters, yet unto His disciples he expounded it plainly. . . .

. . . Thus the Savior Himself explains unto His disciples the parable which He put forth, and left no mystery or darkness upon the minds of those who firmly believe on His words.

We draw the conclusion, then, that the very reason why the multitude, or the world, as they were designated by the Savior, did not receive an explanation upon His parables, was because of unbelief. To you, He says (speaking to His disciples) it is given to know the mysteries of the Kingdom of God. And why? Because of the faith and confidence they had in Him. (Pp. 94–97.)

Why Jesus Associated with Sinners

Christ said he came to call sinners to repentance, to save them. Christ was condemned by the self-righteous Jews because He took sinners into His society; He took them upon the principle that they repented of their sins. (P. 240.)

The Jews Considered Jesus to Be the "Least"

In praise of John the Baptist, Jesus told a multitude that among those born of women there was not a greater prophet than John. He then added: "But he that is least in the kingdom of God is greater than he [John]" (Luke 7:28). The Prophet Joseph was asked what that saying meant. In reply he asked:

Whom did Jesus have reference to as being the least? Jesus was looked upon as having the least claim in God's kingdom, and [seemingly] was least entitled to their credulity as a prophet; as though He had said—"He that is considered the least among you is greater than John—that is I myself." (P. 276.)

Why Jesus Wanted to Gather the Jews

Why gather the people together in this place [Nauvoo]? For the same purpose that Jesus wanted to gather the Jews—to receive the ordinances, the blessings, and glories that God has in store for His Saints. (P. 312.)

Jesus said unto the Jews, "How oft would I have gathered thy children together, even as a hen gathereth her chickens under her wings, and ye would not!"—that they might attend to the ordinances of baptism for the dead as well as other ordinances of the priesthood, and receive revelations from heaven, and be perfected in the things of the kingdom of God—but they would not. . . . God ordained that He would save the dead, and would do it by gathering His people together. (P. 310.)

Responsibility that Jesus Placed upon the Jews

Hence it was that so great a responsibility rested upon the generation in which our Savior lived, for, says he, "That upon you may come all the righteous blood shed upon the earth, from the blood of righteous Abel unto the blood of Zacharias, son of Barachias, whom ye slew between the temple and the altar. Verily I say unto you, all these things shall come upon this generation." (Matthew 23:35, 36.) Hence as they possessed greater privileges than any other generation, not only pertaining to themselves, but to their dead, their sin was greater, as they not only neglected their own salvation but that of their progenitors, and hence their blood was required at their hands. (Pp. 222–23.)

It was the design of the councils of heaven before the world was, that the principles and laws of the priesthood should be predicated upon the gathering of the people in every age of the world. Jesus did everything to gather the people, and they would not be gathered, and He therefore poured out curses upon them. (P. 308.)

Jesus Followed in the Path of His Father

The following commentaries are on Jesus' statements found in John 5:19, 26; 10:17:

The Scriptures inform us that Jesus said, As the Father hath power in Himself, even so hath the Son power—to do what? Why, what the Father did. The answer is obvious—in a manner to lay down His body and take it up again. Jesus, what are you going to do? To lay down my life as my Father did, and take it up again. Do we believe it? If you do not believe it, you do not believe the Bible. (P. 346.)

As the Father hath power in Himself, so hath the Son power in Himself, to lay down His life and take it again, so He has a body of His own. The Son doeth what He hath seen the Father do: then the Father hath some day laid down His life and taken it again; so He has a body of His own; each one will be in His own body; and yet the sectarian world believe the body of the Son is identical with the Father's. (P. 312.)

What did Jesus do? Why; I do the things I saw my Father do when worlds came rolling into existence. My Father worked out his kingdom with fear and trembling, and I must do the same; and when I get my kingdom, I shall present it to my Father, so that he may obtain kingdom upon kingdom, and it will exalt him in glory. He will then take a higher exaltation, and I will take his place, and thereby become exalted myself. So that Jesus treads in the tracks of his Father, and inherits what God did before; and God is thus glorified and exalted in the salvation and exaltation of all his children. It is plain beyond disputation, and you thus learn some of the first principles of the Gospel, about which so much hath been said. (Pp. 347–48.)

Jesus Not Without Fault in the Eyes of Some

Do you think that even Jesus, if He were here, would be without fault in your eyes? His enemies said all manner of evil against Him—they all watched for iniquity in Him. How easy it was for Jesus to call out all the iniquity of the hearts of those whom He was among! (P. 258.)

The Principle Which Caused Jesus' Crucifixion

Many men will say, "I will never forsake you, but will stand by you at all times." But the moment you teach them some of the mysteries of the kingdom of God that are retained in the heavens and are to be revealed to the children of men when they are prepared for them they will be the first to stone you and put you to death. It was this same principle that crucified the Lord Jesus Christ, and will cause the people to kill the prophets in this generation. (P. 309.)

In explaining the seriousness of sinning against the light, the Prophet said:

When once that light which was in them is taken from them, they become as much darkened as they were previously enlightened, and then, no marvel, if all their power should be enlisted against the truth, and they, Judas like, seek the destruction of those who were their greatest benefactors. What nearer friend on earth, or in heaven, had Judas than the Savior? And his first object was to destroy Him. (P. 67.)

This Generation Would Crucify Jesus

This generation is as corrupt as the generation of the Jews that crucified Christ; and if He were here to-day, and should preach the same doctrine He did then, they would put Him to death (p. 328).

I have not the least idea, if Christ should come to the earth and preach such rough things as He preached to the Jews, but that this generation would reject Him for being so rough (p. 307).

Jesus' Post-Mortal Ministry

Jesus in the World of Spirits

Here then we have an account of our Savior preaching to the spirits in prison, to spirits that had been imprisoned from the days of Noah; and what did He preach to them? That they were to stay there? Certainly not! Let His own declaration testify. "He hath sent me to heal the broken-hearted, to preach deliverance to the captives, and recovering of sight to the blind, to set at liberty them that are bruised" (Luke 4:18). . . . It is very evident from this that He not only went to preach to them, but to deliver, or bring them out of the prison house. (P. 219.)

I will say something about the spirits in prison. There has been much said by modern divines about the words of Jesus (when on the cross) to the thief, saying, "This day shalt thou be with me in paradise." King James' translators make it out to say paradise. But what is paradise? It is a modern word: it does not answer at all to the original word that Jesus made use of. Find the original of the word paradise. You may as easily find a needle in a haymow. Here is a chance for battle, ye learned men. There is nothing in the original word in Greek from which this was taken that signifies paradise; but it was—This day thou shalt be with me in the world of spirits: then I will teach you all about it and answer your inquiries. (P. 309.)

Jesus Christ became a ministering spirit (while His body was lying in the sepulchre) to the spirits in prison, to fulfill an important part of His mission, without which He could not have perfected His work, or entered into His rest. After His resurrection He appeared as an angel to His disciples. . . .

. . . Jesus Christ went in body after His resurrection, to minister to resurrected bodies. (P. 191.)

Jesus and Adam

Adam, who was the first man, . . . the Ancient of Days, . . . is Michael . . . to whom Christ was first revealed, and through whom Christ has been revealed from heaven, and will continue to be revealed from henceforth (p. 167).

Christ is the Great High Priest; Adam next (p. 158).

Speaking of Jesus' role at the future conference at Adam-ondi-Ahman, the Prophet said:

The Son of Man stands before him [Adam], and there is given him glory and dominion. Adam delivers up his stewardship to Christ, that which was delivered to him as holding the keys of the universe, but retains his standing as head of the human family. (P. 157.)

This, then, is the nature of the Priesthood; every man holding the Presidency of his dispensation, and one man holding the Presidency of them all, even Adam; and Adam receiving his Presidency and authority from the Lord, but cannot receive a fullness until Christ shall present the Kingdom to the Father, which shall be at the end of the last dispensation (p. 169).

Second Coming of Jesus Christ

The Son of God shall burst the veil, and appear in all the glory of his Father, with all the holy angels (p. 42).

I testify of these things, and that the coming of the Son of Man is nigh, even at your doors. If our souls and our bodies are not looking forth for the coming of the Son of Man; and after we are dead, if we are not looking forth, we shall be among those who are calling for the rocks to fall upon them. (P. 160.)

Jesus Christ never did reveal to any man the precise time that He would come. Go and read the Scriptures, and you cannot find anything that specifies the exact hour He would come; and all that say so are false teachers. (P. 341.)

The Rule of Christ in the Millennium

Christ and the resurrected Saints will reign over the earth during the thousand years. They will not probably dwell upon the earth, but will visit it when they please, or when it is necessary to govern it. (P. 268.)

Jesus Is the Perfect Example of a Saved Being

Where shall we find a prototype into whose likeness we may be assimilated, in order that we may be made partakers of life and salvation? or, in other words, where shall we find a saved being? for if we can find a saved being, we may ascertain without much difficulty what all others must be in order to be saved. . . . We conclude, as to the answer of this question, there will be no dispute among those who believe the Bible, that it is Christ: all will agree in this, that he is the prototype or standard of salvation; or, in other words, that he is a saved being. And if we should continue our interrogation, and ask how it is that he is saved? the answer would be—because he is a just and holy being; and if he were anything different from what he is, he would not be saved; for his salvation depends on his being precisely what he is and nothing else; for if it were possible for him to change, in the least degree, so sure he would fail of salvation and lose all his dominion, power, authority and glory, which constitute salvation; for salvation consists in the glory, authority, majesty, power and dominion which Jehovah possesses and in nothing else; and no being can possess it but himself or one like him. (*Lectures on Faith* 7:9.)

CHAPTER 18

How Jesus Dealt with People

J esus is the creator of the planet on which we live, the creator of the stars we see in the heavens. He is the firstborn son of God in the spirit, the Only Begotten of the Father in the flesh. He atoned for Adam's fall and for our own sins. He is our only Savior, and the final judge of mankind. By comparison the rest of us are so insignificant that we might ask ourselves, who are *we* to interpret Jesus? Yet we rely upon the scriptures and the words of the Brethren, we have the witness of the Holy Ghost, and insofar as we follow that, as Paul said, "we have the mind" of the Lord (1 Corinthians 2:16). When we speak by the inspiration of the Holy Spirit, we say the same things Jesus would say if he were present (see 2 Nephi 32:3). We have been counseled to "trifle not with sacred things" (D&C 6:12), and Jesus has said that men must "beware how they take [his] name in their lips," because "that which cometh from above is sacred, and must be spoken with care, and by constraint of the Spirit; and in this there is no condemnation" (D&C 63:61, 64). With this caution in mind we will examine what has been revealed to us about how Jesus Christ dealt with people while on earth.

The Greatest Person to Live on Earth

There is no doubt that Jesus is the greatest teacher and the greatest example the world has ever known. This is because he is the greatest being that has lived on this earth. He was literally a God living among mortal men. A great Christian gentleman, Dr. Earl V. Pullias of the University of Southern California, wrote, "One can be no greater as a teacher than he is as a person" (*Toward Excellence in College Teaching* [Dubuque, Iowa: W. C. Brown Co., 1963], p. 44). President Harold B. Lee expressed a corollary to this when he said, "You cannot lift another soul until you are standing on higher ground than he is. . . . You cannot light a fire in another soul unless it is burning in your own soul. You teachers, the testimony that you bear, the spirit with which you teach and with which you lead, is one of the most important assets that you can have, as you help to strengthen those who need so much, wherein you have so much to give." (CR, April 1973, pp. 178–79.)

Jesus is the greatest of all teachers because he is the greatest of all persons who have lived on this earth. He stood on the higher ground, and he excelled in every way.

Factors Necessary for Great Teaching

In order for great teaching to occur, certain factors have to be present. I have listed four.

First, one must have something important to teach. The most important truth and subject matter is the gospel of Jesus Christ. Hence Jesus Christ was engaged in the most important work in the world. True religious doctrines will have a more lasting effect, change more people's lives, and do more good in the world than all the secular philosophies and man-made programs ever devised.

Second, there should be a purpose for the instruction.

Third, there must be somebody to teach.

Fourth, one must have an effective way of communicating. In this category are methods, vocabulary, examples, use of objects, models, and audio-visual aids. It includes also recognizing the opportune time, and giving the proper level of instruction based on the readiness of the learner. The material must be appropriate for the occasion, and should be conveyed in so plain a manner that no one can misunderstand. We must teach by the Spirit so that we not only inform but also inspire. And we must testify that we know that what we have taught is true, so that the words will go into the heart and not just into the head.

Using the books of Matthew, Mark, Luke, and John, which are testimonies about Jesus, we will look at some of the events in Jesus' mortal ministry and see what we can learn about him as a communicator. We will supplement the KJV with latter-day scripture—especially with the JST, because it makes Jesus a more vivid figure than other Bibles do.

Jesus' Teaching Was an Organized Plan

Jesus came to earth with a preassigned mission, and as he grew to maturity that mission became completely clear to him. He knew exactly what he needed to accomplish, and he used various communicative methods to get it done. The most prominent tasks he needed to accomplish appear to have been:

1. To prepare himself spiritually. No one deed would suffice, and there would of necessity be many deeds all during his life. The final experience before beginning his public ministry was the forty days in the wilderness, immediately after his baptism, in which he communed with his Heavenly Father (JST Matthew 4:1–10; Mark 1:12–13; JST Luke 4:1–14). The JST gives us by far the best picture of this experience.
2. To bear witness of the gospel (John 7:7; 9:39–41; 15:22; 18:37).
3. To show mankind the only true way toward eternal salvation (John 14:6).
4. To establish the kingdom of God among men on the earth through the restoration of the gospel and the priesthood and converting the honest in heart (includes the training of the Twelve).

5. To withstand temptation and live without sin (Matthew 4:3–11; Hebrews 2:4–18; 4:15; Alma 7:10–13; *Lectures on Faith* 5:2).
6. To testify against wickedness and false traditions (JST John 7:24; Matthew 15:3–6; Mark 7:9–13; 2 Nephi 10:3–5).
7. To make an atonement with his blood and give his life for the world (Luke 24:45–48; John 10:15; Mosiah 3:16–19; D&C 38:4; 45:3–5).
8. To bring to pass the resurrection of all mankind from the dead (John 5:25–29; 2 Nephi 9:21–22; Mormon 9:13).

Teaching was not an end in itself to Jesus, it was a way of accomplishing his purposes. Teaching was a means to advance the gospel and to establish the kingdom of God on the earth.

The record of Jesus' public ministry shows an organized plan: (1) During the first year after his baptism he taught the multitudes, most of whom had already been introduced to the gospel by John the Baptist. From among those who followed him, he chose the ones he would make the leaders. (2) After calling the Twelve and the Seventy, Jesus' efforts were directed less toward the masses and more toward training these new officers. The so-called Sermon of the Mount was given to the disciples only, at a missionary preparation meeting, and not as a public discourse. (3) After this instruction the Twelve and the Seventy were soon sent on missions by Jesus while he was still on earth. This gave them valuable experience at a time while Jesus was still around to counsel them. To properly train the teachers is of prime importance in building the kingdom, and Jesus attended to it personally. (4) No doubt the missionary practices of the early Church were patterned after the methods they had observed when Jesus taught. Jesus spent much of his last two years of mortal life training those who would be the leaders in the Church. (5) The last week of his mortal life he spent instructing the Twelve, and also testifying boldly against the dealings of the Jewish religious leaders. (6) His entire ministry was orderly and purposeful, directed toward accomplishing his mission on the earth.

I have observed at least twenty-seven different ways by which Jesus taught or communicated with people. This idea was first suggested to me over forty years ago in a master's thesis written by Glenn L. Pearson, a former BYU faculty member ("Missionary Methods and Doctrines of the Primitive Church as Determined by a Study of the New Testament," unpublished M.A. Thesis, BYU, 1951, pp. 1–444). Through the years I have continued to learn from the scriptures and have enlarged, adapted, and rearranged what Brother Pearson originally suggested. The twenty-seven are as follows:

1. Used simple declaration. Matthew 5, 6, 7; John 7:14–18.
2. Spoke with forthrightness and authority (not second-hand). Matthew 7:28–29.
3. Performed miracles as a teaching activity. Matthew 21:18–22; Mark 2:8–12; 6:51–52.
4. Spoke consoling words. Mark 5:36; Luke 7:43–50; John 8:10–11.
5. Used irony (almost sarcasm). Matthew 9:10–13; Mark 2:15–17; Luke 5:27–32; 15:1–7; John 8:39–44.
6. Used subtlety and wile. John 4:15–19.
7. Prophesied. Matthew 24:3–51; 12:36–42.
8. Quoted from the Old Testament. Matthew 19:3–6; 22:31–32; John 10:34.
9. Appealed to the Old Testament for precedence. Matthew 12:1–8.
10. Taught the multitudes and Jewish rulers with parables to veil the mysteries from them. JST Matthew 13:1–52; 21:34; Luke 15:1–32; 16:1–31.
11. Used logic. Matthew 12:24–28; Mark 3:22–26; Luke 13:14–17.
12. Employed object lessons. Matthew 18:1–6; 22:16–22; Luke 5:4–10.
13. Used colorful, attention-getting figures of speech. Matthew 18:6; 23:15–33; Mark 14:21; Luke 7:24–28; John 5:14.
14. Asked questions to direct the listener's thinking. Matthew 16:13–15; Luke 7:24–26; 22:35; 24:13–26.
15. Asked questions of those who asked him questions. Luke 10:25–28.
16. Bargained by means of questions. Matthew 21:23–27.
17. Used invective and censure. Matthew 11:20–24; 23:1–39.
18. Used witty reply and repartee. Matthew 22:15–46; John 4:16–19; 10:31–32.

19. Sometimes posed a doctrinal problem. Matthew 17:24–25; 22:41–46; Luke 7:40–42.
20. Candidly corrected those who were in error. Matthew 22:29.
21. Used debate and argument (beyond mere discussion). John chapters 7–8.
22. Was selective in what he taught in different groups. Matthew 7:6; 13:10–11.
23. Refused to give signs. Matthew 12:38–40.
24. Changed the subject, thus avoiding the full force of the issue. Matthew 22:30–32.
25. At least one time refused to say anything. Luke 23:7–11.
26. Sometimes must have communicated by facial expression or other body language, or a pause, or a quick response.
27. Taught by the Spirit—the power of the Holy Ghost. Luke 4:1, 14, 15.

Communication Other Than by Words

In making a list of Jesus' teaching methods it became apparent to me that his methods were adapted to the particular need of the occasion. While our basic sources for information—Matthew, Mark, Luke, and John—are effective testimonies, they are incomplete biographies and therefore often lack supporting details. A person often communicates much without uttering a word: by facial expression, a raised eyebrow, a wink, a gesture, a stare, a smile, a frown, a movement of the body, and so forth, all of which generally go unrecorded and therefore are sometimes not perceived in the sacred record. Mark says that Jesus "looked upon [the Pharisees] with anger" (Mark 3:5). We read that Jesus "did smile upon" the people (3 Nephi 19:25, 30). In each of these instances, the countenance conveyed a message in addition to any words spoken. We cannot avoid wondering how many more times a situation was enhanced by a glance, a step forward, a raised hand, a louder or softer tone of voice, an inflection or emphasis on a word, words spoken rapidly, a long silent pause, a quick retort, and so on. Jesus' entire personality, all that he is physically, mentally, spiritually, and emotionally, would combine to convey the particular communication of the moment. The live teacher is the most effective audio-visual aid there is.

From our previous listing, let us now examine some of the various teaching methods the Savior used.

Straightforward Speech

Jesus repeatedly turned ordinary events into teaching experiences. Often, perhaps *most* often, he simply said what he meant and said it straightforwardly. His instruction to the Twelve seems to be a good example of that. Those who heard were "astonished" with the forthrightness of it, for he spake "as one having authority from God, and not as having authority from the Scribes" (JST Matthew 7:36–37). The scribes were learned, and had studied much, and when attempting to teach they could quote myriad sources and give a waterfront of opinions, but they had no clear declaration or testimony of what was really right. Jesus didn't teach his disciples in that manner. He gave the answer, he declared the doctrine in simple, direct terms, and spoke with the authority of God. His hearers noted the difference between him and the scribes, and were astonished.

Miracles

Jesus also used miracles as a teaching technique. We are impressed with his wide variety of miracles. He healed people of diseases, also of physical structural ailments such as a withered hand; also of blindness, deafness, and inability to speak. He cast out devils, calmed storms, multiplied food, walked on water, got a coin out of a fish's mouth, cursed a tree, reattached a severed ear, and raised persons from the dead. These acts demonstrated that he had power over diseases, over the unseen world of the spirits, over the world of nature and physical things, including the weather; he could overcome the law of gravity, and could even restore life to dead bodies. He cured broken hearts and healed souls as well as mended physical bodies. The wide scope of these activities surely taught his disciples that "all power [was] given unto [him] in heaven and in earth" (Matthew 28:18; D&C 93:17). Jesus spoke to the elements and they obeyed.

That Jesus used healing miracles as a teaching device is illustrated in Mark 2:1–12 and Matthew 9:1–8. A man who suffered from palsy was let down through the roof, upon a bed, in the midst of a crowd of people. Although it was evident that the man was suffering from a physical ailment and was unable to walk, Jesus' first word to him was, "Son, thy sins be forgiven thee." This greatly agitated the scribes who were sitting there, and they reasoned in their hearts: "This man [Jesus] speaks blasphemies; who can forgive sins but God only?" Jesus then said to them, "Is it not easier to say, Thy sins be forgiven thee, than to say, Arise and walk?" (JST Matthew 9:5; JST Mark 2:7). It is as if he said to them, "You cannot determine from the physical sight whether his sins are forgiven or not, but you can see if he gets up and walks." Then Jesus made this clarifying statement as to his purpose: "But that ye may know that the Son of man hath power on earth to forgive sins, I say unto thee [to the one sick with palsy], Arise, and take up thy bed, and go thy way into thine house." It is very clear from the way this miracle is reported, particularly in the JST, that Jesus used the healing of the body, which they could see with their physical eyes, to illustrate his ability to heal a soul, which they could not see. He used this miracle as a teaching device. It surely worked well, for the people were all amazed and said, "We never saw it on this fashion." I suppose one could say it was a case of moving from the known to the unknown, from the visible to the invisible, from the physical to the spiritual dimension.

Subtlety

Jesus also used subtlety, and wile—the *surprise* element. He said to the woman at Jacob's well, "Go, call thy husband, and come hither." The woman answered, "I have no husband." Jesus said, "Thou hast well said, I have no husband: for thou hast had five husbands; and he whom thou now hast is not thy husband: in that saidst thou truly." The woman said unto him,

"Sir, I perceive that thou art a prophet." (John 4:16–19.) But the real message to this teaching moment is that, while sitting at a well where water could be drawn, Jesus told her that he was the Messiah, and he made a comparison of earthly water to "living water." He said that if someone drank the water that was drawn from the well, that person would thirst again, but he [Jesus] had water to give of which one could drink and never thirst again. The woman doubted he could provide such water, because he had neither rope nor bucket and the well was deep. She also asked if he thought he was greater than Jacob himself, the ancient patriarch who gave them the well.

The whole episode compares the secular things to the spiritual. The woman was engrossed in the worldly things—the flesh, the natural water, the rope, the bucket. She could not see past those, and could hardly grasp the idea of the "living water," and even her response when she *began* to believe was that she would like some of that special kind of water, so that she would never have to come to the well again to draw. She was still thinking physically. It took some time until she could appreciate that the "water" that Jesus could give would be like a *flowing* well "springing up into everlasting life." (John 4:6–14.)

Using the Scriptures

Jesus taught from the scriptures. He read from them, quoted them, and explained them to his hearers. On numerous occasions he quoted Isaiah, Moses, or the Psalms, or cited events from the book of Kings. Jesus often reminded his audience of events recorded in the Old Testament, and used the Old Testament to cite a precedent in actions of David, or Moses, or Abraham. He also used the Old Testament to teach doctrine, such as the laws governing marriage and divorce, the doctrine of the resurrection, and particularly his own Messiahship.

Use of Logic

Jesus also used logic or reasoning as a teaching method. We can see him using plain "common sense" to arrive at conclusions about proper daily behavior. For example, Jesus was in the synagogue on the Sabbath day, and there was a man with a withered hand. The Pharisees, anticipating that Jesus would heal him, questioned: "Is it lawful to heal on the sabbath days?" This they asked, seeking a chance to accuse and find fault with him. Jesus reasoned with them. "Would you rescue a sheep that had fallen into a pit?" "How much is a man better than a sheep?" "Wherefore, it is lawful to do well on the sabbath days." Then he healed the withered hand—and he did it right then and there, where everyone could see him do it. (Matthew 12:9–14.) The Pharisees were so frustrated by his power, which exposed the shallowness of their own reasoning, that they "were filled with madness; and communed one with another what they might do to Jesus" (Luke 6:11).

Later—it appears to have been on the same day—he cast an evil spirit out of a man, and many people observed the remarkable change that came over him that was healed. The Pharisees said, "This fellow doth not cast out devils, but by Beelzebub the prince of the devils." Again Jesus used logic or common sense to help them arrive at a proper understanding. Said Jesus: "Every kingdom that is divided against itself is brought to desolation; and every city or house divided against itself, shall not stand. And if Satan cast out Satan, he is divided against himself; how shall then his kingdom stand? And if I by Beelzebub cast out devils, by whom do your children cast out devils?" (JST Matthew 12:20–22.)

Irony and Satire

Jesus sometimes used irony, satire, or justifiable sarcasm when dealing with the Pharisees, Sadducees, and scribes. He seems to have encouraged publicans and sinners to come and sit down with him and his disciples while they were eating. The Pharisees saw a chance to find fault at this, so they asked the disciples, "Why eateth your Master with publicans and sinners?" Jesus knew their intentions and replied, "They that be whole need not a physician, but they that are sick; . . . for I am not come to call the righteous, but sinners to repentance." (Matthew 9:10–13; Mark 2:15–17; Luke 5:27–32.) A casual reading of this event may not uncover the force of the Savior's remarks, but a little meditation on the subject will do so. Who in this world does not need the teachings and the saving power of Jesus? Who among all mankind could be truly righteous without the atonement of Christ? Can anyone be redeemed without the Redeemer? Is there any other way? Is there any other salvation? When Jesus said he was sent only to the sick, that was true, but who among all mankind is not sick? Were those self-righteous, complaining Pharisees spiritually whole and well? Were not they sinners also? Were they not spiritually very sick with self-righteousness? They were unquestionably sicker and in greater need of Jesus' healing power than were those "sinners" whom they despised. When Jesus said to the Pharisees, "I am not come to call the righteous, but sinners to repentance," he was in fact condemning the Pharisaic brand of self-righteousness which had blinded their hearts and eyes to the reality of their own sinful condition.

Another instance of Jesus' use of this type of language is found in Luke 15:1–7, and is spoken in connection with the parables of the lost sheep, the lost coin, and the lost son. The setting is this: The publicans and the sinners drew near to hear Jesus teach; the Pharisees and scribes murmured, saying, "This man receiveth sinners, and eateth with them." Jesus then told the Pharisees and scribes a parable wherein a man who had a hundred sheep and lost one of them went into the wilderness to find that one lost sheep, and having found him, rejoiced mightily over the recovery. Jesus' rebuke of the self-righteous attitude of the Pharisees is found in the words, "I say unto you, that likewise joy shall be in heaven over one sinner that repenteth, more than over ninety and nine just persons, which need no repentance."

If we were to take this statement literally at face value, it would put a premium on sin. The comment about more joy over one sinner than over ninety-nine righteous persons, is not a simple, straightforward declaration of fact; it is a rebuke of the Pharisees' self-important, self-righteous attitude, because they were certain they needed no repentance for themselves. Truly, they were "righteous"—self-righteous. Are we really and literally to believe there is more joy in heaven over *one* sinner that repents than over ninety-nine truly righteous persons such as Enoch, the brother of Jared, Nephi, Joseph Smith, Abraham, and the like? What tremendous odds—99 to 1! Remember the words of Samuel that say, "Hath the Lord as great delight in burnt offerings and sacrifices, as in obeying the voice of the Lord? Behold, to obey is better than sacrifice." (1 Samuel 15:22.) What the Savior really conveyed to the Pharisees was: "There is more joy in heaven over one of these despised publicans who honestly repents than there is over ninety-nine self-righteous persons like you, who in your own estimation need no repentance."

Let us take note of how the Prophet Joseph Smith perceived the Savior's words on this occasion:

> The hundred sheep represent one hundred Sadducees and Pharisees, as though Jesus had said, "If you Sadducees and Pharisees are in the sheepfold, I have no mission for you; I am sent to look up sheep that are lost; and when I have found them, I will back them up and make joy in heaven." This represents hunting after a few individuals, or one poor publican, which the Pharisees and Sadducees despised. . . .
>
> . . . Like I say unto you, there is joy in the presence of the angels of God over one sinner that repenteth, more than over ninety-and-nine just persons that are so righteous; they will be damned anyhow; you cannot save them. (TPJS, 277–78.)

It may bother some to hear that Jesus would speak this way, because it is at variance with the popular misconception that he was timid, bland, and colorless in his personality and spoke only pleasant things in a nice way. I think the record given by the New Testament is quite clear, but it has often been misread and misinterpreted. Sarcasm and satire are literary forms that are unmistakable in their meaning when experienced live. The words say one thing, but mean another thing, and are dependent on the tone of the voice and the context if they are to be correctly understood. When reduced to writing, the background and context are often lost, and as a result the force of the conversation is also lost. The careless reader may even get just the *opposite* meaning, which many do with these examples we have been discussing. They think Jesus is saying kindly things, whereas in reality he is denouncing the Pharisees and Sadducees in very strong terms. There can be no mistaking the fact that the Pharisees, in the live situation, knew they were being scolded by the Master.

There is not a single case in the four Testimonies that ever presents Jesus as impatient, critical, or unkind to people who were humble, teachable, and willing to change their lives. He forgave transgressions and he mingled with publicans and sinners on condition of their repentance. He cast out devils, healed the lame, raised the dead, fed the hungry, opened the eyes of the blind, gave hearing to the deaf, and restored the sick to health, if they only had the faith that he could do it. But he was a terror to the workers of iniquity and to the deceptive, the self-righteous, the hypocritical. In dealing with the repentant he was the gentle yet firm Messiah. To the proud, the haughty, and the arrogant, he was absolutely indomitable and irrepressible, and a constant threat to their craftiness.

Jesus was capable of exerting a tremendous physical and emotional impact on those he met and dealt with. Many people, when they saw and heard him, thought he was one of the Old Testament prophets come to earth again—perhaps Elijah, or Jeremiah (see Matthew 16:14; Mark 8:27–29; Luke 9:18–19). His personality was every bit as powerful and strong as the truth he taught.

Colorful, Unusual Metaphors

Jesus used colorful, attention-getting figures of speech. We find these in conversation with his disciples, in teaching the multitudes, and in censuring the Jewish rulers. Some examples are as follows: When he called fishermen into his service he said, "I will make you fishers of men" (Matthew 4:19). If one knowingly gives offense (which means to lead someone away from the faith), said Jesus, "it were better for him that a millstone were hanged about his neck and that he were drowned in the depth of the sea" (Matthew 18:6). That is, it would have been better for the person to have died, rather than to have committed that sin. Of Judas who betrayed him, Jesus said, "it had been good for that man if he had not been born" (Matthew 26:24).

John the Baptist was praised by Jesus as a "burning and a shining light" and of being "much more than a prophet" (John 5:35; Luke 7:26). James and John he surnamed the "sons of thunder" (Mark 3:17), while the Jewish rulers he called "hypocrites," "blind guides," "children of hell," "like unto whited sepulchres, full of dead men's bones," "a generation of vipers" (Matthew 23:13, 15, 16, 27, 33).

To a man who had been cured of a physical ailment, Jesus said, "sin no more, lest a worse thing come unto thee" (John 5:14), not meaning that every physical ailment is the direct result of sin, but rather that sin would lead to a loss of salvation, which is worse than having a physical affliction. Of those Pharisees and scribes who had such great inconsistency in their beliefs, he said they "strain at a gnat, and swallow a camel" (Matthew 23:24). To others he declared, "if thy hand offend thee, cut if off: . . . if thy foot offend thee cut it off; . . . and if thine eye . . . offend thee, pluck him out" (JST Mark 9:43–47). The JST explains that these are figurative expressions having reference to friends and associates; it being better to be without present friends and companions if they are the kind that would lead us astray.

Jesus Bore Testimony of Himself

In bearing testimony of himself and his Messiahship, Jesus declared, "I am the bread of life" (John 6:35). He likewise said, "I am the door of the sheepfold. All that ever came before me who testified not of me are thieves and robbers." (JST John 10:7–8.) And further, "many righteous prophets have desired to see these days which you see, and have not seen them; and to hear that which you hear, and have not heard (Matthew 13). "The queen of the south" shall condemn this generation on the day of judgment, "for she came from the utmost parts of the earth to hear the wisdom of Solomon; and, behold, a greater than Solomon is here" (Luke 11:31); likewise, the "men of Nineve" shall condemn this generation in the day of judgment, "for they repented at the preaching of Jonas; and behold, a greater than Jonas is here" (Luke 11:32). After telling the

Pharisees he was the Messiah, he said, "If ye believe not that I am he, ye shall die in your sins" (John 8:24).

There is no question that the message came through, for the Pharisees asked, "Art thou greater than our father Abraham?" (John 8:53.) Jesus replied, "Abraham rejoiced to see my day. . . . Before Abraham was, I am. [Or in other words, "Yes, I am greater than Abraham; I am the Lord Jehovah."] Then they took up stones to cast at him." (John 8:56–59.) That they intended to stone him indicates they got the message that Jesus claimed to be the Messiah, the Son of God, the great Jehovah. This was further certified at the cross when passersby "reviled him, wagging their heads, and saying, . . . If thou be the Son of God, come down from the cross" (Matthew 27:39–40). And the chief priests, scribes, and elders said, "He trusted in God; let him deliver him now, if he will have him: for he said, I am the Son of God" (Matthew 27:41–43).

There can be no doubt that Jesus was successful in putting his point across to both Saint and sinner. They didn't always believe him, but they knew what he said about himself.

Visual Aids

Jesus used objects, models, or visual aids to reinforce his words. When the Apostles had fished all night and caught nothing, Jesus told them to cast their nets on the other side of the ship. When they did so, the nets came up full of fish. All were astonished, and then Jesus, with his object lessen vividly in place, said to Peter: "Fear not: from henceforth thou shalt catch men" (Luke 5:4–10). The purpose of a model, or object, or visual aid is to increase the learner's perception. We see Jesus doing this with persons who are blind or deaf. If the person is deaf, Jesus sometimes puts His fingers into his ears. Thus the person not only sees Jesus, but feels him (Mark 7:33). If the person is blind, Jesus sometimes puts his hands over the eyes, or places clay on them. This at least would increase the perception, for although the blind person could not see, he could hear Jesus and feel his touch also (Mark 8:22–25; John 9:6). We cannot know all the reasons why Jesus did these things, but it appears to have been to increase the perception, attention, and experience of the afflicted person.

On another occasion, when his disciples asked who was the greatest in the kingdom of heaven, he set a little child before them and declared that to become great a person must become converted and be as humble as a little child. He also warned against "offending" "one of these little ones which believe in me." The word that is translated "offend" needs some clarification. To "offend" does not mean, in this case, simply to displease the child or to make it unhappy; literally, it means to "cause to stumble" or depart from the gospel. Jesus' statement about offending little children is a warning against false teachings, and a warning that teachers must be concerned about the influence they have on students. The teacher who plants doubt in place of faith in the minds of his students, who criticizes the Brethren, or who makes light of sacred things and fosters a spirit of cynicism, risks the possibility of offending the Lord's "little ones." So exercised was Jesus on this point that he said, "whoso shall offend one of these little ones which believe in me, it were better for him that a millstone were hanged about his neck and that he were drowned in the depth of the sea" (Matthew 18:6).

Such descriptive language tells us that the Lord has strong feelings against the teacher who is cynical and who by example teaches others to be the same. He called this the "leaven of the Pharisees" and warned us to beware of it (Matthew 16:6, 12). He said that a person receiving this kind of faithless doctrine becomes "two-fold more the child of hell" than he was before he was taught (JST Matthew 23:12). Better that the sheep have no shepherd than to be in the care of wolves. The problem with a cynic is that he feels little if any responsibility for the consequences of what he gives to others. He fails to sense the problems he causes. Such a teacher is a wolf in sheep's clothing. The image of a wolf is well chosen, for the word *cynic* itself comes from a word meaning "dog-like." You can see him with his nose to the ground running around, sniffing out something to complain about or some cherished belief to discredit.

Asking Questions

We mentioned earlier that Jesus could turn ordinary events into teaching situations. One way that he would do that was by asking questions. In this way he could get people talking, and therefore involved. For example, we hear him asking the Twelve, "What was it that ye disputed among yourselves by the way?" (Mark 9:33.) They were wondering who was the greatest among them. As soon as he could get them talking or at least thinking about it, then he could teach them. On another occasion he asked the Twelve, "Whom do men say that I the Son of man am?" (Matthew 16:13). In this case Jesus was making a point clear by contrast—"Who do *other* men say I am; and who do *you* say I am?" Later, on the day of his resurrection, as he walked along the road to Emmaus with two disciples (who didn't recognize him) he asked, "Why are you so sad today?" They replied, "Haven't you heard about the things that have happened in Jerusalem the last few days?" And Jesus asked, "What things?" Then the disciples rehearsed the manner of the crucifixion of Jesus and of the reported resurrection. By these questions Jesus set up the structure for a whole afternoon's discussion of the mission of the Messiah, and it gave him the opportunity to teach of his atonement, and to show that the scriptures testified of him. This experience caused their hearts to burn within them. (Luke 24:13–32.)

Sometimes he asked questions in return to those who asked him. When a "certain lawyer asked, What shall I do to inherit eternal life?" Jesus said to him, "What is written in the law? how readest thou?" When the man answered his question himself from the scriptures, Jesus said, "Thou hast answered right." (Luke 10:25–28.)

Bargaining with Questions

At least one time Jesus bargained with his enemies by means of questions. The Jewish rulers wanted to know by what authority Jesus did what he did, and who gave him that authority. He had just the day before driven the money changers out of the temple, so they were very sensitive and aware of him at this point. When they inquired as to his authority he said, "I also will ask you one thing, which if ye tell me, I in like wise will tell you by what authority I do these things" (Matthew 21:23–24). He then asked them to tell him by what authority John the Baptist did his work—was it of heaven or of men? By this type of question they were forced into a dilemma. He knew they would be. If they admitted John's authority was of God, he would say, "Why didn't you then believe him?" If they said John's authority was of man, they were afraid of the reaction and displeasure of the people, who received John as a prophet. So they attempted to save face, and said, "We cannot tell." Jesus promptly replied, "Neither tell I you by what authority I do these things." (Matthew 21:25–27.) However, he did deliver a powerful blow to their egos when he said to them that John's authority was of heaven and that the publicans and harlots who believed John would go into heaven before they (the Pharisees) would (verses 28–32).

Posing a Doctrinal Problem

Jesus knew how to deal effectively with the cunning craftiness of the Pharisees, the scribes, and the Sadducees. He sometimes asked them doctrinal questions which they, as religious leaders, ought to have been able to answer, but of which they seemed to be ignorant. An example is seen in his interview with Nicodemus, a Pharisee and a "ruler of the Jews" (John 3:1–12). When Jesus spoke to him about being born again, Nicodemus asked how a man could "be born when he is old? can he enter the second time into his mother's womb, and be born?" It seems obvious from this retort that Nicodemus was being a little facetious, if not ridiculous. When Jesus explained the birth of water and of the Spirit, Nicodemus replied, "How can these things be?" Jesus answered, "Art thou a master of Israel, and knowest not these things?" Evidently a religious ruler in Israel—a master of the heritage the Jews claimed from Abraham, the chosen people, the elect of God—was expected to know about the spiritual rebirth. Jesus' words had a note of reproof which must have pricked Nicodemus. It is as if Jesus said, almost incredulously: "Nicodemus, how can you not know these things? Either you are feigning ignorance of the doctrine of rebirth so as to justify your own lack of spiritual progress, or you are amazingly uninformed on this elementary subject." In either case, Jesus' words were not complimentary to Nicodemus.

A later, more vivid exchange of words on a doctrinal matter between Jesus and the Pharisees occurred just three days before the Crucifixion. After a day of challenging debate between Jesus and the Jewish rulers on various subjects such as Jesus' authority, the question of resurrection, eternal marriage, apostasy, and such things, Jesus posed a very significant theological question. He initiated the discussion by asking the Pharisees: "What think ye of Christ? whose son is he? They say unto him, The Son of David." What this question meant was when the Messiah comes, who will he be? What is his lineage? The Jews, knowing the prophecies (such as Isaiah 9:6, 7), quickly replied, He will be a descendant of David. Jesus then asked the difficult question: "How then doth David in spirit [or by the spirit] call him Lord?" "If David then call him Lord, how is he his son?"

The Jewish leaders could not answer this puzzling question. Furthermore, the scripture says: "And no man was able to answer him a word, neither durst any man from that day forth ask him any more questions." (Matthew 22:41–46.)

There can be no doubt that Jesus knew that this line of questioning would totally baffle the spiritual leaders of Jerusalem. The answers are simple enough to anyone who knows the eternal plan of salvation and the doctrine of premortal existence, and that every mortal is a dual being—a spirit body plus a physical body. David, who lived approximately 1000 B.C., worshipped the God of Israel, who was called Jehovah, and who was at that time a spirit being. When it came time for the Messiah to be born, Jehovah, the God of Israel, came to earth and was born into a physical body through Mary, a descendant of David. Hence Jesus the Christ, the Messiah, was both the Lord of David and the descendant of David. That situation is rather a fundamental concept within the Father's plan, but Jesus knew that the unbelieving and self-righteous Pharisees didn't understand it, even though there was enough information in their scriptures and their spiritual heritage that they should have understood it. This was not a riddle that Jesus posed, for a riddle is a situation that is clothed in mystery and guesswork. Jesus put this problem to them to demonstrate how little doctrine they really knew.

Adversarial Situations

Many of the examples in the scriptures are adversarial in nature, because they arose while Jesus labored with the hard-hearted, cynical, and conniving Jewish rulers. Some might wonder why Jesus engaged in this combative activity with those who were so opposed to him. Why didn't he just ignore them? This type of confrontation actually constituted part of his mission. Note this explanation by the Prophet Joseph Smith:

> The Melchizedek High Priesthood [is] no other than the priesthood of the Son of God. . . . It is also the privilege of the Melchizedek Priesthood to reprove, rebuke, and admonish, as well as to receive revelation. . . .
> I frequently rebuke and admonish my brethren. . . . Such a course of conduct is not calculated to gain the good will of all, but rather the ill will of many . . . the higher the authority, the greater the difficulty of the station; but these rebukes and admonitions become necessary, from the perverseness of the brethren, for their temporal as well as spiritual welfare. They actually constitute a part of the duties of my station and calling. (TPJS, 112–13.)

On the basis of what the Prophet has said on this subject, we conclude that it was necessary that Jesus, as one possessing all the powers of the Melchizedek Priesthood, testify against sin and wickedness, and rebuke those responsible for that wickedness. Were he to fail to do that, they would not have been challenged to repent in this life, nor would they be left without excuse in the day of judgment. Rebuking others is a prerogative of those holding the priesthood keys. The rest of us had best not use this method so directly.

To the disciples and the believers, Jesus performed acts of kindness, talked about prayer, explained the need they had for the Holy Ghost, and taught in the synagogues and in the court-yard of the temple. To the woman with an issue of blood, he said, "Be of good comfort: thy faith has made thee whole; go in peace" (Luke 8:48). To the woman who bathed his feet with her tears and dried them with her hair, he said, "Thy sins are for-given. . . . Thy faith hath saved thee." (Luke 7:48–50.)

Teaching by the Spirit

Jesus taught with the Spirit, using the scriptures. When he quoted the law, the prophets, and the Psalms in all things con-cerning himself, the believers' hearts burned within them (Luke 24:25–32). It was the Spirit that made this happen. When Peter testified that he knew that Jesus was the Christ, the Son of God, Jesus said, "Flesh and blood hath not revealed it unto thee, but my Father which is in heaven" (Matthew 16:17). In other words, "flesh and blood" represents the learning of the world by worldly methods through one's mortal senses. Learning from "my Father in heaven" represents learning by the spirit of reve-lation. There is an essential difference between the knowledge of the world and the knowledge of the Spirit. Knowledge by revelation saves one's soul. Worldly knowledge, even if correct, does not cleanse the soul. The Spirit reveals things absolutely essential to one's salvation that cannot be learned through the mortal physical senses. Such things are learned through the Spirit or they are not learned at all.

The Jewish leaders thought a person had to go to their school in order to learn to preach. This is illustrated by the amazement of the Jewish rulers about Jesus' endless wisdom. He had not gone through their training and curriculum, nor had he attended their schools, and yet he knew so much about the scriptures and about men and things. In what appears to be a mixture of surprise and dismay over Jesus' success as a teacher, the rulers marvelled and cried out, "How knoweth this man letters, having never learned? Jesus answered them and said, My doctrine is not mine, but his that sent me." (John 7:15–16.) It was not that Jesus had "never learned," but that his learning came by revelation from the Father, rather than from the schools and philosophy of the worldly wise. The Pharisees and Sadducees had facts, but they were without the conviction and witness of the Holy Ghost, and thus they were "ever learning, and never able to come to the knowledge of the truth" (2 Timothy 3:7). Without the Spirit they could not understand the things of God, even when they read the scriptures. The Father gave Jesus the Spirit without measure (John 3:34). Hence he taught by the power of the Holy Spirit; it had been with him all his life, and it gave him divine wisdom, even by the age of twelve.

Jesus taught by example. He prepared himself for his ministry and for the work he had to do. He fasted, he prayed, he read the scriptures, and he taught. Those who knew him would have observed these things about him and learned from him. Even though he was divine and the Son of God, he would not have had spiritual power unless he had been obedient, and had worked to develop it. When the disciples were unable to cast out a certain type of evil spirit, Jesus told them that was because their faith was not strong enough. He cast out the spirit, and explained that such power required prayer and fasting (Matthew 17:21). Does not this episode show us that it was by fasting and prayer that Jesus obtained his power and spiritual strength?

Jesus' Effect upon People

Jesus caused wonder and astonishment among the people. Generally those who witnessed his miracles and heard his discourses were much amazed. Some of their reactions were as follows:

1. "We never saw it on this fashion." Mark 2:12 (when he healed palsy).
2. "What manner of man is this?" Mark 4:41 (when he calmed a storm).
3. They were astonished beyond measure. Mark 5:42; 6:51 (when he raised the dead; also when he calmed a storm).
4. "We have seen strange things today." Luke 5:26 (when he healed palsy and forgave sins).

5. "Never man spake like this man." John 7:46 (said by the officers when they returned to the chief priests without arresting him).
6. There was a division because of him. John 10:1–19 (when he said he was the Son of God).
7. "These are not the words of him that hath a devil." John 10:21 (when he healed a blind man).
8. "He hath done all things well." Mark 7:37 (when he healed the deaf and dumb).
9. "When Christ cometh, will he do more miracles than these which this man hath done?" John 7:31 (when he preached at the feast of tabernacles).
10. "All things that John spake of this man were true." John 10:41 (said by many of the multitude after listening to Jesus' discourse).

He Used Parables to Veil Truth

No discussion of Jesus as a teacher would be complete if his parables were not included. We have already mentioned several of the parables that Jesus directed to the Jewish rulers, and noted that these had an element of censure and condemnation in them. The parables of instruction to the multitudes, such as those of the sower, the ten virgins, the talents, and the pearl of great price have a little less of this element, but nonetheless are somewhat hidden in their meaning. It is possible that many of the Pharisees and scribes and also the multitudes did not at first catch the full impact of the message he spoke to them in parables, even when he chided them. Parables were used by Jesus not for the purpose of making the spiritual points crystal clear but as a device to conceal and shadow the deeper meaning from the proud, the lazy, and the self-righteous. The parable of the sower illustrates this, by dealing with different kinds of soils. The soils represent the different degrees of readiness and productivity of the people.

Although many have thought that the parables were intended to make the truths of the kingdom easily available, the truth of the matter is that the parables were intended to conceal the finer points of doctrine from those who did not value them. When Jesus was asked by the disciples why he spoke to the multitudes in parables, he replied: "Because it is given unto you to know the mysteries of the kingdom of heaven, but to them it is not given. . . . Therefore speak I to them in parables: because they seeing see not; and hearing they hear not, neither do they understand." (Matthew 13:10–13.)

It is common among teachers in and out of the Church to misuse the parables, and to fail to note what Jesus said about why he used them. But the New Testament is quite clear on this matter. It has been my experience that if a person already knows the doctrine, it can usually be found somewhere in a parable, but it is next to impossible to learn it for the first time from the parable alone. Jesus was selective in what he taught to different groups. He did not give away the mysteries to those who had no interest in them, and who would not search for and meditate upon and seek to live worthy of the higher truths. Jesus' purpose in withholding information can be seen as merciful, because it prevents the people from receiving information upon which they will later be judged. But it is more than that. It is also an act of justice. No man can be saved in ignorance. The rule is: "Ask, and it shall be given you; seek, and ye shall find; knock, and it shall be opened unto you: for everyone that asketh receiveth; and he that seeketh findeth; and to him that knocketh it shall be opened" (Matthew 7:7–8).

Jesus did not refuse to teach the unbelieving, the indifferent who would not seek, or even the rebellious, but he gave them the lesser part because of their lack of readiness. No doubt they would eventually reach a time later when they would regret their slothfulness and pride, and mourn their lost opportunity. This will occur, if not in this life, then in the spirit world. Such will be true to some extent of all of us. The principle of readiness is basic in the psychology of teaching and is nowhere better illustrated than in Jesus' use of parables. (A more complete discussion of Jesus' use of parables is found in chapter 15, "The Parables of Jesus.")

We have a love for the New Testament, especially as it has been enhanced through latter-day revelation and the teachings of the Brethren. There is joy in learning about the Savior, his compassion, his courage, his humility, and his assertiveness. He is our greatest hero. We marvel that in his greatness he also has time for smaller things: He knows each of us, he knows our names, and our joys, weaknesses, and trials. He knows and he cares. Through latter-day revelation we can more perfectly find the true Messiah.

CHAPTER 19

Sacred Events on the Holy Mount

In acknowledging that Jesus was the Son of God (see Matthew 16:16), Peter was no doubt speaking for the Twelve. His declaration is often called "the great confession." A week later Peter, James, and John received the keys of the holy priesthood upon the Mount of Transfiguration. These two events are doctrinally and historically related.

The events that took place on the Mount of Transfiguration are among the most significant of all religious history. Few things are more significant to an understanding of the establishment of the kingdom of God on the earth in the time of the New Testament and the operation of the keys of the priesthood on the earth and in the heavens. Since the New Testament does not present the matter in all its salient aspects, the subject must be supplemented by doctrinal information received by latter-day revelation.

"Upon This Rock I Will Build My Church"

About a week before the experience on the mount, Jesus asked the Twelve, "Whom say ye that I [the Son of man] am?"

Answering for them, Peter said: "Thou art the Christ, the Son of the living God." Jesus confirmed Peter's testimony, stressing that such knowledge was not of human origin, that is, not from "flesh and blood," but of God. The Lord also said: "Thou art Peter, and upon this rock I will build my church." (Matthew 16:13–18.) Since the name Peter means "a rock," there is some parallelism here. Jesus said, in effect: "You say I am Christ; I say you are Peter; I am bedrock, you are a smaller rock."

Many discussions have asked what was meant by this statement, and especially what is meant by the rock on which the Church will be built. Some have taken these words to mean that Peter was the rock; others, that the testimony of Jesus, such as Peter had, was the rock, and that this kind of divine revelation and knowledge would be the foundation upon which the Church would be built. Still another view is that Christ himself is the rock.

The Prophet Joseph Smith declared that the rock upon which Jesus would build his church was the rock of revelation (see TPJS, 274).

An examination of the Doctrine and Covenants shows that in this dispensation the Lord frequently has referred to his gospel and also to himself as a rock or the rock upon which the Church would be established: For example:

Christ, the rock	D&C 50:44
The gospel is the rock	D&C 6:34; 10:69; 11:16; 11:24; 18:4, 5, 17; 33:12–13

It was a common Hebrew metaphor to refer to God, or the Messiah, as the Rock, as is shown in the following biblical references:

Deuteronomy 32:4, 31	He is our Rock.
1 Samuel 2:2	There is no rock like our God.
2 Samuel 22:2–3....................	The Lord is my rock.
Psalm 42:9.........................	God is my rock.
1 Corinthians 10:1–4..............	Christ is the spiritual Rock.
Ephesians 2:20	Jesus Christ is the chief cornerstone.

Psalm 118:22; Matthew 21:42..... The stone which the builders rejected is become the head of the corner.

Whatever one concludes as to the Lord's meaning of the term *rock*, it is readily seen that there is a common element in all of the usages listed above, and that common element is Jesus Christ. In each instance it is either the gospel of Christ, the testimony of Christ, the revelation of Christ, or Christ himself that is the rock. Presumably even those who make the interpretation that Peter is the rock would acknowledge that it was not simply Peter as a human being that distinguished him, but Peter the witness for Jesus Christ.

Keys of the Kingdom Promised

In continuing his conversation with the Twelve, Jesus said to Peter: "And I will give unto thee the keys of the kingdom of heaven: and whatsoever thou shalt bind on earth shall be bound in heaven: and whatsoever thou shalt loose on earth shall be loosed in heaven" (Matthew 16:19).

It was common to the Hebrews to refer to power and authority as keys. For example: "And the key of the house of David will I lay upon his shoulder: so he shall open, and none shall shut; and he shall shut, and none shall open (Isaiah 22:22; see also Revelation 3:7).

Giuseppe Ricciotti, a current Catholic scholar, speaks of the symbolism of keys representing authority:

> The symbols of the keys and of binding and loosing are typically Semitic. Even today in Arab towns men go about the streets with a set of huge keys tied together with a small cord and dangling conspicuously on either side of the shoulder. They are landlords parading their authority in that particular fashion. The figure of binding and loosing (cf. Matthew 18:18) retains here the meaning it had in contemporary rabbinic terminology, where it occurs frequently. The rabbis bound when they prohibited something and loosed when they permitted it. Rabbi Sechonya, who flourished around A.D. 70, used to preface his lessons with the following

prayer: "May it please thee, O Yahweh, my God and God of my father that . . . we may not declare impure what is pure and pure what is impure; that we may not bind what is loosed nor loose what is bound." (Giuseppe Ricciotti, *The Life of Christ* [Milwaukee: The Bruce Publishing Company, 1944], pp. 404–5.)

More than two years earlier, Jesus had spoken of Simon Peter as a stone, but without explanation (John 1:42). The JST adds the comment at that point that Peter would be a seer. But now the promise that Peter would be given "the keys of the kingdom of heaven" sheds enlightenment on the earlier declaration. Peter was to be the chief Apostle, the prophet, seer, and revelator, holding all the keys and gifts of the holy priesthood. Not upon Peter simply as a man, but upon the keys, the powers, the authority, and the testimony of Christ that Peter possessed was the Church to be built.

Keys of the Priesthood Given on the Mount

About one week after the great confession and the Savior's promise that the keys of the kingdom would be given, Jesus took Peter, James, and John onto the high mountain, and there he was transfigured before them. The Savior's body and clothing became very white and shiny and "glistering" (Luke 9:29), which means they sparkled brilliantly. Moses and Elias (Elijah) appeared in glory and spoke to Jesus about his forthcoming atonement and death, which he would accomplish in Jerusalem. The Father spoke out of a cloud, testifying to the three apostles that Jesus was the Son of God. These things are recorded in Matthew 17, Mark 9, and Luke 9, and Peter makes reference to the event in 2 Peter 1:16–18. It is evident, however, that the biblical record is incomplete as to what really took place on the mount. The Prophet Joseph Smith affirmed: "The Savior, Moses, and Elias, gave the keys [of the priesthood] to Peter, James and John, on the mount, when they were transfigured before him." (TPJS, 158.)

The transmission of the keys is probably the most important thing that transpired on the mount. The promise of the keys, given a week earlier, was now fulfilled. The three Apostles, with Peter at the head, now held the keys of the holy priesthood, the same keys which Moses and Elijah held and which had power to bind and to loose, both on earth and in heaven.

The Twelve had been given the Melchizedek Priesthood more than a year earlier when they were ordained Apostles and sent on missions (see Matthew 10), but the keys were not transferred to them for the fulness of the kingdom and the organization of the Church upon the earth until the time on the mount, which was in October, six months before the Lord's death. The keys are the directing and presiding power in the priesthood.

It appears from the foregoing statement of the Prophet Joseph Smith, "when they were transfigured before him," that the three Brethren were likewise transfigured and shrouded in glory, as were Jesus, Moses, and Elijah. This would seem proper as they were seeing things and engaged in business not natural to the mortal existence.

Comparison with Events in the Kirtland Temple in Ohio

There are numerous similarities between the establishment of the Church and the restoration of priesthood keys and powers in the latter days and that which is recorded in the New Testament. Since we have more precise information about the present dispensation, it can serve as a guide in understanding the development and sequence of events in the meridian of time. This is shown in the following:

Meridian of Time	*Fulness of Times*
Twelve Apostles called, ordained, and sent on missions. The Seventy also called. A.D. 31 (Luke 6 and 10; Matthew 10.)	Melchizedek Priesthood restored May or June 1829.
	Twelve Apostles and the Seventy called and ordained 1835.
Keys of the kingdom given to Peter, James, and John on the Mount of Transfiguration by Moses and Elijah in A.D. 33. (Matthew 17, Mark 9, Luke 9.)	Keys of priesthood restored by Moses, Elias, and Elijah in 1836 in the Kirtland Temple.

The similarity of the events on the Mount of Transfiguration with those of the Kirtland Temple seems to certify that the main accomplishment of the visitation of the holy beings on the mount was the bestowal of priesthood keys, in order to establish the dispensation of the meridian of time on a solid and complete foundation, with power to preach the gospel, perform the ordinances, call persons to the ministry, seal up the faithful to eternal life, and communicate all the gifts, powers, and graces of the gospel of Jesus Christ.

It is remarkable that this most important and significant event is all but lost in the biblical account. In this respect, latter-day revelation is an indispensable help in understanding the New Testament.

Why Elijah?

The Prophet Joseph Smith explained the postmortal mission of Elijah in these words:

> Elijah was the last Prophet that held the keys of the Priesthood, and who will, before the last dispensation, restore the authority and deliver the keys of the Priesthood, in order that all the ordinances may be attended to in righteousness. It is true that the Savior had authority and power to bestow this blessing; but the sons of Levi were too prejudiced. "And I will send Elijah the Prophet before the great and terrible day of the Lord," etc., etc. Why send Elijah? Because he holds the keys of the authority to administer in all the ordinances of the Priesthood; and without the authority is given, the ordinances could not be administered in righteousness. (TPJS, 172.)

Elijah, as a mortal, had lived approximately 850 years B.C. in and around the country of Samaria and was a prophet to the northern kingdom of Israel in the days of King Ahab and Queen Jezebel. The account of his translation is given in 2 Kings 2:9–12.

Moses a Translated Being

Although it is recorded in Deuteronomy that Moses died and supposedly was buried by the hand of the Lord (Deuteronomy 34:1–8), it is certain that he did not die but was translated. If it were not so he could not have appeared on the Mount of Transfiguration to lay on hands and bestow keys of the holy priesthood. Since this event took place before the resurrection of Jesus, and since Moses had lived thirteen centuries before Christ, it follows that in A.D. 33 Moses was a translated being, even as Elijah. Perhaps this is why "no man knoweth of his sepulchre" and why it was assumed that he "was buried by the hand of the Lord" in Moab (Deuteronomy 34:5–6; Alma 45:19); for since he was translated, there was no place of burial.

Dramatic Effect

The Lord had the authority to confer the keys upon the Apostles had he chosen to do so alone. That he chose to do so in company with Moses and Elijah says much about the order of the kingdom and the effectiveness of Jesus as a communicator.

Moses and Elijah are prophets of renown and respect in the Old Testament records, and were objects of veneration among the Jews in later generations. It was their privilege as bearers of the sacred priesthood and keys of presidency to confer those necessary powers on the heads of the First Presidency of the Church in the meridian of time. Jesus, who as Jehovah presumably had called Moses and Elijah in the Grand Council and foreordained them to their work in the kingdom of God, and who had led and blessed them through their mortal lives, honored their great service and their priesthood callings by using them to assist him in conferring the keys on the three chief Apostles.

Furthermore, it was a great object lesson for Peter, James, and John to personally meet these ancient prophets about whom they had read in the sacred scriptures, and to see first-hand their worship and respect of Jesus, and then to feel the hands of Moses and Elijah on their heads as the keys were conferred. No doubt the three Brethren knew that all the prophets worshipped Jesus, and that there was only one plan of salvation and one Redeemer. But to actually stand in the presence of two such glorified beings as Moses and Elijah and see them with Jesus and be literally ordained by them was an experience they would never forget. And, marvelous and spectacular as all this was, it was crowned with the audible voice of God the Father bearing witness of his approval of the occasion, and that he was well pleased in his beloved Son (Matthew 17:5).

Peter makes reference to this experience some thirty years later: "For we have not followed cunningly devised fables, when we made known unto you the power and coming of our Lord Jesus Christ, but were eyewitnesses of his majesty. For he received from God the Father honor and glory, when there came such a voice to him from the excellent glory, This is my beloved Son, in whom I am well pleased. And this voice which came from heaven we heard, when we were with him in the holy mount." (2 Peter 1:16–18.)

The Mount

The precise mount of the Transfiguration is not specified in the scriptures, but it is evident that it was in the northern part of Israel, probably not far from Caesarea Philippi (see Matthew 16:13). The location is believed to be either Mount Hermon, several miles to the northeast, or Mount Tabor, just west of the Sea of Galilee.

High mountain peaks have often been the places where the Lord has communed with his prophets. We have only to think of Mount Sinai with Moses (Exodus 19–20), another (unidentified) mountain with Moses (Moses 1:1, 42), the brother of Jared on Mount Shelem (Ether 3:1), Enoch on Mount Simeon (Moses 7:2–4), and Nephi receiving revelation on a high mountain (1 Nephi 11:1), to realize that there is a pattern in this. Each of these events occurred on separate mountains, but all were the sites of unusual spiritual experiences in which the Lord was present. A dedicated temple is the usual house of the Lord—often called the mountain of the Lord's house—and is the place where he communes with his servants, but mountain peaks have been used in the absence of a sacred temple. Perhaps the Lord chooses such peaks because they have not been polluted by sinful men.

That the Lord chose a mountain to confer the keys of the priesthood on his Apostles indicates further that the temple in Jerusalem was defiled and no longer was the sacred house of the Lord.

John the Baptist at the Mount

JST Mark 9:1–4, suggests that John the Baptist was also present on the Mount of Transfiguration. The original manuscript of the JST reads precisely as the printed editions do for these verses.

John would be a spirit only, since he had been slain some months before and the Savior's resurrection had not yet taken place. Just what John the Baptist's mission could be at this event is not clear, but perhaps there were many holy and angelic beings present for a number of reasons. Elder Bruce R. McConkie expressed his understanding of the event as follows: "It is not to be understood that John the Baptist was the Elias who appeared with Moses to confer keys and authority upon those who then held the Melchizedek Priesthood. . . . Rather, for some reason that remains unknown—because of the partial record of the proceedings—John played some other part in the glorious manifestations. . . . Perhaps he was there, as the last legal administrator under the Old Covenant, to symbolize that the law was fulfilled." (DNTC, 1:404.)

A Vision of the Glorified Earth

In addition to the foregoing events, it is learned from latter-day revelation that Peter, James, and John, while on the mount, saw a vision of the earth as it will appear in its glorified state. "Nevertheless, he that endureth in faith and doeth my will, the same shall overcome, and shall receive an inheritance upon the earth when the day of transfiguration shall come; when the earth shall be transfigured, even according to the pattern which was shown unto mine apostles upon the mount; of which account the fulness ye have not yet received" (D&C 63:20–21). This circumstance is also referred to by the Prophet Joseph as follows: "They saw the glory of the Lord when he showed the transfiguration of the earth on the mount" (TPJS, 13).

In view of what has been revealed, which is only a partial account, we conclude that the happenings on the Mount of Transfiguration are among the most historically and doctrinally important in the New Testament, especially as pertains to the priesthood and the establishment of the Church of Jesus Christ in that dispensation.

CHAPTER 20

Jesus and the Law of Witnesses

$\mathbf{M}$oses declared the word of the Lord as it pertains to the establishment of fact in matters of controversy. This principle has come to be known as the law of witnesses and is worded as follows: "At the mouth of two witnesses, or three witnesses, shall he that is worthy of death be put to death; but at the mouth of one witness he shall not be put to death" (Deuteronomy 17:6).

And also: "One witness shall not rise up against a man for any iniquity, or for any sin, in any sin that he sinneth: at the mouth of two witnesses, or at the mouth of three witnesses, shall the matter be established" (Deuteronomy 19:15).

These two passages formed the basis for the law of witnesses in the house of Israel through Old Testament times. This practice is referred to also in the New Testament as the approved way of settling a question or establishing a point among the people. Jesus told his disciples that when they wished to settle a difference between brethren they were to "take with thee one or two more, that in the mouth of two or three witnesses every word may be established" (Matthew 18:16). Paul also alludes to this law (see 1 Timothy 5:19; 2 Corinthians 13:1, Hebrews 10:28).

249

Giving witness is the form of asserting a testimony or a statement of evidence in a dispute or when there is a question to be resolved or a point of information to be established beyond doubt. The force of multiple witnesses is illustrated in the New Testament with regard to Jesus Christ. To begin with, we have not just one record of Jesus' mortal life, but four, and they are rightly named "The Testimony of St. Matthew," "The Testimony of St. Mark," and so forth. Furthermore, there were many and varied testimonies or presentations of evidence as to the unique birth of Jesus into mortality. In the testimony of Luke we read of the angel coming to Zacharias, and later to Mary (Luke 1:5–56), and in the record of Matthew we read of the angel coming to Joseph (Matthew 1:18–21), announcing the forthcoming birth of Jesus. When the birth occurred, the shepherds in the field near Bethlehem were told by an angel that the Savior was born nearby, and was lying in a manger. The shepherds—more than one—went to Bethlehem, found the baby, and "made known abroad the saying which was told them [by the angel] concerning this child" (Luke 2:8–17).

When Jesus was presented at the temple after the forty-day purification period specified by the law of Moses (see Leviticus 12) both Simeon and Anna saw him and they knew by the Holy Ghost that this infant was the Christ (see Luke 2:22–39).

In the Testimony of Matthew we read of the visit of the wise men to the Messiah. How many wise men there were we are not told, but it was more than one; and on the basis that three gifts were given it has been assumed there were three men. They came from a land east of Palestine, and were guided by a new star in the sky. It had been months since the birth of the Savior, and he was living in a house rather than in the stable of his birth. After finding the Christ child and presenting their gifts, the wise men returned home to their own land, being directed by a sacred dream. They had sought the Messiah and they had found him, and being protected on their journey they returned to their people as valid witnesses that the Messiah had indeed been born into the world. (JST Matthew 3:1–12.)

At the Mount of Transfiguration, Moses, Elias (i.e., Elijah), and Jesus conferred the keys of the holy priesthood upon not just one but upon all three of the Brethren—Peter, James, and John (see Matthew 17; see also the discussion of this event in chapter 19, "Sacred Events on the Holy Mount").

At the tomb when Jesus rose from the dead there were two angels present, no doubt as witnesses of this all-important event (JST Matthew 28:2; see also the discussion of this topic in chapter 23, "Death and Resurrection"). These two angels testified to the women at the tomb that the Lord was risen indeed.

Law Proves Jesus and the Father
Are Separate Individuals

In John 5:31 we find an important account of Jesus invoking the law of witnesses. The whole episode of John 5 is an encounter between Jesus and the Jewish rulers, with legal implications. The rulers, of course, did not accept Jesus as the Son of God. Jesus said: "If I bear witness of myself, my witness is not true." In plainer terms, the meaning of this statement is: "If I am the *only* witness of my sonship, my witness is not legally valid and binding."

Jesus then spoke of John the Baptist as a witness for him (vss. 32–34). He further declared that he had additional witness beyond the testimony of John. He identified this further witness as the testimony of his divine works; the testimony that the Father had given of him (vs. 37), and also the testimony of the scriptures (vs. 39), especially those things written by Moses (vss. 45–47). A short time later as recorded in John chapter 8, the Pharisees verbally attack Jesus and say: "Thou bearest record of thyself; thy record is not true [i.e., not legally valid]" (John 8:13). Jesus replied: "I am not alone, but I and the Father that sent me. It is also written in your law, that the testimony of two men is true. I am one that bear witness of myself, and the Father that sent me beareth witness of me." (John 8:16–18.)

The Jews, in total disbelief, jeeringly asked him, "where is thy Father?" (John 8:19.)

The validity of the Lord's argument that he was the Son of God rests squarely on the fact that the Father is a separate and distinct person from Jesus, else the law of witnesses would not be complied with. That Jesus declared that his Father and he were separate witnesses should go far in persuading any believer in the Bible that such is literally so. If it were not so, Jesus would not have proved his case and the Jews would have had wherewith to disbelieve him.

CHAPTER 21

Spiritual Strength and Courage of Jesus

Jesus Christ is the literal Son of God, the firstborn in the spirit and the Only Begotten of the Father in the flesh. He has the greatest biological inheritance and is the most magnificent being ever to live on this earth. The scriptures contain many accounts of wondrous miracles he performed, such as walking on the water, calming a violent storm, healing the sick, restoring sight to the blind, restoring the dead to life, turning water into wine, reading people's thoughts, and even getting a coin from a fish's mouth. Oh to be like Jesus and to have such powers!

It may seem that these characteristics came as natural endowments because he was the literal Son of God. But I do not think they were that easily obtained. In order to develop the spiritual dimension, Jesus had to discipline his thoughts and actions in the same way as any of us must do. There is no doubt he brought into mortality his great spiritual capacity from his premortal life. Yet it seems that at first these were rendered somewhat dormant because he took on him the nature of mortality when he was born in the flesh. His divinity began to be awakened in him as a youth. (See the discussion of this matter in chapter 10, "Mary and Joseph.")

Because he was fathered in the flesh by the immortal Elohim, Jesus had power over death in a way that no one else has ever had in mortality. He alone had power over death while he was a man on the earth. Yet he was mortal in some ways and of necessity had to struggle against the limitations of mortality. He was totally successful in winning the struggle, but the scriptures show that it was not easy.

Jesus' Spiritual Preparation

Even though Jesus was the Son of God by divine appointment, he had to keep the commandments and be sinless in order to make an atonement that would benefit others. He had to remain sinless, even as he was tempted and could sense the pull and attraction of sin. Note Paul's words: "For verily he took not on him the nature of angels; but he took on him the seed of Abraham." That means that he did not come into this world with a wall around him that would shield him from pain and sorrow and temptation; rather, he came with the feeling, warmth, concern, and sensitivity common to other human beings. "Wherefore in all things it behoved him to be made like unto his brethren, that he might be a merciful and faithful high priest in things pertaining to God, to make reconciliation for the sins of the people. For in that he himself hath suffered being tempted, he is able to succour them that are tempted." (Hebrews 2:16–18.) Paul also wrote that Jesus "was in all points tempted like as we are, yet without sin. Let us therefore come boldly unto the throne of grace, that we may obtain mercy, and find grace to help in time of need." (Hebrews 4:15–16.)

Isaiah wrote that the Messiah would be a "man of sorrows and acquainted with grief," "oppressed . . . and afflicted" (Isaiah 53:3, 7).

An angel told King Benjamin the Savior "shall suffer temptations, and pain of body, hunger, thirst, and fatigue, even more than man can suffer, except it be unto death; for behold, blood cometh from every pore, so great shall be his anguish for the wickedness and the abominations of his people" (Mosiah 3:7). Alma said Jesus would take upon him "the pains and sicknesses of his people" (Alma 7:11).

The Prophet Joseph Smith taught that Jesus "descended in suffering below that which man can suffer; or, in other words, suffered greater sufferings, and was exposed to more powerful contradictions than any man can be" (*Lectures on Faith* 5:2). Because Jesus knew more he felt more; he understood more; he suffered more; and he could be tempted more than any other person. It seems that the number and severity of the temptations that one experiences are in proportion to one's knowledge and perception. A person with greater capacity may be called on to endure greater temptations. On the other hand, the joys and the rewards for that same person are also greater.

Jesus was obedient to the Father. He said, "The Father hath not left me alone; for I do always those things that please him" (John 8:29). Jesus drew strength from his Father in the same way that we can draw strength from Jesus. He used vivid description when he said that his disciples were to take up the cross and follow him. What does it mean to take up one's cross? "Then said Jesus unto his disciples, If any man will come after me, let him deny himself, and take up his cross and follow me. And now for a man to take up his cross, is to deny himself all ungodliness, and every worldly lust, and keep my commandments." (JST Matthew 16:25–26.) The foregoing passages of scripture show that Jesus denied himself of things that his mortal nature may have desired and yet were wrong for him; and he became spiritually strong as a result of that denial.

Perfect Example of Self-Mastery

Evidences of the achievement of self-mastery in Jesus' life are found throughout the scriptures. For example, after his baptism Jesus went into the wilderness for forty days, during which time he fasted and prayed and communed with God (JST Matthew 4:1–2). The Savior's communion with his Father, made possible by his fasting and prayers, strengthened him spiritually.

Consider another episode in Jesus' life. In Galilee the disciples tried to cast out an evil spirit, and they could not. The Savior, however, was successful in doing so. When the disciples asked Jesus why they had failed, he explained that they didn't have enough faith. He also said that evil spirits of that type "goeth not out but by prayer and fasting" (Matthew 17:21). Jesus' success in casting out that evil spirit demonstrates that he had the necessary faith, which he had developed by prayer and fasting.

Spiritual strength and self-mastery are rooted in personal prayer. The record says that before choosing the Twelve, Jesus prayed all night unto his Father (see Luke 6:12–13). Why would he have done that if it were not necessary for his spiritual well-being? No doubt such prayer would aid him in choosing the Twelve in accordance with his Father's will. At the time of his greatest ordeal in the Garden of Gethsemane, when he bled at every pore and took upon himself the sins of mankind, he prayed. And then, as the scriptural account tells us, "there appeared an angel unto him from heaven, strengthening him" (Luke 22:43).

That the experience of earth life, and the self-discipline that is necessary required constant and deliberate effort, even for Jesus, seems to be evident in the following expression from the Savior to his disciples: "I have a baptism to be baptized with; and how am I straightened till it be accomplished!" (Luke 12:50). The "baptism" he refers to is not the water baptism he received from John in the Jordan, but is symbolic of the demands of his mission. "Straightened" means "hard pressed." This is a very telling passage of scripture; and it greatly enhances our appreciation and love for the Savior that he was faithful and true even when it was difficult. When Jesus appeared in glory to the Nephites, he told them: "I have suffered the will of the Father in all things from the beginning" (3 Nephi 11:11). What I want to emphasize here is *how* the Savior received this spiritual strength: He got it through obedience, prayer, and fasting. We have every reason to believe that Jesus' spiritual strength came to him as a result of his triumphant struggles to overcome the drag of mortality. That is, his attainment and development of spiritual power came through his deliberate effort and from his receiving strength from his Father.

For the Savior, then, the price was his complete obedience and dedication to the Father's will; he did not allow himself any deviation or straying from that path of obedience. In order to be able to save the world, he had to be the one who would be sinless, who would be perfect in his self-denial and his self-mastery. He had to become the person able to save himself as well as others. This Jesus did, as he worked out his own and our salvation, ultimately paying the highest price imaginable—the sacrifice of his own life. The price of the world's redemption was so high that only a God could bring about our deliverance. Jesus Christ, through his voluntary atoning sacrifice, "purchased [us] with his own blood" (Acts 20:28; see also Hebrews 9:12).

Jesus' mortal life was destined to be difficult from the start. Lucifer, his archenemy from the premortal life, would see to that. It was no doubt Lucifer's influence that led Herod the Great to attempt to kill the infant Jesus. And immediately after the Lord's baptism Lucifer sought to overcome him, first by an attempt to plant doubt in Jesus' heart as to his calling and his divinity, and then by trying to buy his allegiance with the riches of the world. In addition Jesus had to endure the never-ending criticism from the spiritual and political leaders of the Jews, who found fault with almost everything he said and everything he did, and who were systematically plotting his death. He did not smile and say gentle things in all cases, for in Mark 3:5 we read that when his enemies eagerly watched for him to heal a man on the Sabbath in the synagogue, hoping they would find something on which to accuse him, "he looked round about on them with anger." Then he healed the man. He knew that in doing so on the Sabbath it would evoke criticism. Jesus had to combat sophisticated wickedness in high places, because ofttimes the power and influence of the highest officials was arrayed against him.

There is also evidence of Jesus' sometimes being weary and seeking rest and solitude, but often not finding the quiet he desired, because many people were coming to him, wanting his help. In these cases his compassion overruled his physical and mental weariness (see John 4:6; Mark 1:45; 6:30–34; JST Mark 7:22–23).

Even those who believed he was the Christ were sometimes slow to understand him. For example, on at least one occasion after a period of many healings and great popularity, Jesus and the Twelve went into a house as multitudes of people gathered without. It appears that Jesus went out and talked with the crowds. But his "friends" (whoever that may have been) came to lay hold on him, to lead him away, for they said he was "beside himself," which literally means they thought that he was out of his senses (Mark 3:21). On another occasion, after he had taught the multitudes in parables, the disciples asked him the meaning. He replied: "Are ye also yet without understanding?" (Matthew 15:16). When they asked him specifically about the parable of the sower he asked them: "Know ye not this parable? and how then will ye know all parables?" (Mark 4:13). Later when the disciples could not cast the evil spirit out of a man, Jesus said aloud, "O faithless and perverse generation, how long shall I be with you; how long shall I suffer you?" (Matthew 17:17). When the three Apostles slept while he suffered in the Garden, Jesus asked, "Could ye not watch with me one hour?" (Matthew 26:40).

The constant pressure from his enemies combined with the sometimes lack of appreciation from his friends would have frustrated a lesser man. I do not think Jesus was ever frustrated, but these passages of scripture seem to imply that he experienced moments of exasperation and disappointment.

The unusual demands of his ministry, made more difficult by persecution from enemies, the disloyalty of some of his followers, and the lack of appreciation from friends, required that Jesus have the utmost spiritual strength and courage in order to complete his assigned work.

Why Jesus Contended with His Enemies

Someone might ask, "Why did the Savior contend with the priests, who were so encrusted with priestcraft and selfishness? Why not just ignore them?" Jesus surely would have had less trouble if he had not spoken so openly to his enemies in their wickedness. We need to consider that he had no enemies except for the gospel's sake. It was his righteousness and his true doctrine that made them angry. If he had not corrected them, those wicked persons could have charged him with negligence on the day of judgment. But as he did challenge them, they are left without excuse, as he said: "If I had not come and spoken unto them, they had not had sin: but now they have no cloke for their sin" (John 15:22).

Jesus would not be the Redeemer if he had failed to rebuke the rebellious people among whom he lived. One of his basic responsibilities was to testify against sin and wickedness. He had to mark the way for all to see. To fail to speak harshly against sin would be interpreted by the people as condoning it.

Jesus' spiritual maturity and courage enabled him to do "all things well" (Mark 7:37) and to complete every task with the right amount of firmness and love and gentleness. It enabled him to endure to the end, and to tread the winepress of redemption alone.

CHAPTER 22

Jesus and the Jewish Rulers

The relationship between Jesus and the Jewish rulers was often adversarial. It was inevitable that differences would exist, for Jesus brought the pure doctrine and philosophy of heaven, whereas many of the people and their rulers were saturated in selfishness, materialism, priestcraft, and the pleasures of the flesh. The principle on which this conflict arose is expressed as follows: "And this is the condemnation, that light is come into the world, and men loved darkness rather than light, because their deeds were evil. For every one that doeth evil hateth the light, neither cometh to the light, lest his deeds should be reproved. But he that doeth truth cometh to the light, that his deeds may be made manifest, that they are wrought in God." (John 3:19–21.)

Such conflict is not limited to Jesus only, for his true prophets and Apostles always find themselves at variance with the ways and desires of the natural, fallen world of mankind. Such differences began in the premortal life with the rebellion of Lucifer and the war in heaven; and it has continued on the earth to this day. The conflict was especially sharp and visible in the New Testament because Jesus is the purest and greatest of all men, and the Jews of that particular time and place were among the most wicked of all time (2 Nephi 10:3).

The doctrine taught by Jesus called for a higher standard of personal integrity and purity of life than most unrepentant mortals are willing to tolerate. Jesus told those Jews, who regarded themselves as the favorites of heaven, that they were in fact the enemies of the very God they claimed to worship. Since they could neither ignore, nor silence, nor tolerate him, they sought to destroy his influence, and eventually to remove him altogether.

It was necessary that Jesus testify of their wickedness so as to give them a chance to repent, and also, in case they persisted, to leave them without excuse on the day of judgment. It was also necessary that Jesus proclaim against the false doctrine and works of the corrupt leaders as a clear message to the people. To have kept silent in the midst of such flagrant corruption and public misdeeds would be to condone the leaders' wicked behavior and send the wrong message to the masses of the people. There were some among the leaders who were favorable to Jesus. Apparently Joseph of Arimathaea, and to some extent Nicodemus, were disciples. There may have been others. Certainly there were some who knew Jesus was right, but who lacked the courage to publicly agree with him. The record indicates, however, that there were a substantial number of the leaders who openly and repeatedly opposed the Savior. The JST adds this comment: "And the common people heard him gladly; but the high priest and the elders were offended at him" (JST Mark 12:44).

When wicked persons seek to destroy a righteous prophet, there are several avenues available. Often they attempt to refute his doctrine. When that fails they attack his character. We find the following items with regard to the Jewish rulers and Jesus. These attacks were made primarily during the last two years of his ministry.

Accusations Made Against Jesus' Character

1. Some of his friends once thought he was "beside himself." Mark 3:21.

2. A Sabbath breaker. John 5:16.
3. A gluttonous man and a winebibber. Matthew 11:19; Luke 7:34.
4. A friend of publicans and sinners. Luke 7:34.
5. One who deceiveth the people. John 7:11–12.
6. A false witness. John 8:13.
7. Is possessed of a devil. John 8:48; 10:20.
8. He is a Samaritan. (This was an insult intended to say he was a sympathizer with an "inferior" people.) John 8:48.
9. A sinner. John 9:24.
10. He is mad. John 10:20.
11. A blasphemer. John 10:32–33.
12. He perverteth the nation. Luke 23:2, 14.
13. He stirreth up the people. Luke 23:5.
14. He forbiddeth to pay tribute to Caesar. Luke 23:2.
15. He is guilty and worthy of death. JST Matthew 26:67.

Throughout his public ministry Jesus let the Jews know where they needed improvement. As early as the Savior's instruction to the Twelve in the first year of his ministry he told them that the scribes and Levites and Pharisees were hypocrites (JST Matthew 7). Toward the end of his ministry these reminders became more frequent and more pointed. The record contains the following:

Jesus' Declarations Against the Jewish Rulers

1. Ye transgress the law of God by your tradition. Matthew 15:3.
2. Ye are hypocrites. Matthew 15:7.
3. Ye teach for doctrines the commandments of men. Matthew 15:9.
4. Ye are blind leaders of the blind. Matthew 15:14.
5. Ye are a wicked and adulterous generation. Matthew 16:1–4.
6. Ye do err, ye neither know the scriptures, nor the power of God. Matthew 22:29.
7. Ye bind heavy burdens on men's shoulders but will not touch them with one of your fingers. Matthew 23:4.

8. Ye do your works to be seen of men. Matthew 23:5.
9. Ye shut up the kingdom of heaven against yourselves and also shut it for others [by false teaching and example]. Matthew 23:13.
10. Ye devour widows' houses. Matthew 23:14.
11. For a pretense ye make long prayer. Matthew 23:14.
12. Your converts are twice as bad as they were before you taught them. JST Matthew 23:12.
13. Ye are blind guides. Matthew 23:16.
14. Ye are fools and blind. Matthew 23:17.
15. Ye have omitted from your lives the weightier matters of the law: judgment, mercy, and faith. Matthew 23:23.
16. Ye strain at a gnat and swallow a camel. Matthew 23:24.
17. Ye are full of extortion and excess. Matthew 23:25.
18. Ye outwardly appear righteous, but inwardly are full of hypocrisy and iniquity. Matthew 23:28.
19. Ye are serpents, a generation of vipers. Matthew 23:33.
20. Ye will kill the prophets and those sent to you. JST Matthew 23:29, 37.
21. Ye have taken away the key of knowledge—the fulness of the scriptures. JST Luke 11:53.
22. Ye know neither Moses nor the prophets; if ye had known them ye would have believed me. JST Luke 14:36.
23. Ye justify yourselves before men. Luke 16:15.
24. Ye deny the written scriptures. JST Luke 16:20.
25. Ye condemn him [Christ] whom the Father hath sent. JST Luke 16:20.
26. Ye have said in your hearts there is no God. JST Luke 16:21.
27. Ye pervert the right way. JST Luke 16:21.
28. Ye persecute the meek. JST Luke 16:21.
29. In your violence ye seek to destroy the kingdom [of God]. JST Luke 16:21.
30. Ye are adulterers. JST Luke 16:21.
31. Ye have made my Father's house a house of merchandise and a den of thieves. John 2:16; Matthew 21:13.
32. Ye shall die in your sins. John 8:24.
33. Ye seek to kill me. John 8:37.
34. My word hath no place in you. John 8:37.

35. Ye are children of the devil. John 8:44.
36. Ye will do the lusts of your father. John 8:44.
37. Ye are not of God. John 8:47.
38. Ye are liars when you say you know God. John 8:55.
39. Ye are not my sheep. John 10:26.

With such a catalog of sins and errant behavior charged against the Jewish leaders, it is little wonder that the more hardened among them plotted to kill Jesus. They didn't want to secretly slay him, they wanted to publicly discredit and disgrace him, and if possible get the Roman government to execute him. Therefore they watched and goaded him, hoping to catch him in his words, that they might have a reason to accuse him (see Mark 12:13; Luke 11:53–54). We will now examine instances where the Pharisees, Sadducees, priests, and political leaders sought occasion to slay him.

Why the Jews Sought to Kill Jesus

1. Because he baptized so many people and was so popular; even more so than John the Baptist. JST John 4:1–2.
2. They attempted to throw Jesus over a cliff in Galilee because he compared them unfavorably to non-Israelites. Luke 4:28–30.
3. For healing on the Sabbath day. John 5:16.
4. For saying that God was his Father. John 5:18.
5. Because he told them the truth. John 8:40.
6. The Jews sought to stone Jesus for saying he was the God of Abraham, therefore that he was Jehovah the God of Israel. John 8:59.
7. They sought to stone Jesus for saying he was the Son of God. John 10:32–38.
8. The Jews wanted Jesus crucified for saying he was the Son of God. John 19:7.

This chapter concludes with a detailed chronology of the efforts put forth by the Jewish rulers to arrest, imprison, humiliate, and slay the Lord Jesus Christ.

Formal Attempts to Destroy Jesus

The Jewish leaders made several formal attempts to arrest and dispose of Jesus before the feat was actually accomplished. The record shows that the Pharisees, particularly, held several councils and consulted with others to plot the death of Jesus. When he was finally betrayed by Judas and taken captive, it was the culmination of more than two years of planning. The dates are approximate, but the following arrangement is probably as accurate as can be determined with the available information. The sequence is important.

A.D. 30
Judea

The Pharisees sent a formal delegation of priests and Levites from Jerusalem to the Jordan River to question John the Baptist of his activities. They asked him if he was the Christ. This was a few days after Jesus' baptism. He was in the wilderness at this time. John 1:19–28.

A.D. 30
Late
fall,
Judea

The Jewish leaders were angry with Jesus because he has made so many baptisms through his disciples. The JST (John 4:1–4) states that the Pharisees sought to kill Jesus at this time. This was several months earlier than the first mention in any other Bible of a desire to kill Jesus.

A.D. 31
Early
spring,
near
Dead
Sea

John is imprisoned by Herod. He was probably somehow betrayed or delivered up by the Pharisees. This is suggested by an alternate reading of Matthew 4:12 which states, "when Jesus heard that John had been delivered up, he withdrew into Galilee."

A.D. 31
April,
Jerusalem

The Jews sought to kill Jesus because he healed a man on the Sabbath and also because he said God was his Father. (This is the earliest mention in the KJV of an attempt to kill Jesus.) He reminded them that the Jews had sent a delegation to John and that John bore witness of him.

(It should be noted that when the record of John makes reference to the "Jews" it is the Jewish rulers and leaders that are usually meant and not the Jewish people as a whole. In this instance it would be the Pharisees, since they were the ones who had sent the delegation to John the Baptist.) John 5:15–36.

A.D. 31
April,
Galilee

The Pharisees in Galilee, offended because Jesus healed a man on the Sabbath, took council with the Herodians of how they might destroy Jesus. The Pharisees were strange confederates with the Herodians, but united in a common cause against Jesus. Matthew 12:9–14; Mark 3:1–6; Luke 6:6–11.

A.D. 31
Early winter,
near the
Dead Sea

John the Baptist was beheaded in prison, at the command of Herod. Jesus was in Galilee at the time. Mark 6:14–29; Matthew 14:1–13. John had been imprisoned just less than a year.

A.D. 32
April,
Capernaum

A formal delegation of scribes and Pharisees from Jerusalem came to Jesus in Galilee. They questioned him as to why his disciples ate with unwashed hands contrary to the traditions of the elders. Jesus told them that what comes out of the heart is more important than food in the mouth. He told them they broke the laws of God, which was worse than breaking the traditions of the elders. They were much offended by Jesus' reply. Jesus told his disciples that the Pharisees were blind leaders of the blind. Matthew 15:1–14; Mark 7:1–13.

A.D. 32
Summer,
Galilee

In response to a request from the Pharisees and Sadducees that he show them a sign from heaven (to prove his divine ministry), Jesus said that a wicked and adulterous generation seeks after a sign. He observed that they were able to discern the signs of the weather but not the signs of the times. He warned the disciples to beware of the leaven of the Pharisees and of the Sadducees, which was their false doctrine. Matthew 16:1–12.

A.D. 32 Fall, Northern Galilee, Mount of Transfiguration
Jesus told Peter, James, and John that John the Baptist had been rejected by the Jews, who had done to John whatsoever they wanted. Also that the Son of Man would suffer in like manner from the Jews. Since the Pharisees played such a prominent part in the arrest of Jesus, it appears from this passage that the Pharisees had also played a major role in the capture of John the Baptist. See entry for A.D. 31, early spring, above. Matthew 17:12–13.

A.D. 32 Autumn, Galilee
For a short time Jesus stayed primarily in Galilee because the Jews in Judea planned to kill him if he went there. John 7:1.

A.D. 32 October, Jerusalem
Jesus attended the Feast of the Tabernacles. The Pharisees and chief priests sent officers to arrest him. The officers returned without arresting him, saying they have never known such a man as Jesus. The chief priests and Pharisees were angry. Then Jesus told the Jewish rulers he knew they sought to kill him. They denied it, but then took up stones to cast at him. John 7:2, 32–49; 8:1–59.

A.D. 32 October, Jerusalem
On the Sabbath, Jesus healed a man born blind. When the Pharisees heard of it they made an extensive investigation and announced that anyone who spoke favorably of Jesus would be cast out (excommunicated) from the synagogue. The healed man did so and was cast out by them. Jesus lectured the Pharisees on spiritual blindness and told them they were without excuse in their sins. John 9:1–34.

A.D. 32 December, Jerusalem
At the Feast of Dedication in Jerusalem the Jews sought to stone Jesus because he said he was the Christ, the Son of God. Almost humorously Jesus asked, "I have done many good

works; for which one do you stone me this time?" They said, "for making yourself a God." They sought to take him but he escaped and went to the Jordan, where John had first baptized. John 10:22–42.

A.D. 33
Early
spring,
Jordan or
Perea

The Pharisees warned Jesus to depart out of the country, for Herod sought to kill him. This was probably a trap of some kind, since the Pharisees would not seek to protect Jesus from Herod. He gave them a message to give to Herod, thereby showing that he knew they were in contact and in collusion with Herod. Luke 13:31–33.

A.D. 33
Late
March,
near the
Jordan or
Perea

Jesus heard that Lazarus was sick. He told the Twelve he was going to Bethany in Judea to heal him. They reminded Jesus that the Jews recently sought to stone him in Judea. The intense feeling of the Jews against Jesus is shown by the fact that Thomas suggested to the Twelve that they go with Jesus "and die with him," showing that they expected to be killed by the Jews if they entered the vicinity of Jerusalem. John 11:1–16.

A.D. 33
Late
March,
Bethany,
Feast of
Passover

Jesus raised Lazarus from the dead and it was known in all the area. "From that day forth [the Pharisees and chief priests] took counsel together for to put Jesus to death." Jesus left the area of Bethany and went into the wilderness with his disciples. The Pharisees and Sadducees gave a commandment that if any knew where Jesus was he was to show it to the rulers, that they might take him. Many people were converted by Lazarus' testimony, so the chief priests consulted that they might put Lazarus to death also. John 11:17–57; 12:1–11.

A.D. 33
April,
Jerusalem

Many of the chief rulers believed on Jesus but would not openly confess him because of their fear of the Pharisees, lest they be put out of the synagogue. John 12:42–43.

A.D. 33
April,
Jerusalem,
two days
before
Passover

The Pharisees and Herodians again sought to catch Jesus in his talk to have wherewith to accuse him. Chief priests and scribes sent forth spies to watch Jesus and to catch him in some way so they might deliver him to the governor. They asked him about tribute to Caesar. He put them to silence by saying they ought to render to Caesar that which was Caesar's. Throughout the day the Pharisees and Sadducees issued alternate "hard" questions to catch him. He put them all to silence by his answers. After this series of public humiliations, no man dared ask Jesus any more questions. Matthew 22:15–46; 26:1–2; Mark 12:13–17; Luke 20:19–26.

A.D. 33
April,
Jerusalem,
two days
before
Passover

Jesus publicly scolded the Pharisees and scribes for their lack of spirituality and their sins. He called them hypocrites, serpents, vipers, children of hell, whited sepulchers, and wicked men. Matthew 23.

A.D. 33
April,
Jerusalem

Judas, knowing of the plots and machinations to take Jesus, offered to deliver him to the chief priests and Pharisees for money. He came to Jesus in the Garden of Gethsemane with a band of men, officers, chief priests, and captains of the temple, armed with lanterns, torches, and weapons. They bound Jesus and took him to Annas and Caiaphas. Jesus declared that he was betrayed into the hands of sinners. Matthew 26:14–16, 47–50; Mark 14:41; John 18:1–13. It should be noted that Jesus could not be taken until he was willing. No man took his life from him without his consent. John 10:17–18.

A.D. 33
April,
Jerusalem,
before the
Sanhedrin

Jesus was tried before a night meeting of the Sanhedrin contrary to their own rules of procedure. Many of the procedural rules were violated by the very group whose business was to provide law, order, and justice. False witnesses were brought to testify. To the Jewish Sanhedrin, Jesus was accused of blasphemy for saying he was the Son of God. The charge was changed to treason by the same officers when he was taken before the Roman tribunal, since blasphemy of the God of Israel would mean nothing to a Roman court. Matthew 26:57–75; Mark 14:53–72; Luke 22:54–71; John 18:13–27.

A.D. 33
April,
Jerusalem,
before
Pilate

When Pilate was determined to let Jesus go and insisted that he found "no fault in him" "the chief priests and elders vehemently accused Jesus and also persuaded the multitude" to shout, "crucify him, crucify him." When it appeared as though Pilate was about to release Jesus, the crafty leaders of the Jews maneuvered Pilate into an awkward position by saying to him, "If thou let this man go, thou art not Caesar's friend: whosoever maketh himself a king speaketh against Caesar." Pilate reminded them that Jesus was their king. In reply the chief priests uttered their final word of self-degradation by saying: "We have no king but Caesar." The clever and experienced priests were too much even for Pilate, and they extracted Jesus' sentence of death from him. Matthew 27:1–38; Mark 15:1–27; Luke 23:1–33; John 18:28–38.

A.D. 33

Jesus was crucified. Not satisfied with his death, the chief priests and Pharisees came to Pilate and arranged for a guard of soldiers to be set at the tomb to prevent the theft of his body and therefore the appearance that he had been resurrected. When the soldiers later told the chief priests about the angels who rolled away the stone, and that Jesus really was resurrected at the tomb, they gave them money to say that the disciples stole Jesus' body in the night. The guards accepted the money and did as they were told by the priests and elders. Matthew 27:62–66; 28:1–15.

The foregoing entries illustrate what kind of enemies Jesus had to deal with in his ministry. These were the pretended spiritual leaders of the Jews. It is easy to see that if Jesus had been anything less than he was in physical, spiritual, and moral excellence, he could not have accomplished the task of establishing the kingdom of God on the earth in the midst of such priestcraft and self-righteousness. Jesus spoke with understatement when he said he was betrayed "into the hands of sinners." The rulers of the Jews were probably as violent and hard-hearted a group as have ever been assembled at a given time and place. It seems appropriate to repeat at this point the prophetic statement of Jacob concerning the conditions in Palestine in the time of Jesus:

> Wherefore, as I said unto you, it must needs be expedient that Christ—for in the last night the angel spake unto me that this should be his name—should come among the Jews, among those who are the more wicked part of the world; and they shall crucify him—for thus it behooveth our God, and there is none other nation on earth that would crucify their God.
>
> For should the mighty miracles be wrought among other nations they would repent, and know that he be their God.
>
> But because of priestcrafts and iniquities, they at Jerusalem will stiffen their necks against him that he be crucified. (2 Nephi 10:3–5.)

The Prophet Joseph Smith said that if Jesus had come to earth and preached the same "rough things" and the "same doctrine" in the Prophet's day as he did to the Jews, that generation too would put him to death (TPJS, 307, 328). It is noted that while the KJV is quite clear in depicting Jesus' troubles with the Jewish leaders, the JST and the Book of Mormon are even more explicit and pronounced. These later sources give us a more detailed and enhanced concept of the magnitude of the conflict than we could have obtained from the KJV alone.

CHAPTER 23

Death and Resurrection

In the early morning on the first day of the week, just outside the walls of Jerusalem, Jesus Christ came forth alive from the stone cavern in which his body had been entombed three days earlier. His lifeless corpse had been taken down from the cross, hastily wrapped in a linen cloth, and laid on a stone ledge within a cave hewn out of solid rock. A few hours after death his body had become as cold, inflexible, and rigid as the stone on which it lay. But now all that had changed. He who once was dead was now alive, warm, energetic, radiant, and glorious. Jesus himself described the change in these words: "I am he that liveth, and was dead; and behold, I am alive for evermore" (Revelation 1:18).

Before the resurrection of Christ, others had been raised from the dead by the marvelous power of God. For example, the son of the widow of Zarephath was revived by Elijah's instrumentality (1 Kings 17:17–24); the son of the Shunammite woman was brought back by Elisha's prayers and ministrations (2 Kings 4:18–37); and Jesus himself had raised three from the dead: a twelve-year-old girl (Mark 5:35–43); a widow's only son (Luke 7:11–17); and Lazarus (John 11:1–46). But each of these had been restored from death only to mortal life, whereas Jesus was raised to immortality, never to die again. Mortals have blood in their veins; resurrected bodies do not have blood (TPJS, 199–200, 367; 1 Corinthians 15:50). In Jesus' resurrection, death was conquered permanently. He would never grow old, never again experience physical pain, never suffer bodily disease, disorder, or any of the physical maladies and limitations of mortality.

The Miracle of Resurrection

The coming forth of Jesus Christ in the resurrection is part of the greatest event that has happened on this earth since the fall of Adam—the Atonement. Indeed it is related to the Fall, for Adam's fall brought death into the world, and Jesus' atonement and resurrection were necessary to conquer death, so that everything that has ever lived and died on this earth, or which shall yet live and die on this earth, can come forth in due time in a resurrection whose effects are permanent. The English word *resurrection* comes from two Latin terms: *re*, to do again; and *surgere*, or surge, meaning a thrust of power, energy, or life. Thus to re-surrect means that, having been dead, one gets up again in everlasting life.

Jesus had been slain three days before his resurrection. Events immediately leading to his death include a trial before the Jewish Sanhedrin and another trial before the Roman governor, Pilate. These were touched upon in the previous chapter. The precise charges that resulted in his execution are reiterated here for emphasis.

The Death of Jesus Christ

Jesus was condemned by the Jewish Sanhedrin to die as a blasphemer for saying that he was Jehovah, and also the Son of God. Under the Jewish legal system blasphemy was a capital crime, and punishment was usually by stoning. Since the Roman government had taken away from the Jews the legal right to exercise capital punishment, the Jewish rulers took Jesus to the Roman governor Pilate in hope of getting a sentence of death from him. However, blasphemy against the God of Israel was of no consequence to a Roman official, and was certainly not a capital offense in Roman law. So the crafty, designing Jewish rulers changed the charge to treason, saying to Pilate that Jesus made himself a king and was therefore a rival of the Roman emperor. They didn't really believe it themselves, but they feigned alarm and pretended loyalty to the Empire in order to make Jesus appear as a criminal in the mind of Pilate. They wanted Jesus to be found guilty of treason in a Roman court.

A charge of treason was so serious that Pilate was obligated to investigate, so he questioned Jesus about his kingdom. The dialogue is recorded in John 18:33–38: "Then Pilate entered into the judgment hall again, and called Jesus, and said unto him, Art thou the King of the Jews? Jesus answered him, Sayest thou this thing of thyself, or did others tell it thee of me?" (That is, Jesus asked, "Are you speaking as a Roman official or are you simply repeating what the Jews have said? Are you asking an ecclesiastical question or a political question?")

"Pilate answered, Am I a Jew? Thine own nation and the chief priests have delivered thee unto me: what hast thou done?" (Pilate's response, "Am I a Jew?" means, "I am not asking as a Jew, I am asking politically as a Roman official." Therefore, Jesus responds:)

> My kingdom is not of this world: if my kingdom were of this world, then would my servants fight, that I should not be delivered to the Jews: but now is my kingdom not from hence.
>
> Pilate therefore said unto him, Art thou a king then? Jesus answered, Thou sayest that I am a king. To this end was I born, and for this cause came I into the world, that I should bear witness unto the truth. Every one that is of the truth heareth my voice.
>
> Pilate saith unto him, What is truth? And when he had said this, he went out again unto the Jews, and saith unto them, I find in him no fault at all.

What all this means is: "Yes, I am a king, and eventually my kingdom shall fill the whole earth, but not now. Therefore, I have not set up a kingdom on earth to rival or threaten the present Roman Empire."

We know that ultimately Jesus' kingdom *is* "of this world," for he said that the meek shall inherit the earth (Matthew 5:5; D&C 88:17), and the promise is that the faithful shall become kings and priests unto God and "shall reign on the earth" (Revelation 5:10). The time will come when the kingdom spoken of by Daniel (2:44–45) will fill the whole earth and will replace all the kingdoms of the earth. This is also what the Twelve had in mind when they asked Jesus, "Wilt thou at this time restore again the kingdom to Israel?" (Acts 1:6). Jesus answered, in effect, "Not at this time—but later" (see v. 7). Hence Jesus answered Pilate as he did, and Pilate recognized that the kingdom of Jesus was no political threat to the Empire, so he endeavored to release him.

The Jewish rulers were not about to let their well-laid plans be thwarted. They had schemed to achieve this moment for over two years. So they said to Pilate:

> If thou let this man go, thou art not Caesar's friend: whosoever maketh himself a king speaketh against Caesar.
>
> When Pilate therefore heard that saying, he brought Jesus forth, and sat down in the judgment seat in a place that is called the Pavement, but in the Hebrew, Gabbatha.
>
> And it was the preparation of the passover, and about the sixth hour: and he saith unto the Jews, Behold your King!
>
> But they cried out, Away with him, away with him, crucify him. Pilate saith unto them, Shall I crucify your King? The chief priests answered, We have no king but Caesar.
>
> Then delivered he him therefore unto them to be crucified. And they took Jesus, and led him away.
>
> And he bearing his cross went forth into a place called the place of a skull, which is called in the Hebrew Golgotha:
>
> Where they crucified him, and two other with him, on either side one, and Jesus in the midst. (John 19:12–18.)

The chief priests were expert in priestcraft and in the art of extortion. They knew that Pilate was morally weak and they recognized the right moment to coerce him. They maneuvered him into an awkward position in relation to the Emperor when they challenged him with the outcry, "whosoever maketh himself a king speaketh against Caesar." They were too much even for the Roman governor, and they were able to get Pilate to issue the official order of Jesus' death, and even the help of the Roman soldiers to carry it out. Crucifixion was a Roman form of execution.

That Jesus would be crucified on a cross rather than to die by stoning, or some other way, had been known among the prophets since the beginning. Enoch saw it in vision (Moses 7:55) as also did Nephi (1 Nephi 11:33) and others (Ether 4:1). Jesus lived on the cross probably three hours, evidently corresponding to the three hours of terrible destruction experienced in the Western Hemisphere (see 3 Nephi 8:19). Crucifixion usually did not cause death so quickly, and it appears that Jesus actually died of a ruptured heart (see James E. Talmage, *Jesus the Christ*, pp. 668–69). A soldier thrust a spear into his side, making a large hole, from which "blood and water" came out (John 19:33–34). When the soldiers found Jesus already dead, they did not break his legs to create shock, to hasten death, as was the usual custom (John 19:31–33).

Jesus died in the afternoon, the Sabbath would begin at sundown in a matter of three or four hours, and the burial needed to be done in that short time. Joseph of Arimathaea, a member of the Sanhedrin and a believer in Christ, went to Pilate and obtained permission to get Jesus' body. Joseph wrapped the body in a clean linen cloth and placed it in his (Joseph's) own tomb. "Linen" implies white cloth. Throughout the scriptures when white cloth is meant it is usually called "linen" (see Exodus 26:1). No doubt other faithful persons assisted in getting the body off the cross and placing it in the sepulchre. Some women helped to prepare the body for burial (probably by washing away the blood), but in the short time available did not do as much as they desired to do. Jesus' body was quickly wrapped, a cloth or "napkin" was tied around the head to hold the jaw in place, the body was laid to rest in the tomb, and a stone was rolled over the doorway.

Some of the Pharisees who knew that Jesus had taught the doctrine of resurrection and had said that he himself would be resurrected three days after his death, went to Pilate and asked that a seal be placed on the stone, and guards be placed there also, to prevent the disciples from stealing the body and saying that he had risen (Matthew 27:62–66). By these various events (the soldiers finding him already dead, the sealing of the stone, etc.) the fact of Jesus' death and the security of the tomb were thus well established among the unbelievers, as well as among his disciples. There could be no question in anyone's mind who was there, that Jesus was completely dead, and that the tomb containing his body was completely secure.

While Jesus' body lay in the tomb, his spirit, alive and well, was in the world of spirits, preaching, and organizing a mission for the teaching of the gospel to those who had departed from this life without it (D&C 138). There he would remain until the time for his resurrection in three days.

The Resurrection

After the Sabbath was over, on the first day of the week, several women who were desirous of finishing the burial preparations came back to the tomb with spices and ointment. They talked among themselves as they walked toward the sepulchre and wondered aloud how they would remove the stone that covered the door (Mark 16:1–3; Luke 23:55–56). They were astonished to find the stone already moved and also to find that the body of Jesus was gone. The two angels who had moved the stone and were still present told the women that Jesus was not there any longer, for he had risen from the dead. A resurrected, glorified being is not hampered by earthly walls or solid rock. The stone was not rolled away so that Jesus could get out, but so that mortals could see in, and enter, and see for themselves that his body was gone.

The angels told the women that before Jesus died he had appointed a meeting in Galilee where he would meet the Brethren. They asked the women to remind the Brethren of that appointment (see Matthew 28:7, 16–18; Mark 16:7). This meeting in Galilee apparently culminated in over five hundred persons seeing the resurrected Lord all at one time (1 Corinthians 15:6), and was perhaps similar to the happening on the western continent as recorded in the Book of Mormon (3 Nephi 11).

On the day of the resurrection Jesus met with at least ten of the Twelve (Judas was dead, and Thomas was absent) and invited them to handle his body and remove all doubt in their minds as to his literal resurrection. "But they were terrified and affrighted, and supposed that they had seen a spirit. And he said unto them, Why are ye troubled? and why do thoughts arise in your hearts? Behold my hands and my feet, that it is I myself: handle me, and see; for a spirit hath not flesh and bones, as ye see me have. And when he had thus spoken, he shewed them his hands and his feet." (Luke 24:37–40.) The same day he ate fish and honeycomb with them (see Luke 24:41–43).

A week later, Thomas being present, Jesus again showed the Apostles his body and called particular attention to the wounds. The relative size of the wounds is illustrated by Jesus' instructing Thomas to feel the nail holes with his finger, but to thrust his hand into the hole in his side. (John 20:24–27.)

That Jesus literally rose from the grave in the most real physical sense, with the same body of flesh and bones he had on earth, is demonstrated in many ways. First, the angels said that he had risen. Second, the women and then the Brethren noted that the body was no longer in the tomb. Third, the women held Jesus by the feet (Matthew 28:9). Fourth, the Apostles felt his resurrected body with their own hands and saw the nail holes and the hole from the spear. Fifth, Jesus ate real food. Sixth, after he showed them his hands and feet, he "breathed on them" (John 20:22). It would be unthinkable for a *spirit* to be able to breathe on mortals, but since a resurrected body is an absolutely tangible physical being, why not? Luke records in the book of Acts that Jesus showed himself alive "by many infallible proofs" (Acts 1:3). These proofs, as we have noted, include hearing, seeing, touching, and being breathed upon, all in addition to the witness of the Holy Spirit. Such evidences attest not only to Jesus' having *a* body but also that it was the *same* body he possessed at death—the body which was nailed to the cross. The evidence that he was resurrected and alive must of necessity be as clear and definite as the evidence that he had died.

The scriptures affirm that the resurrection is a restoration in which the body is restored to the spirit. Unless one receives the same body one had at death it would not be a restoration, but a replacement. Latter-day scripture is especially clear that the same body one has on earth is the one that will be received in the resurrection (see Alma 11:42–45; 40:22–24; Mormon 6:21; D&C 88:28).

The Apostles Preach Resurrection

The resurrection of Jesus Christ greatly enlivened the Apostles. Jesus had spoken to them before of his death and resurrection, but now that they had seen it actually occur they understood it better. Furthermore, after they received the witness of the Holy Ghost the Twelve became fearless testifiers and spokesmen for the Lord, openly affirming his resurrection wherever they went. It is impressive to note just how vigorously Peter and the others declared the resurrection of Jesus. A few instances will illustrate:

1. Peter defined the calling of an Apostle to replace Judas as one who was "a witness of [Christ's] resurrection" (Acts 1:22).
2. On the day of Pentecost, Peter announced that God had raised up Jesus from the dead, and that the Apostles were witnesses of it (see Acts 2:22–24, 32).
3. Peter said he was able to heal a lame man, not through his own power, but by the power of Jesus Christ who was the "Prince of life," whom God had raised from the dead (see Acts 3:12–16).
4. Peter and the Apostles were put in prison by the Jews because they had preached so much about Jesus and the resurrection of the dead (see Acts 4:1–3, 10).
5. With "great power gave the apostles witness of the resurrection of the Lord Jesus" (Acts 4:33).
6. After being released from prison by an angel, Peter declared to the Jewish rulers that God had raised from the dead the same Jesus whom they had killed. He said that the Apostles and the Holy Ghost all bore witness of his resurrection. (See Acts 5:30–32.)
7. Paul also became a major witness of the resurrection of Jesus, and made mention of the resurrection in all his epistles except in the short personal letter to Philemon.

The Jewish population should have been willing to accept the doctrine of the resurrection, since many of their ancient prophets had spoken of it: Job (19:25–27), Isaiah (26:19), Ezekiel (37:1–14), and Daniel (12:2). The Nephite prophet Abinadi says that all of the ancient prophets knew of the resurrection and had declared that the Messiah would bring it about (Mosiah 13:33–35).

The resurrection of Jesus, and thus also of all mankind, is a fundamental doctrine of the gospel of Jesus Christ, and it is necessary that whenever and wherever the gospel is preached the doctrine of the resurrection be preached along with the first principles (TPJS, 149).

Why the Resurrection Is So Important

With so much scriptural emphasis on the resurrection, it is natural to wonder why it is so important. Why could we not simply continue into eternity as spirit beings without the physical body? In the New Testament the account of Jesus' resurrection is beautifully given; but it is in latter-day revelation that we learn why it was so important.

The resurrection of our individual bodies is important because our Heavenly Father has a resurrected body of flesh and bone (see D&C 130:22), as has our Heavenly Mother. It would be possible to continue in eternity as spirit bodies without the physical body, but as such we could not reach the fulness of salvation. A spirit body without a resurrected physical body cannot obtain a fulness of joy (see D&C 93:33–34). The revelations inform us that the spirits of mankind in the world of spirits, where they go when they depart from this mortal life, wish to have their bodies, and look upon the long absence from their bodies as a bondage (D&C 45:17; 138:50).

The Prophet Joseph Smith discussed the eternal significance of the body, and also of the devil's dilemma in having no body: "We came to this earth that we might have a body and present it pure before God in the celestial kingdom. The great principle of happiness consists in having a body. The devil has no body, and herein is his punishment. He is pleased when he can obtain the tabernacle of man, and when cast out by the Savior he asked to go into the herd of swine, showing that he would prefer a swine's body to having none." (TPJS, 181.)

And also: "Perhaps there are principles here that few men have thought of. No person can have this salvation except through a tabernacle. . . . The greatness of [Lucifer's] punishment is that he shall not have a tabernacle. This is his punishment." (TPJS, 297.)

Resurrection Is a Priesthood Ordinance

Paul, in his great treatise on resurrection in 1 Corinthians 15, poses two questions: "How are the dead raised up? and with what body do they come?" (v. 35.) He then proceeds to answer these questions in the remainder of the chapter and explains that all will rise from the dead, but not with the same glory (verses 29–42). Yet, says Paul, regardless of the degree of glory, all will receive a body that is immortal and incorruptible (vss. 42–44). We have already discussed the important fact that in the resurrection each receives the same body which was the "natural body," the body our spirit lived in during mortality (D&C 88:28). It will, of course, have become immortal by then.

In response to Paul's question as to "How are the dead raised up?" we have the further teachings of Apostles and prophets in this dispensation that resurrection is a priesthood ordinance, and will be conducted in an orderly, assigned manner, agreeable to the established order of the kingdom. Both President Brigham Young (JD 6:275; 15:136–39) and Elder Erastus Snow (JD 25:34) taught that the resurrection will be conducted much as other things are done in the kingdom, by those in authority and by delegation. The procedure is that as one cannot baptize himself, nor can he baptize others until he himself is baptized and ordained, so one cannot resurrect himself, but will be called forth by someone in authority. Men will be given the keys of this ordinance after they are resurrected, and then they can resurrect others. President Young also indicates that the Prophet Joseph Smith will be the first person resurrected in this dispensation. He will receive the keys and give them to others.

In general conference of April 1977, President Spencer W. Kimball quoted President Brigham Young: "We are in possession of all the ordinances that can be administered in the flesh; but there are other ordinances and administrations that must be administered beyond this world. I know you would like to ask what they are. I will mention one. We have not, neither can we receive here, the ordinance and the keys of resurrection." (JD 15:137; CR, April 1977, p. 69.)

Any doctrine or ordinance as fundamental to man's eternal salvation as the resurrection of the dead is of necessity regulated and performed by the keys of the Melchizedek Priesthood. It is also part of the patriarchal order of the family. So far as the celestial kingdom is concerned, the resurrection is a family event. We would at first naturally suppose that Jesus would resurrect himself, but perhaps he did not. Jesus did not baptize himself. The clear rendering of Acts 2:22–24, 32; 3:12–15; 5:30–32 (as cited above) represents Peter saying on three separate occasions that *God* raised up Jesus from the dead. If we read those passages literally and combine that concept with the teachings of President Young and Elder Snow, that only a resurrected being can perform a resurrection, we may gain an insight into the resurrection process as a patriarchal family order in which a righteous resurrected father would resurrect his son, and so forth.

A curious observation in John 20:4–7 indicates that as Peter and John looked into the empty tomb they saw the linen clothes in which Jesus had been wrapped. The napkin which had been about his head was in a separate place, neatly folded. Something about the arrangement of the linen was sufficient to attract the attention of these two Brethren and also rate a special notice in John's testimony. Whatever else is meant, the impression is that Jesus had come forth from the dead in orderly, dignified fashion, and took time to fold the clothing.

After Jesus' resurrection, many of the Saints whose bodies were in their graves around Jerusalem arose and came into the city and appeared to many (Matthew 27:52–54). A similar resurrection took place in the western hemisphere (3 Nephi 23:9–13).

The Law of Resurrection

Resurrection is necessary because of the fall of Adam. The law governing the resurrection is stated in Alma 11:42–45, and specifically provides that all shall rise from the dead, the body restored to the spirit, no parts missing, and the resurrected person restored to the presence of God for judgment. That a judgment should come after the resurrection of the body is reasonable, because we will be judged of the deeds done while in the body (Alma 5:15). In the most absolute and definite terms it is stated that once a person is resurrected, that person can never die a physical death again; the spirit and the body are united, never to be divided (Alma 11:45).

Such fundamental guidelines to the process of resurrection can direct our thinking and enlarge our comprehension of the eternal plan of salvation. For example, the question is often asked; "Is Jesus the Savior of worlds in addition to this earth?" The correct answer is "Yes," according to the scriptures (D&C 76:24; 88:24–62) and the teachings of the Brethren. Next question: "Did Jesus have to suffer and die on any other worlds to redeem them, as he did on this earth?" The answer, based on the provisions of Alma 11, cited above, can only be, "No." The fact that he was born, died, and resurrected on this earth—these being one-time events—demonstrates that he had never done these things elsewhere, or he would not have been able to do them here. And having done them on this earth, he cannot repeat them anywhere else. We see how unique our own world is in the universe. This earth is called God's footstool (D&C 38:17). On this earth Jesus Christ obtained his only physical body, and on this earth he was resurrected with that same body, and on this earth he will stand again and reign in his body throughout eternity (see D&C 130:9).

Jesus Had Complete Power over Death

Since the Fall has captured all mankind (without any exception) in the grip of its two deaths, and there is none who escape, how was Jesus able to conquer death when no one else could do so? Paul says Jesus "led captivity captive" (Ephesians 4:8). That is, death has captured all mankind, but Jesus captured the captor. It is because Jesus is the "Only Begotten of the Father," the "Son of God in the flesh" (1 Nephi 11:18, 21) that he can conquer death. He had a special supernatural power "given unto him from the Father" (Helaman 5:11; Mormon 7:5–6) that other men do not have. He was not dominated by death as we are, because he was the Son of God in the flesh. Giving his life was "not . . . a human sacrifice," nor a "sacrifice of man," but the infinite sacrifice of a God (Alma 34:10). Jesus, because of his paternity, had life in himself. His body of flesh and bones was fathered by an immortal God, and power over death was transmitted to Jesus biologically. He was a God on earth with power over death, and he would not have had to die in and of himself.

Jesus spoke of his unique power over death: "For as the Father hath life in himself; so hath he given to the Son to have life in himself" (John 5:26). And, "Therefore doth my Father love me, because I lay down my life, that I might take it again. No man taketh it from me, but I lay it down of myself. I have power to lay it down, and I have power to take it again. This commandment have I received of my Father." (John 10:17–18.)

If Jesus had been subject to death, and in the natural course of events would have died anyway, he wouldn't really have given his life in the fullest sense. He would only have given *time*. However, since he did not have to die at all it follows that, as he willingly laid down his life in the Atonement, he did indeed give his life to pay the debt of sin.

Perhaps it was this complete power over death that led Jesus to speak of dead persons as only "asleep." Thus he spake of Jairus's twelve-year-old daughter (Mark 5:39–43), even though the onlookers knew that she was very dead, and for which statement they laughed him to scorn. Jesus was ever the teacher, and having a full awareness of his own power over mortal death, to him all dead persons actually only "sleep," since death is not final. Likewise, of Lazarus, who was both dead and buried, Jesus said he "sleepeth" (John 11:11). Without the knowledge of the gospel, mankind in general naturally looks upon death as final and decisive, while sleep is but temporary. In Jesus' method of teaching the people that death, too, is temporary, it was an effective attention-getter to speak of those he was about to bring back to life as merely sleeping.

Jesus visited with the Brethren at intervals for forty days after his resurrection and then ascended to heaven from a point on the Mount of Olives near the village of Bethany. Two angels appeared and conversed with the eleven Apostles and told them "that this same Jesus" would return from heaven in a time to come. Since Jesus had his resurrected body at the time of ascension (Acts 1:9–12; Luke 24:50–52), it is clear that he will still have the same body at the time of his return.

Appearances of Jesus After the Resurrection

1. To Mary Magdalene. Mark 16:9–10; John 20:1–18. Early morning on the day of resurrection.

2. To the other women. Matthew 28:9–10. Early morning on the same day as above. They held him by the feet.

3. To two disciples on the way to Emmaus. Mark 16:12–13; Luke 24:13–32. Afternoon, the same day.

4. To Peter. Luke 24:34. Sometime the same day as above.

5. To ten Apostles. Mark 16:14; Luke 24:26–40; John 20:19–25. The evening of the day of resurrection. Thomas absent. Judas absent also. Jesus showed them his hands and his feet, and explained that a spirit did not have flesh and bones as he had. Then he ate fish and honeycomb before them, and they saw him do it.

6. To the eleven. John 20:26–31. A week later; Thomas present. Thomas felt the nail marks in his hands and feet; thrust his hand into the wound in Jesus' side.

7. To the seven disciples, beside the Sea of Galilee. John 21. Sometime after no. 6.

8. To the Eleven (and five hundred). Matthew 28:16–20; 1 Corinthians 15:6. A mountain in Galilee.

9. To James. 1 Corinthians 15:7. Time and place unknown.

10. To the Eleven on Ascension Day. Mark 16:19; Luke 24:44–51; Acts 1:3. Near Bethany.

11. To Paul. Acts 9:1–9; 22:6–10; 1 Corinthians 9:1; 15:8. Near Damascus, about A.D. 35.

12. To John on the island of Patmos. Revelation 1:9–18. About A.D. 96.

Note: The statement in Acts 1:3, that Jesus "showed himself alive . . . by many infallible proofs, being seen of them forty days, and speaking of the things pertaining to the kingdom of God" along with Acts 10:41 and Acts 13:31 implies that our Lord made many appearances besides those recorded, and that his post-resurrection ministry was much more extensive than we know.

PART V

Unto All Nations

During Jesus' life on earth the gospel was taught almost exclusively to the Jews, for he had instructed the Twelve not to teach among the Samaritans or the Gentiles. After his resurrection the Lord directed the Brethren to enlarge the scope of their ministry to include all nations. However, it was to be done in an orderly and systematic way. They were to wait until they received the gift of the Holy Ghost, then preach first to the Jews, next to the Samaritans, and finally to the Gentiles. This outreach is chronicled in the book of Acts.

It should be noted that extending the gospel to other nationalities did not mean that it was withdrawn from the earlier ones. Hence the gospel was still taught among the Jews even after it was extended to the Samaritans and the Gentiles.

The book of Acts is a brief account of about thirty years of missionary effort following the ascension of Jesus Christ into heaven. Far from containing the complete record, Acts is focused on a limited geographical area in the countries along the northern and western shores of the Mediterranean. Although our knowledge of the outreach of the Church begins with Acts, it is enriched in both history and doctrine by the epistles penned by the early leaders, especially Peter and Paul.

Of major significance is the special council held in Jerusalem about the year A.D. 49 or 50, as a result of doctrinal and cultural problems that arose when the gospel of Jesus Christ was taught directly to people of Gentile lineage. The decision of the council is a model of tact and restraint, and was effective in allowing the expansion of the Church to go forward among the Gentiles without the encumbrance of the law of Moses.

The missionary methods, the priesthood order in the Church, the doctrinal teachings, and the fact that the Church was led by the Spirit, are clearly illustrated in the Acts and the epistles. Emphasis is on the saving grace of Jesus Christ, and the reality of Jesus' resurrection from the dead.

CHAPTER 24

The Church After
the Ascension of Christ

The compilation known as the book of Acts presents our first glimpse of the Church after the departure of Jesus. It is generally understood to have been written by Luke, and is in reality a sequel to the book of Luke. Both the book of Luke and the book of Acts are addressed to an acquaintance named "Theophilus" (Luke 1:3; Acts 1:1). The book of Acts makes reference to the book of Luke as the "former treatise" of "all that Jesus began both to do and teach" (Acts 1:1), whereas Acts deals with the work and development of the Church after Jesus had ascended into heaven. Acts picks up the story where Luke and the other Testimonies end, and is in fact a testimony of Christ in and of itself. It is more than a simple recitation of historical information, for it is a presentation of facts so arranged as to tell a dramatic and moving story. It makes use of particular events in the early Church that effectively illustrate how the outreach of the Church (which was at first almost exclusively offered to none but Jews) was extended to include active missionary work among the Gentiles.

The complete title of the book of Acts is The Acts of the Apostles, and while it is true that all of the twelve Apostles are mentioned at least once, it is not a record of the "acts" of all of the apostles, but of only a few: a little of James and John, somewhat more of Peter, and a great amount of Paul.

Acts is a short account of the missionary plan of the Church, first to the Jews in Judea, then to the Samaritans, and finally to the Gentiles throughout the Mediterranean world. It covers not more than thirty years, and can be divided naturally into three parts: First, chapters 1–14, dealing with the Church from Jesus' ascension to the extension of the missionary effort among the Samaritans and then to the Gentiles. These activities precipitated the problems leading to a special council in Jerusalem. Second, Acts 15, giving an account of the Jerusalem council itself. And third, Acts 16–28, giving an account of Paul's missionary service among Jews and Gentiles; his imprisonments; his formal defense before the angry mob in Jerusalem, then to the Jewish Sanhedrin, and finally before King Agrippa; and then the journey to Rome for trial. Since Paul is the dominant personality in the extension of the Church among Gentile people, he becomes the dominant personality in the book of Acts from chapters 13 through 28. Likewise, fourteen of the twenty-one epistles in the New Testament were authored by Paul.

A Latter-day Perspective About the New Testament

There cannot be any doubt that many, if not all, of the Twelve did extensive missionary service and travel, even though a record of it is not contained in our present New Testament. Jesus commanded the Twelve to go to all nations, teaching the gospel of Christ and baptizing all who would believe (Matthew 28:19–20). Apocryphal sources and early tradition tell us that the original Apostles were true to their commission, traveling throughout the countries of Africa, India, Mesopotamia, the Near East, and so forth, preaching the gospel of Jesus Christ. (See William Byron Forbush, ed., *Foxe's Book of Martyrs* [Universal Book and Bible House, Philadelphia, Pa., 1926], pp. 1–5; also Montague R. James, trans., *The Apocryphal New Testament* [Oxford: The Clarendon Press, 1969], pp. 14–15, footnote; also see the index for various geographic areas such as Persia and India.) Yet the New Testament that has been among Christianity for the past 1800 years focuses primarily on the area immediately surrounding the northern shores of the Mediterranean Sea: Greece, Turkey, Italy, with slight mention of Spain, and contains no record of the ministry of the Twelve in other parts of the world such as Egypt and India.

There is a reasonable explanation for this narrow focus. The New Testament is a record of the work and preaching of then-living prophets and Apostles who went forth with priesthood authority to build up and regulate the Church of Jesus Christ in the first century A.D. Most of the writings and records of travel of those early authorized Brethren have not been preserved for later generations. Why then have the particular missionary records of Paul, Peter, and John been preserved instead of the others? Could it not be that they were preserved in the wisdom of God for the benefit of the Restoration in the last days? Knowing in what areas and among what people the Restoration in the latter days would need to begin, the Lord preserved those sacred records that dealt with the establishment of the Church in southern Europe, and which would move through-out Europe, the British Isles, and into Scandinavia. Although there was an apostasy of the true Church, a form of Christianity survived, and the records also survived to some extent. Thus there was a New Testament as a scriptural witness and a base for the restoration of the fulness of the gospel, which would come through the Prophet Joseph Smith.

Most of the settlers in early North America were from the countries of Europe, and they brought the Bible with them. The Protestant reformation of the sixteenth century based most of its philosophy on the writings of Paul and his emphasis on grace. The Reformation was absolutely necessary in preparation for, and was actually a prologue to, the Restoration in the nineteenth century. The Joseph Smith family, and the Youngs, Kimballs, Pratts, Whitmers, Taylors, Richardses, and other early families in the Church, were of European Protestant stock and were all be-lievers in the Bible. Furthermore, as missionaries of the Church went forth in the late 1830s and immediately thereafter, most of the converts came from such European countries as England, Wales, Scotland, Scandinavia, Germany, and Holland, where Protestantism was firmly in place.

It seems natural that the Lord preserved what he did in the New Testament because it was that part of the history and doctrine of the Church of the first century that would be most useable and serviceable in establishing The Church of Jesus Christ of Latter-day Saints in the dispensation of the fulness of times. The Lord knew and designed that it should be among those in America of European extraction that the restoration in the latter days should first take root. It would then be nourished by converts from Europe. From this beginning the gospel in the latter days will spread to all other nations. Without the New Testament already among the people, it would have been a great deal more difficult than it was for The Church of Jesus Christ of Latter-day Saints to be established in the nineteenth century. It would also have been more difficult without the particular type of New Testament that produced the Protestant reformation of the sixteenth century. Everything seems to have been designed in favor of the restoration of the gospel in the latter days.

Events Leading to the Jerusalem Council

As noted earlier, the causes that produced the Jerusalem council did not develop in a vacuum. The need for such a council was in consequence of several doctrinal and cultural factors that had been at work among the Jews for centuries. It will be necessary to review the activities of the Church as recorded in Acts chapters 1 through 14 in order to feel the thrust and direction of the early Church and see what led to the council itself. It is not likely that at the start many were aware of what the expansion of missionary work would bring by way of doctrinal and cultural problems, but probably some of the leaders of the Church sensed the situation very early. Following is a summation of significant events.

Acts 1. Jesus ascended into heaven from the Mount of Olives after telling the Twelve not to extend their ministry beyond Jerusalem until after they received the Holy Ghost. They would then be empowered to go to Jews, Samaritans, and the "uttermost part of the earth" (Gentiles), in that precise order and sequence (Acts 1:1–12). To fill the vacancy in the Quorum of the Twelve Apostles, Peter called the Eleven together. From those who had followed Jesus since the beginning of his ministry, Matthias was chosen and "ordained to be a witness with us of [Christ's] resurrection." (Acts 1:13–26.)

Acts 2. Jesus was crucified at the time of the annual Passover feast. Three days later he was resurrected. He tarried with the Apostles after his resurrection for forty days, thus making his ascension forty-three days after the Passover. In seven more days the annual feast of Pentecost would take place, having been established by revelation to Moses to be fifty days after Passover (see Leviticus 23:15–16). Gathered in Jerusalem for this particular Pentecost were thousands of Jews from at least fifteen nations throughout the Near East and Middle East (see Acts 2:9–11). They were native to these outlying areas, and spoke the language of their place of birth (Acts 2:5–12). On this occasion the Holy Ghost came upon the Twelve and they spoke in tongues to these visitors from many lands, and miraculously the people understood them. The Apostles taught them the gospel of Jesus Christ. How many thousands were present we do not know, but the record says that from these visitors the Twelve converted and baptized three thousand in that one day (Acts 2:41). After their baptism, these new converts would return to their homelands and thus the Church would have members in widely scattered areas. Missionaries would subsequently be sent to those locations to nourish these new members and build up branches.

It is of particular importance that the record states that those who came from these fifteen nations were both Jews and proselytes—which means that they were not all Jewish by lineage, but some were Gentile converts to Judaism (Acts 2:10). The term *proselytes* as used in the New Testament always means Gentile converts to Judaism. Most of the visitors, of course, would be Jews by lineage, but it is clear that some were of Gentile lineage who had embraced Judaism.

Among the three thousand converts to the Church on that day of Pentecost some would certainly be from among the "proselytes." These would be the first persons of Gentile lineage to join the Church in that dispensation. Jesus had instructed the Twelve two years earlier, when starting on their first missions, not to go among the Gentiles or the Samaritans at that time (Matthew 10:5). Hence Church membership up till this time was exclusively Jewish. But we note this important fact: Even though there were those of Gentile lineage who now came into the Church, they had all previously converted to Judaism, which means they were circumcised, ate kosher food, offered sacrifice, and honored the Sabbath day in proper Jewish style. Although Greek, Galatian, or Roman in lineage, they were religiously Jews. *Kosher* is a Hebrew term meaning ceremonially and ritually clean or correct. Kosher food is that which is in keeping with the dietary laws given in Leviticus 11.

It is significant that the Holy Ghost should come on the day of Pentecost, which was a "feast of harvest, the firstfruits of thy labours" (Exodus 23:16). Just as the paschal lamb of the Passover symbolized the death of the Lord, and thus Jesus was crucified at Passover time, even so receiving the Holy Ghost at Pentecost symbolized that the Holy Spirit is the firstfruit of our faith in Jesus Christ.

Acts 3–6. These four chapters deal with the ministry of the Twelve in and around Judea, among the Jews. The Twelve vigorously testified of Jesus and his resurrection from the dead, and the Church grew rapidly with Jewish converts. Persecution came from the Jewish leaders, because they objected to the success of the Apostles in teaching of the resurrection of Christ. They said the Twelve "have filled Jerusalem" with the doctrine of Christ (Acts 5:28). The Church at this time had strong Jewish ties, culturally, religiously, and geographically. Church growth necessitated administrative adjustments, so seven men were selected to assist the Twelve, primarily in welfare duties. Among these seven are some with Gentile-sounding names such as Stephen, Parmenas, and Nicolas. Nicolas was further identified as a proselyte from Antioch (Acts 6:5), thus affirming that he was a Gentile by lineage who first accepted the Jews' religion and then subsequently was converted to Christ and the Church. Thus at least Nicolas was actually of Gentile lineage, but he had been circumcised and had subscribed to all that pertains to the

Jews' religion and the law of Moses. Before becoming a member of the Church, Stephen was probably a "Hellenized Jew," or one who, though Jewish by lineage and religion, had been reared in a Greek environment and spoke Greek.

It is important at this point to clarify a statement in Acts 6:1 that says there was "a murmuring of the Grecians against the Hebrews, because their widows were neglected in the daily ministration." The Church in Jerusalem at this time was practicing a form of "united order," or economic system in which members held all things in common (Acts 4:34–37; 5:1–11). However, there seems to have been a feeling among the "Grecian" widows that they were neglected, that they did not receive as good treatment as other widows. A Grecian was not a Greek, but was a Jew who spoke Greek as a native language, and hence one who had been reared away from Palestine, as in Alexandria, Egypt, or some other place where there were large collections of Jews who spoke Greek.

The importance of this situation in the Church in Jerusalem is that it is evident there were Jews of the outlying countries— Jews by lineage, but from Greek-speaking areas—who had gathered to Jerusalem. These "Grecians," as they were called, thought they detected some prejudice from the more conservative Hebrews or Aramaic-speaking Jews of Palestine. This might be why the seven who were called to oversee the distribution of food were not strictly Jerusalem-oriented Jews but, as we noted in the case of Nicolas and Stephen, had some Gentile and Greek attachment. Proper priesthood order and procedure in the Church is also evident here: The Twelve made the selection of the seven under the inspiration of the Holy Ghost, and after the men were sustained by the people the Twelve set them apart by the laying on of hands (Acts 6:1–6).

It is also to be noted in Acts 6:6 that the Church grew rapidly in Jerusalem, and "a great company of the priests were obedient to the faith." This means that many of the priests under the Aaronic order, direct descendants of Aaron, joined the Church.

Acts 7. Stephen, one of the seven, was accused by the Jews of having taught that Jesus would destroy Jerusalem and the temple and "change the customs which Moses delivered" to

Israel (Acts 6:14–15). He was subsequently brought before the Sanhedrin and permitted to speak. When he declared that he could see in vision the heavens open, and Jesus "standing on the right hand of God," he was accused of blasphemy and stoned to death. Saul (later known as Paul) witnessed his death. The record says that "devout men" came and buried Stephen (Acts 8:2). "Devout men" are usually regarded by New Testament scholars as Greeks who were favorable to Judaism but not actual proselytes. Being buried by them suggests something of Stephen's Hellenistic background. Stephen is the earliest in the New Testament record who is reported to have said that Jesus would change the Mosaic customs.

Because there were seven men appointed, some have wondered if their office is analogous to that of the seven Presidents of the Seventy in the Church today. This is possible, but appears unlikely, since they were especially appointed to "serve tables," whereas the calling of a Seventy is to administer and travel and teach the gospel. We learn from Luke 10:1, 17 that Jesus had appointed "seventy" in his day. Any Presidents of the Seventy would likely be from among them. It is probably only coincidental that this group consisted of exactly seven men. That they may be of the Seventy is possible; that they were the seven Presidents is less likely, but we just do not know.

Furthermore, many Bibles contain a heading at the top of the page at this point identifying these seven men as "deacons." This interpretation has been made by the editors and translators because these seven are identified as servants or assistants to the Apostles. The English word *deacon* comes from the Greek *diakona*, meaning a servant or an assistant. Although these seven men were surely in that general category, their calling ought not to be equated with the ordained office of deacon in the Aaronic Priesthood in The Church of Jesus Christ of Latter-day Saints today.

Actually, Luke does not give us an account of the work of these seven men in their assignment "to serve tables." He does, however, follow the activities of two of the seven—Stephen and Philip—not in serving tables (a welfare-type assignment), but in preaching the gospel to nonmembers. It might be that Stephen and Philip were called to do missionary work in addition to the welfare assignment. Or they simply may have been reassigned.

The procedure of the Church today may provide an example of such changes in assignment. We understand that most calls to service are temporary in nature, and a person is likely to serve in several different callings over the period of a few years. Thus a man who once was Presiding Bishop is now a member of the Council of the Twelve; one who was a Seventy is now Presiding Bishop; one serving as a ward bishop may later be called as a stake president; and so forth. Nothing suggests that the seven men who were called and set apart to assist in the daily ministration of food were to remain in that capacity and in no other for the remainder of their lives. In fact, it appears that Stephen and Philip were soon engaged in a different capacity. Had they remained only in the original calling we might have heard nothing further of them, since Luke provides a detailed account of only their preaching activities.

Acts 8. Philip, one of the seven, baptized many men and women in Samaria. This was a new extension for the Church, whose members up to this point had not done formal missionary work there. Peter and John came from Jerusalem to lay their hands on the new converts and confer the Holy Ghost. The Church was thus officially established among the Samaritans, but this is only a half-step away from teaching the Jews, because even though the Samaritans were genealogically of Israel mixed with other nations (and thus technically were not Jews), they practiced the law of Moses—hence were circumcised, ate kosher food, offered sacrifice, and so on. In this respect they were ritually similar to the Jews, and the conversion of Samaritans did not challenge allegiance to the law of Moses. Acts chapter 8 also presents the first principles of the gospel (faith in Jesus Christ, repentance, baptism for the remission of sins, and the laying on of hands for the gift of the Holy Ghost) more completely in one setting than in any other section of the Bible (Acts 8:5–25).

Acts 9. Saul, a vigorous persecutor of the Saints, was converted to Jesus Christ by a personal visit in which he saw, heard, and conversed with the resurrected Lord. After that he was baptized and proclaimed his testimony of Christ in the synagogues of Damascus. For Saul to become a follower of Jesus Christ was a major change in his own life and startled many both within and without the Church; but his conversion did not mark a doctrinal or cultural change in the Church, because it did not raise a question as to the law of Moses, since he was already circumcised, ate kosher food, and so on.

The Lord's timetable is clearly seen unfolding in these early chapters of Acts. Saul (Paul) was going to be greatly needed in the Church missionary system in a short time, so the Lord got him converted at this time in order that he would be ready for service when the need arose. When the events in chapters 10 and 11 occurred, Saul was maturing in the gospel and being prepared. Furthermore, somewhat earlier, Barnabas in Jerusalem had introduced him to the Apostles (Acts 9:27). Hence they knew of Saul and he knew them.

Acts 10–11. Peter, being directed by a vision and the voice of the Spirit, was led to a meeting with Cornelius and his family at Caesarea. In Peter's vision he was shown animals that were forbidden to be eaten under the law of Moses, and he was told to kill and eat them. Peter was hesitant because of his long-standing allegiance to the law. But he was made to see that this was a sign to him, from the Lord, that the kosher restriction of the law of Moses was about to end. It took him a few moments, plus the help of the Spirit, to get used to the idea.

Cornelius was a good man, an Italian, a soldier, and was favorable to but not a proselyte to Judaism. He is called "one that feared God," or, in common parlance, a God-fearing man; a believer in many of the things of the Jews, but not a total proselyte, not circumcised, and so on. In a vision an angel had directed him to send for Peter. Peter, already having been prepared by the Lord, was willing to baptize Cornelius. This is the first clear case of a Gentile coming into the Church without having first gone the route of the law of Moses. The conversion and baptism of Cornelius in this manner is a major step—a *full step*—in the Church missionary system. The proper priesthood order of the kingdom is shown in the fact that the Lord brought about this major new procedure through Peter, who was President of the Church holding all the priesthood keys, and was the proper officer through which such direction from the Lord should come.

Many Jewish brethren in the Church objected to this direct-entry process and complained to Peter, but he answered their criticism with a detailed recital of the vision, the angel, the voice of the Spirit to him, and the fact that Cornelius and his family received a manifestation of the Holy Ghost before their baptism (Acts 11). Cornelius did not receive the complete gift of the Holy Ghost before baptism, for such would be contrary to the established order of the kingdom. What Cornelius received was the *power* of the Holy Ghost. The Prophet Joseph Smith clarified this matter:

> There is a difference between the Holy Ghost and the gift of the Holy Ghost. Cornelius received the Holy Ghost before he was baptized, which was the convincing power of God unto him of the truth of the Gospel, but he could not receive the gift of the Holy Ghost until after he was baptized. Had he not taken this sign or ordinance upon him, the Holy Ghost which convinced him of the truth of God, would have left him. Until he obeyed these ordinances and received the gift of the Holy Ghost, by the laying on of hands, according to the order of God, he could not have healed the sick or commanded an evil spirit to come out of a man, and it obey him. (TPJS, 199.)

Even after this landmark conversion of Cornelius, with Peter, the Lord's anointed, directing this phase of the missionary outreach, some Jewish members of the Church remained reluctant to accept the change, and we read in Acts 11:19 that they would preach the gospel to "none but the Jews only."

It is evident that Peter's experience with Cornelius opened the way for Gentiles to come into the Church without becoming Jews first. At Antioch of Syria, a great Gentile city about 310 miles north of Jerusalem, there began to be so many Gentiles join the Church that the Brethren in Jerusalem sent Barnabas to Antioch to oversee this change that was taking place. Barnabas was a good choice for this assignment, because of his varied background: He was a Jew of the tribe of Levi by lineage, reared in Cyprus, a Gentile environment, a convert to the gospel, being "a good man, and full of the Holy Ghost and of faith" (Acts 4:36; 11:20–24). Upon seeing the magnitude of the Gentile conversion in Antioch, Barnabas, being much pleased with the direction the missionary work was going, got Saul (Paul) to come and assist him.

Acts 12. This chapter deals with the martyrdom of James, one of the three presiding Apostles. Although the New Testament does not categorically distinguish between these three presidents and the other members of the Twelve, and does not speak directly of a separate Quorum of the First Presidency, from the viewpoint of the Church today we would easily regard Peter, James, and John as the First Presidency. It was this James, the brother of John, the son of Zebedee, whose martyrdom is recorded in Acts 12:1–3. Other administrative activities are also discussed in this chapter, such as Barnabas and Saul going on a welfare mission from Antioch to Jerusalem (end of chapter 11), and then returning to Antioch with John Mark, Barnabas's nephew or cousin.

Acts 13–14. Saul and Barnabas at Antioch were called and set apart to missionary service by the local authorities, which certainly means that neither Barnabas nor Saul were yet ordained Apostles or members of the Twelve. Taking John Mark, they went to Cyprus (Barnabas's native country), then to many cities in what is now central Turkey but was then called Galatia. It was probably while at Cyprus that Saul changed his Hebrew name to the Latin *Paul*, evidently for public relations purposes (Acts 13:9). This was doctrinally significant and proposed some cultural changes, because it showed they were very interested in conversion of the non-Jews. The Brethren preached first to the Jews, then to the proselytes who came to the synagogues. They taught that the gospel of Jesus Christ was greater than the law of Moses, and that the law of Moses could not save them (Acts 13:38–39). The Jews were furious, but many of the Gentile proselytes left the Jews and joined the Church. The two brethren thereafter directed their chief attention to the Gentiles (Acts 13:45–49). Along the way, for some reason not explained but which was not pleasing to Paul, John Mark left the mission and returned to Jerusalem. John Mark is believed to be the same person who later composed the book of Mark.

Paul and Barnabas established branches of the Church and ordained elders in each of the cities they visited, and then returned to Antioch of Syria with glowing reports of their success among the Gentiles. And of course, they had baptized many Gentiles directly into the Church without benefit of the law of

Moses. The mission occupied about one year, and required fourteen hundred miles of travel by sea and land. (It would be helpful for readers to examine the maps in the appendix section of the Bible and trace the journey of Barnabas and Paul.)

For clarification, it should be noted that there were two cities named Antioch. The larger city was in Syria and was the "second capital" of the Church, the place of Paul's residence between his missions. Each of his missions began there. The other Antioch, called Antioch of Pisidia, was in Galatia and was visited by Paul on his missions.

Acts 15. When word of the success of Paul and Barnabas among the Gentiles reached certain Church members in and around Jerusalem, these Judean brethren, much concerned, went to Antioch on their own, without authorization from the Twelve or any of the presiding Brethren of the Church, and declared to the Gentile Church members at Antioch, "Except ye be circumcised after the manner of Moses, ye cannot be saved" (Acts 15:1). This clearly stated the problem: Was obedience to the law of Moses with all its attendant performances required for salvation, after Jesus Christ had made the Atonement?

Why Circumcision?

It may be helpful at this point to explain why there is so much emphasis and concern about circumcision. It seems to us today such a strange matter to be fighting about in the Church. Circumcision is a very old practice among mankind, even among non-Jewish peoples. However, the Lord Jehovah appointed it the token of the covenant he made with Abraham (Genesis 17). This covenant was to extend throughout Abraham's posterity, and through this covenant were blessings and promises of God's favor to be realized throughout time and eternity. Circumcision was the badge, the sign of identification showing that one was a believer in the true God, and in all the dimensions of the Abrahamic covenant. The token was continued in the law of Moses. The manner in which the word *circumcised* is used throughout the book of Acts and the epistles is generally as a one-word representation for the entire law of

Moses; hence when the Jewish members of the Church insisted that Gentiles be circumcised, they really meant that the Gentiles should obey all of the law of Moses. But now, we must return to the events at Antioch.

Paul and Barnabas contended with these brethren from Judea on this important matter, which was not simply a topic about tradition or custom but involved a fundamental doctrinal issue regarding the atonement of Jesus Christ. The dissension became so great that it was decided that such a matter could be settled officially only by the Twelve (and First Presidency) at Jerusalem.

The significance of the question is threefold:

1. Did Jesus Christ by his earthly ministry and atonement fulfill the law of Moses with all its ordinances and performances? and if so,
2. Do converts from among non-Israelite peoples have to become "Jews" first and obey the law of Moses in order to become baptized members of the Church of Jesus Christ? and
3. Should Church members, Jews and Gentiles, have their children circumcised as a requirement for salvation?

The settlement of these questions would affect how one regarded Christ's mission, and would affect the missionary procedures of the Church. It would also affect the behavior and practices of every family in the Church in relation to their own children for generations yet unborn.

Having surveyed this doctrinal, cultural, and historical background, the setting is laid for us to look at the council which convened in Jerusalem to consider these problems that had arisen in the Church.

The Council Convenes: Acts 15

When Paul and Barnabas arrived in Jerusalem to see the Brethren they were respectfully received and had opportunity to convey to them an account of their success among the

Gentiles. However, there were in Jerusalem many Jewish members of the Church who had been Pharisees before their conversion to Jesus Christ. These would not give up the law of Moses, and insisted "that it was needful to circumcise [the Gentiles], and to command them to keep the law of Moses" (Acts 15:5). Therefore the Apostles and the elders at Jerusalem "came together for to consider of this matter" (Acts 15:6).

The problems confronting the council were manifold. Conflict within the Church is always unfortunate. Moreover, the ever-present persecution from the nonmember Jews could not be overlooked. If the new and little Church opposed the powerful influence of the Jewish establishment with regard to the law of Moses, what would be the consequence? That the Brethren moved with discretion seems apparent in every aspect of the council—in the proceedings, as well as in the decision. Some diplomacy seems to be evident in the role of James. The original James, brother of John and son of Zebedee, had been slain some years earlier (Acts 12) and apparently another James, the Lord's own brother, was called as an Apostle (Galatians 1:19). It appears that, while Peter presided, James played a major role in the council. Being the Lord's brother would give James some influence. Also he was a very conservative-type person. He would seem to be particularly well suited for this role. In a desire to bring together both Jews and Gentiles who were strongly opposed to one another's views on the law of Moses, the selection of James to speak at the conference seems like a good diplomatic choice, no doubt inspired by the Holy Spirit.

After much disputation had taken place in the council, Peter rose up and spoke of the conversion of Cornelius, and others, by his hand, "a good while ago" and reminded the congregation that the conversion of the Gentiles is the work of God, and that God "put no difference between us and them, purifying their hearts by faith." He also stated that both "we" and "they" would be saved by the "grace of the Lord Jesus Christ." (Acts 15:7–11.) This is an important affirmation that without God's grace man's works are drastically insufficient, hence all people will find that salvation is possible only through grace and not alone by their works, whether those works be the law of Moses or the gospel of Jesus Christ.

Following Peter's testimony, the "multitude" in the council listened as Barnabas and Paul told of the "miracles and wonders God had wrought among the Gentiles by them" (Acts 15:12).

After these things, James stated his recommendation that no greater burden than the necessary things of purity and refraining from idol worship and from eating blood should be placed on the Gentiles who wished to come into the Church. This is in effect the "golden rule" in reverse—do not do unto them what we would not want done to us. The law of Moses was not specifically mentioned by James and it is conspicuous by its absence, although the context of the council made it implied. The council also decreed that Paul and Barnabas should return to Antioch, accompanied by two men from Jerusalem, "chief men among the brethren," named Barsabas (also called Judas) and Silas. These two could testify with Barnabas and Paul as to the decision of the council. The Brethren also prepared an epistle to be carried to Antioch and the surrounding area, stating the decision of the council. The content of that epistle is as follows:

> The apostles and elders and brethren send greeting unto the brethren which are of the Gentiles in Antioch and Syria and Cicilia:
>
> Forasmuch as we have heard, that certain which went out from us have troubled you with words, subverting your souls, saying, Ye must be circumcised, and keep the law: to whom we gave no such commandment:
>
> It seemed good unto us, being assembled with one accord, to send chosen men unto you with our beloved Barnabas and Paul,
>
> Men that have hazarded their lives for the name of our Lord Jesus Christ.
>
> We have sent therefore Judas and Silas, who shall also tell you the same things by mouth.
>
> For it seemeth good to the Holy Ghost, and to us, to lay upon you no greater burden than these necessary things;
>
> That ye abstain from meats offered to idols, and from blood, and from things strangled, and from fornication: from which if ye keep yourselves, ye shall do well. Fare ye well. (Acts 15:23–29.)

Upon arriving at Antioch of Syria the Brethren assembled a multitude of Church members, read the epistle, and exhorted the people, who "rejoiced" at the news (Acts 15:30–33).

Such is the report of the proceedings of the council given in Acts 15. However, we learn other interesting details from Paul's later epistle to the Galatians. From the epistle we learn that Paul went up early to Jerusalem to confer privately with the Brethren to learn of their views, and to make certain they were in agreement with what he and Barnabas had done with regard to receiving the Gentiles, "lest by any means I should run, or had run, in vain" (Galatians 2:2). This private meeting is probably what is referred to in Acts 15:4–5, but Paul's epistle gives it a clearer focus and calls more attention to it, by expressing his motive in speaking with the Brethren in private.

Another important factor that we learn from this Galatian epistle is that Paul and Barnabas took Titus, a young Gentile convert probably from Antioch (Galatians 2:4), to the council. Paul apparently saw in Titus living evidence, or "exhibit A," being an uncircumcised Greek who was a model of faith and virtue, and strong in the Spirit. Paul could show the Jewish members of the Church in Jerusalem a living, breathing example of the grace of God given to the Gentiles without the encumbrance of the law of Moses. Paul apparently was successful in his purpose, for he declared, "But neither Titus, who was with me, being a Greek, was compelled to be circumcised" (Galatians 2:3).

The Galatian epistle also assists us in determining the date of the council. In chapter one Paul tells of his conversion to Jesus Christ. In chapter 2:1 he tells of going to Jerusalem with Barnabas and Titus to the council fourteen years later. We do not know the precise year when Paul joined the Church, but it could not have been less than a year or two after the ascension of Christ. Assuming that is so, and that he was baptized in about the year A.D. 35 or 36 (Galatians 1:15–19), fourteen years later would be A.D. 49 or 50. Paul also mentions an event that took place "three years" after his conversion (Galatians 1: 17–19), but a close reading of Galatians chapter 1 seems to show that the three years were within the scope of the fourteen, and not added to it. It is my conclusion that the Jerusalem conference took place about fourteen years after Paul's conversion.

These significant details about the council would be unknown to us if we did not have the Galatian epistle.

Jerusalem Council Decision
Only a Half-Step from the Law of Moses

As forward-reaching and beneficial as was the decision by the Jerusalem council, certain dimensions identify it as only a half-step in the progress of the Church. For one thing, the council did not decisively declare an end to the law of Moses. It is noticeable that in the part of the epistle that gives the decision of the council the words "law of Moses" are not used, nor does it declare that the law is fulfilled by Christ, or has a final and absolute end as a practice in the Church. Furthermore the epistle was not addressed to all members of the Church, but only to the Gentile members in Antioch, Syria, and Cilicia. The council said that observance of the law of Moses was not obligatory so far as the Gentiles were concerned, but it did not address the subject so far as Jewish members were concerned. On the basis of the epistle, Jewish members of the Church could continue to observe the ordinances of the law of Moses as a supposed requirement for salvation.

Why would the Brethren have been so ambiguous and non-declarative? They seemed to have said as little as they could about the matter. Was it not that they wished to avoid a division in the Church and not alienate the strict Jewish members? Likewise they would not want to invite persecution from non-member Jews. James seems to have these factors in mind when after announcing the moderate decision he says to the council: "For Moses of old time hath in every city them that preach him, being read in the synagogues every sabbath day" (Acts 15:21).

The decision of the council was favorable to Paul, Barnabas, Titus, and the Gentiles who were already in the Church and also those who would yet join, but it also left the Jewish members free to continue the practice of the law of Moses if they cared to do so. It should be noted that the council did not say that the Gentiles *could not* or *must not* practice the law of Moses, but only that they *need not* do so for salvation.

By wording the decision in the way they did, the Brethren probably avoided an open schism in the Church, and no doubt also avoided some of the ire that would have come from the Jews had the decision been more pronounced. There must have been many who would have preferred a stronger declaration, but the Brethren acted in the wisdom requisite for their situation. However, in avoiding a major division in the Church, they also created in effect two types of practice within the Church: the Jewish practice with the law of Moses, and the Gentile practice without the law of Moses.

It is interesting to note that not long after the council adjourned, when Paul departed from Antioch on his second mission, he came to Lystra and wanted Timothy, a Greek convert, to accompany him. Since Timothy's mother was a Jewess, but his father was a Greek, he had not been circumcised. Paul therefore circumcised Timothy so that he would be more acceptable to the Jews in that area among whom he would do missionary work. Coming so soon after the council, this may seem contradictory to Paul's standards, but it is fairly simple: In the case of Timothy it was an expediency because of Jewish tradition and culture. He did not want the messenger to stand in the way of the message. If circumcision had been regarded as a necessity for Timothy's own salvation, Paul would not have done it.

Aftermath of the Council

The effects of the moderate decision of the council were far-reaching and long lasting. About ten years later, as Paul returned to Jerusalem at the end of his third mission—this one among the Gentiles of Greece, Galatia, and Asia (Galatia and Asia being in present-day Turkey)—he was greeted by the Brethren, who rejoiced at his great success among the Gentiles of the Roman Empire but cautioned him about preaching strong doctrine, especially about the law of Moses, in Jerusalem. It is obvious that even a decade after the council, Jewish Church members in Judea were still observing the law of Moses. The record as told by Luke reads:

> And when we were come to Jerusalem, the brethren received us gladly.
> And the day following Paul went in with us unto James; and all the elders were present.

And when he had saluted them, he declared particularly what things God had wrought among the Gentiles by his ministry.

And when they heard it, they glorified the Lord, and said unto him, Thou seest, brother, how many thousands of Jews there are which believe; and they are all zealous of the law:

And they are informed of thee, that thou teachest all the Jews which are among the Gentiles to forsake Moses, saying that they ought not to circumcise their children, neither to walk after the customs.

What is it therefore? the multitude must needs come together: for they will hear that thou art come.

Do therefore this that we say to thee: We have four men which have a vow on them;

Them take, and purify thyself with them, and be at charges with them, that they may shave their heads: and all may know that those things, whereof they were informed concerning thee, are nothing; but that thou thyself also walkest orderly, and keepest the law.

As touching the Gentiles which believe, we have written and concluded that they observe no such thing, save only that they keep themselves from things offered to idols, and from blood, and from strangled, and from fornication.

Then Paul took the men, and the next day purifying himself with them entered into the temple, to signify the accomplishment of the days of purification, until that an offering should be offered for every one of them. (Acts 21:17–26.)

There is no question that Peter and the Brethren knew that the law of Moses was fulfilled by Christ. The doctrinal question was settled: The law was not any longer a requirement for salvation now that Jesus had made the Atonement. Missionary work among the Gentile nations could go forth directly and without impediment.

But there remained a conflict between culture and doctrine. The Brethren were clear on the matter, but the long-standing culture and tradition persisted among many Jewish members of the Church even after the doctrinal question had been settled. There is generally a lag between revelation and actual practice. Latter-day scripture leaves no doubt that the law of Moses was fulfilled in Christ (3 Nephi 15:4–5; Moroni 8:8; D&C 74), yet we see that the moderate decision of the council allowed it to linger among Jewish Christians.

The account of the Jerusalem council in the book of Acts gives our present generation an informative model as to how both Church members and nonmembers react when revelation confronts tradition and long-standing custom. Only living prophets could correctly handle the situation then. Only living prophets can do so now.

CHAPTER 25

Paul's Missionary Methods

W e will now continue a brief overview of Acts, highlighting particular historical and doctrinal items that occurred as the Church continued onward after the Jerusalem council. This portion of Acts covers Paul's second and third preaching missions, then his three defenses before (1) the mob at the temple courtyard; (2) the Jewish Sanhedrin; and (3) King Agrippa and the Roman procurator, Festus; and finally his tumultuous journey to Rome. We will dwell at length on the second mission as contained in Acts 16–18 so as to illustrate missionary methods and doctrine.

Acts 16. We learn from the concluding verses of Acts 15 that after the Jerusalem council, Barnabas, Paul, Silas, and Judas return to Antioch of Syria and give a report on what had occurred in the council. Paul proposes to Barnabas that they visit the area of their first mission (as recorded in Acts 13–14) and "see how they do." He no doubt wants to tell them of the decrees of the council. Barnabas agrees to go and determines to bring John Mark. Paul, however, is not favorable to having Mark come because he had departed from them early on the first mission. Unable to come to a satisfactory arrangement, Barnabas takes

Mark and sails to the island of Cyprus, while Paul chooses Silas and travels inland throughout parts of Syria and on to Cilicia, Derbe, and Lystra, the latter two places being cities visited on the previous mission.

At Lystra the young Timothy (spoken of in the previous chapter), joins the company and at Paul's request is circumcised so he will be more acceptable to the Jews among whom he will preach (Acts 16:1–3). It is probable that Paul had converted Timothy during his first mission two or three years before. We are acquainted with Paul's absolute refusal to accept circumcision as a requirement for salvation, but now we see his adaptability in attending to this ritual only to make Timothy socially acceptable.

As the company of missionaries travel through these Gentile cities they tell of the decrees of the Jerusalem council. It seems reasonable that a copy of the letter would be left with every branch of the Church in the area. Although these cities of the Roman Empire are largely of Gentile population, there are many Jews scattered throughout all the area, and Paul finds a synagogue in almost every city. He seems to begin his contact at the synagogue in each new place (see Acts 17:1–2).

Paul's plan is to preach in Asia (present-day western Turkey) and Bithynia (present-day northern Turkey) but is "forbidden of the Holy Ghost." He therefore travels westward to Troas, where he is directed by a vision to leave the area and go to Macedonia. He obeys and sails to Philippi.

It is at Troas that an interesting change occurs in the narrative style, for the text begins to speak of "us" and "we," indicating that the author, Luke, is present. Such tell-tale signs of his presence in the company come and go as the record progresses, suggesting that he did not accompany Paul in every instance. He apparently met Paul at Troas and accompanied him to Philippi.

At Philippi there was no synagogue, because it was originally a Roman colony or military outpost, and had very few Jews. Therefore, Jews and others met by the riverside. Here Paul baptizes some converts (Acts 16:12–15). The city of Philippi was named after its founder, Philip, father of Alexander the Great, who had ruled this area more than 350 years earlier.

The spirit of discernment is demonstrated at Philippi by Paul when he casts an evil spirit out of a woman, even though she says good things about the missionaries, even declaring that they are "servants of the most high God." On the surface she seems to be supportive, but she is motivated by "a spirit of divination" (Acts 16:16–18), and has brought her masters much gain by soothsaying. After the evil spirit is gone, her masters' source of income is also gone, so they physically and verbally attack the missionaries. Paul and Silas are publicly stripped, beaten, and cast into jail, for "being Jews" and "troubling" the city with their teachings. All this is done without a trial or the formal procedure required by Roman law.

In prison Paul and Silas pray and sing hymns and the other prisoners hear them. At midnight an earthquake opens all the prison doors, "and everyone's bands were loosed," but no one flees. That night the missionaries preach the gospel of Jesus Christ, and the jailer and his household are converted and baptized. When the city magistrates send word in the morning to release Paul and Silas, Paul refuses to go. His bold and courageous response is that they have been unjustly and illegally beaten, jailed, and publicly humiliated, and they are not going to leave secretly. He wants the magistrates to come personally to release them. Paul also adds the convincing bit of information that he and Silas are Roman citizens. This brings the magistrates to the jail, and the missionaries receive a proper release. They are also asked to leave the city.

At first it might seem as though pride and stubbornness cause Paul to demand such personal attention, but there is a more substantial reason. It is widely known by the people that Paul and Silas are ministers of the gospel of Christ. Since they have been publicly arrested, beaten, and jailed, it is necessary for the benefit and good name of the Church that their names be cleared, at least with the authorities. In order that future missionaries and Church members be without a negative and false reputation the situation has to be corrected. This is a legal matter, and it takes a man of Paul's disposition and courage to recognize the need and bring it about.

In the account of the imprisonment no mention is made of Timothy or Luke. Perhaps they were not imprisoned because

they are of Greek lineage, whereas Paul and Silas were specifically accused of "being Jews" (Acts 16:20).

Acts 17. Paul and company leave Philippi and travel westward to Thessalonica, a city named after Thessalonica, sister of
Alexander the Great. As no mention is made of Luke at this
point, it appears that he remained at Philippi. Leaving Luke to
be in charge of the Church at Philippi is a good arrangement,
since he had not been jailed, and was himself a Greek, and
could be valuable to the Church in that area. The conclusion
that Luke remained at Philippi is not argued from mere silence
alone but is strengthened by the fact that the "us" and "we"
passages do not occur anymore in the narrative, after Philippi,
until several years later during the third mission, when Paul returns to Philippi and the "we" passages reappear, showing that
Luke is in the company again at that juncture (see Acts 20:1–5).

Paul, Silas, and Timothy remain at Thessalonica at least
three weeks, with Paul reasoning in the synagogue with the
Jews and the Greeks. His missionary approach is to show from
the scriptures that Jesus is the Christ, and that he suffered and
died and now has risen from the dead. (Acts 17:1–3.) Among the
Jews some believe and some do not, but many of the Gentiles
believe. Persecution becomes so severe that Paul and Silas leave
by night for the nearby Berea, while Timothy apparently stays
in Thessalonica. Paul goes to the synagogue at Berea and makes
many converts among both Jews and Greeks. When the Jews at
Thessalonica hear of Paul's success at Berea, they come there
and stir up so much trouble that Paul leaves by ship for Athens,
while Silas stays at Berea and Timothy at Thessalonica. It is evident that in every location the greatest enmity of the Jews is
shown against Paul, more so than against the others, probably
because he is so effective in using the scriptures to declare the
mission of Jesus Christ and the fulfillment of the law of Moses.

When Paul arrives at Athens, he sends word to Silas and
Timothy to come at once and join him. While waiting for their
arrival, which will take several weeks, he preaches in the synagogue of the Jews. He is greatly stirred within himself when he
encounters the idolatry and philosophy of the Greeks.
However, he is very resourceful, and when he sees an altar dedicated "To the Unknown God," he tells the people that he

knows that unknown God, and proceeds to preach to them Jesus and the resurrection. The doctrine of the resurrection of the dead is so new and puzzling to Greek thinking that many of them mock, but some are curious, and a few believe. All of this apparently occurs before Silas and Timothy arrive.

Acts 18. After the experience with the philosophers at Athens, Paul visits Corinth. Here he meets a faithful couple— Aquila, a Jew, and his wife, Priscilla, who for the next few years became prominent in the life of Paul and the progress of the Church. Paul has a special attachment with the couple, for they are tentmakers, the same occupation as was Paul. He stays with them for a time, awaiting the arrival of Silas and Timothy. Paul reasons in the synagogue every Sabbath, and "testified to the Jews that Jesus was Christ" (Acts 18:4–5). Paul and his company remains at Corinth for "a year and six months" with much success, mostly among the Greeks.

After a time the company decide to return to Antioch of Syria, and so begin the long journey. The first part of the trip is by sea from Athens to Ephesus. Paul does not remain in Ephesus long, but while there he "reason[s] with the Jews" at the synagogue. Paul expresses an urgency to get to Jerusalem to attend "this feast," before returning to Antioch. The particular feast is not specified. (Acts 18:19–21.)

Sometime in the latter part of the second mission, probably from Athens or Corinth, Paul composes his two epistles to the Thessalonians that are in the New Testament. These are the earliest epistles we know of from Paul.

Nothing is said in the scriptures about the purpose and events of Paul's visit to Jerusalem and the "feast" he was so anxious to attend at the end of this second mission. The visit must have been brief. It is barely mentioned in Acts 18:22, which states only that after he had landed at the coastal city of Caesarea, "and had gone up, and saluted the church, he went down to Antioch." This passage may need some explanation: always in the Bible one goes "up" to Jerusalem, and "down" to anywhere else. This is due to the topography of Palestine, Jerusalem being at a high point of about 2,600 feet above sea level. The verse cited means that Paul went from Caesarea to Jerusalem, visited the brethren, and then went on to Antioch.

Even though the word *Jerusalem* is not categorically stated at this point, it is necessarily implied.

The second missionary journey included a distance of at least three thousand miles and required about two years.

When Was Paul Ordained an Apostle?

Although the scripture is silent about Paul's activities with the Brethren at this juncture in Jerusalem, there may be more than is at first discernible from a casual reading. We mentioned Paul's first two epistles having been written near the end of the second mission. In neither of these epistles does Paul introduce himself or declare that he is an Apostle in the ordained sense. The salutation in both cases reads: "Paul, and Silvanus [Silas], and Timotheus [Timothy], unto the church of the Thessalonians" (see 1 Thessalonians 1:1; 2 Thessalonians 1:1). However, the next epistles written by Paul, which were written during the third mission, emphatically state that he is an Apostle, and read as follows: "Paul, called to be an apostle of Jesus Christ through the will of God . . . unto the Church of God which is at Corinth" (see 1 Corinthians 1:1; 2 Corinthians 1:1). The difference between the introductory statements of the first two epistles and the next two is dramatic, and prompts the supposition that Paul was ordained to the apostleship while at the "feast" in Jerusalem between the second and third missionary journeys. Most of Paul's epistles written after this time begin with a solid declaration that he is an Apostle—Philemon and Hebrews are the exceptions.

Many students of the New Testament feel that Paul was an Apostle at an earlier time than I have stated above. There is some evidence for an earlier date. In at least two instances the word *apostle* is applied to Paul, one even as early as the first mission (Acts 14:4), and the other in the second mission (1 Thessalonians 2:5–6). In the case of Acts 14:4, Luke is writing long after the time, and it would be a simple anachronism for him to refer to Paul as an apostle. In the case of 1 Thessalonians 2:5–6, the word *apostle* might be used in the sense of a special witness of Christ, which Paul was ever since his vision on the

Damascus road, and not in the more formal ordained sense. In the early records of The Church of Jesus Christ of Latter-day Saints, the Seventy are sometimes referred to as the "seventy apostles," showing that the office of Seventy is an apostolic-type calling. Therefore, the occasional use of *apostle* with reference to Paul's first and second missions does not seem as persuasive as the much stronger evidence found in the opening lines of 1 and 2 Corinthians (as cited above) in which Paul states unequivocally for the first time, that he is "called to be an apostle."

Paul's Missionary Methods

Missionary methods of the Church in the New Testament were first established by Jesus. He went to the synagogues and the marketplaces. The first Apostles followed his lead.

There is a distinct pattern to Paul's missionary approach. He almost always began his activities in each city at the Jewish synagogue. Paul had conversed with the resurrected Lord. He had a perfect knowledge of Christ's reality, and was so well acquainted with the Old Testament that he had no fear or reluctance to engage in discussion and to "reason" with the Jews on the meaning and purpose of the law of Moses and the teachings of the prophets about the Messiah (Christ) to come.

Not only would Paul's activity at the synagogue give him opportunity to engage the Jews in conversation but it also put him in direct contact with Gentile proselytes, which was a door to the larger work among the Gentiles. The "proselytes" he would meet at the synagogue would have family and friends (Gentiles) who had not joined the Jews' religion. The proselytes could give him access to them in a type of referral system.

The first Gentiles to come into the Church of Christ in New Testament times were those who had already converted to the Jews' religion. This gave them a common background and familiarity with the prophets of the Old Testament. In like manner, as missionaries of The Church of Jesus Christ of Latter-day Saints have gone to traditionally non-Christian cultures such as in the Far East and Africa, the first converts have come from those who have been converted first to Catholic or Protestant churches, which has given them a familiarity with the Bible and thus made it easier for them to respond to the fulness of the gospel as restored in the last days through the Prophet Joseph Smith.

After Paul and his companions had converted and baptized a number of people in an area, they would then ordain elders and organize branches (Acts 14:23).

Paul was in every way an administrator and Apostle. He taught, baptized, ordained, called people into service, transferred missionaries, excommunicated when necessary, wrote letters, travelled, and also conducted a welfare program throughout the large area of his personal visits (see 2 Corinthians 9; Romans 15:25–28).

Acts 19–21. The third mission begins at Antioch and covers the area of Galatia, Asia, Macedonia, and Achaia (Greece). Paul's missionary methods are the same as before. Being a strong leader, he visits the synagogues and reasons with the Jews, testifying that Jesus is the Christ. He writes epistles to branches of the Church he has earlier visited—most of which he originally organized; he calls many missionaries into service and transfers them from place to place. (Such methods are recommended in latter-day revelation as examples in guiding the Lord's church in our present dispensation—see D&C 84:106–8.) Paul's greatest success is among the Gentiles, although there is considerable opposition and persecution from both Jews and Gentiles. The third mission covers a distance of at least 3,500 miles and occupies three and a half years and more.

Among the notable experiences on the third mission are: (1) rebaptizing twelve men at Ephesus who thought they were members of the Church but had been "baptized" by someone without proper priesthood authority (Acts 19:1–7); (2) raising Eutychus from the dead at Troas when he fell asleep about midnight during Paul's long sermon, and fell three flights to the ground—after reviving him, Paul continued to preach until daybreak (Acts 20:7–12); (3) Paul's warning to the elders from Ephesus that an apostasy would come in their church after his departure (Acts 20:17–38).

The third mission ends at Jerusalem, when Paul visits the Brethren and reports his success among the Gentiles. They rejoice at his ministry but counsel him to be seen at the temple with some Jewish brethren, so that the Jews of the city will see that he is an "orderly" person and "keepest the law" (Acts 21: 17–24). Paul conforms to the wishes of the Brethren and all goes well for about a week until some Jews from Asia recognize him at the temple, and they raise such a commotion that Paul is arrested by the Roman officers as a protection, because the Jews are about to kill him. The soldiers bind Paul with two chains, and put him on the stairs overlooking the temple area, from which he addresses the angry mob in the Hebrew (or Aramaic) language. The KJV uses the word *Hebrew*, but it is generally understood that ever since the return from Babylon the Jews in Palestine spoke Aramaic (which is similar to Hebrew) as their common tongue.

Acts 22. From the stairs Paul eloquently tells of his early life as a Jew, then as a persecutor of the Christians, then of his vision of Jesus Christ on the road to Damascus, followed by his subsequent unceasing labors as a disciple of the Christ whom he once opposed. He affirms that this same Jesus, who is both Lord and Christ, had commanded him to preach to the Gentiles. When he says these things to the already angry mob at the temple courtyard they became even more exercised because he makes Jesus a divine being, and also because he says that the command to preach to the Gentiles was from God. Such ideas they consider blasphemy, and they shout, "Away with such a fellow from the earth: for it is not fit that he should live" (Acts 22:22).

Paul is again rescued by the Roman soldiers and this time is put in prison. The Romans do not know what Paul has done that has made the Jews so angry, so the next day he is brought before the Jewish high court known as the Sanhedrin, consisting of seventy members or judges and a high priest, to be examined formally by them.

Acts 23. Paul stands on trial before the highest court of the Jewish nation. At this instant he must have reflected on the fact that nearly twenty-five years before, at the time of his vision on the Damascus road, the Lord Jesus said that he would proclaim the name of Christ "before Gentiles, and kings, and the children of Israel" (Acts 9:15). Since that day he has had many experiences before mobs, magistrates, and lesser rulers. Now he stands before the all-important Jewish high court.

Paul's discourse is much shorter on this occasion than the one he had given the day before to the mob. He probably intended to make a longer presentation on this once-in-a-lifetime opportunity, but two things happen in this closed, private meeting that precipitate a short session. First, as he begins to speak to the court he says: "Men and brethren, I have lived in all good conscience before God until this day." The court does not accept this self-evaluation. Here stands the man that the Jews see as a traitor to their religion, an enemy to the law of Moses, and a threat to the religion of their fathers. To hear him speak of his "good conscience" agitates the high priest so much that he commands that Paul be smitten on the mouth. Paul doesn't take this silently, and retaliates with a bold accusation: "God shall smite thee, thou whited wall: for sittest thou to judge me after the law, and commandest me to be smitten contrary to the law?" Those in attendance are so shocked at Paul's words that they ask: "Revilest thou God's high priest?" Paul replies: "I wist [knew] not, brethren, that he was the high priest."

It is difficult to believe that Paul really didn't know that the man was the high priest, if for no other reason than that the high priest was the regular presiding officer of the court and sat in a conspicuous place of honor in front of the other judges, who were seated in a half-circle. Paul's reply may have been a form of sarcasm. Perhaps what he really meant was something such as: "Oh, is he the high priest? How is one to know? I would not have guessed it from his illegal actions." This episode at the very start of the session was of itself an unsettling influence.

The second disruptive occurrence follows soon afterward, when Paul, seeing that one part of the council consists of Sadducees and the other of Pharisees, senses an opportunity to pit the judges against one another. He cries out, "Men and brethren, I am a Pharisee, the son of a Pharisee: of the hope and resurrection of the dead I am called in question" (Acts 23:6). This declaration is especially provocative because the Sadducees and Pharisees are often suspicious of each other on doctrinal grounds and differed markedly on the subject of resurrection. Paul knows this, and his words have the desired effect: The meeting is thrown into confusion. Luke's description of the event is sufficiently expressive as to need no further explanation:

And when he had so said, there arose a dissension between the Pharisees and the Sadducees: and the multitude was divided.

For the Sadducees say that there is no resurrection, neither angel, nor spirit: but the Pharisees confess both.

And there arose a great cry: and the scribes that were of the Pharisees' part arose, and strove, saying, We find no evil in this man: but if a spirit or an angel hath spoken to him, let us not fight against God.

And when there arose a great dissension, the chief captain, fearing lest Paul should have been pulled in pieces of them, commanded the soldiers to go down, and to take him by force from among them, and to bring him into the castle. (Acts 23:7–10.)

Paul may not have wanted to entirely end the session so abruptly. Possibly all he wanted was to gain the favor of the Pharisees, who he hoped would see him as a brother and give him an opportunity to declare the gospel of Christ and obtain a favorable verdict of the court. Whatever his intention, the session was soon over and Paul was rescued again by the Roman soldiers and imprisoned.

Acts 24–25. The Roman governor, Felix, keeps Paul in prison, first at Jerusalem and then at Caesarea for two years, hoping that Paul will give him money for his release (Acts 24). In the meantime Felix is replaced by Festus. Paul appeals to Festus to be sent to Rome, to Caesar's court, because he feels that he cannot get a fair trial in Jerusalem, or Caesarea, or anywhere in Palestine because of the strong Jewish influence, and also because of the Roman officials' willingness to please the Jews. Paul insists that he has broken no law of the Empire, or of the Jews, and rightly should not be judged in a Jewish court. Because he is a Roman citizen, Paul has a strong case for appealing to Rome. Festus is willing that Paul be sent to Caesar, but a problem exists: He has no official crime to charge Paul with that would be admissible in a Roman court. Since King Agrippa (Herod Agrippa II, great-grandson of Herod the Great) is in Caesarea, Festus tells him about Paul, and that he is at that very time in prison, but there is no legitimate accusation against him. Agrippa desires to hear Paul himself, and a meeting is arranged for the following day. (Acts 25.)

Paul's Magnificent Defense Before Agrippa and Festus

Acts 26. Paul's discourse to King Agrippa, Festus, and other dignitaries at Ceasarea is one of the great events of the New Testament and of all religious literature. Though he is a prisoner shackled in iron chains, he is magnificent in bearing and composure. As is his custom, he begins his discourse with diplomacy and with background information to establish a common bond with his hearers. He acknowledges that Agrippa is an expert in the things of the Jews and asks that the king hear him patiently. Paul reviews his early life in Jerusalem as a Pharisee and says that he ought to be accepted by the Jews, since he has only taught what the prophets also taught. Since the topic of resurrection is a point of conflict between Paul and the Jews, and between Paul and the Gentiles also, he asks Agrippa: "Why should it be thought a thing incredible with you that God should raise the dead?" (Acts 26:8.) Paul then reviews his conversion on the road to Damascus, his personal conversation and interview with the resurrected Jesus, and his diligence since that time in fulfilling the Lord's command to him to testify of Jesus Christ and the resurrection to both Jews and Gentiles.

One of the most dramatic moments of his defense comes immediately after mentioning the resurrection of the dead. Festus loudly interrupts and says: "Paul, thou art beside thyself: much learning doth make thee mad" (Acts 26:24). "Beside thyself" literally means, "you are out of your mind." Paul, with firm dignity replies: "I am not mad, most noble Festus; but speak forth the words of truth and soberness. For the king knoweth of these things." (Acts 26:25–26.)

Then, addressing the king, Paul says forcibly:

> King Agrippa, believest thou the prophets? I know that thou believest.
>
> Then Agrippa said unto Paul, Almost thou persuadest me to be a Christian.
>
> And Paul said, I would to God, that not only thou, but also all that hear me this day, were both almost, and altogether such as I am, except these bonds. (Acts 26:27–29.)

As an aftermath of the defense, Festus and Agrippa discuss the matter and say that Paul has done nothing worthy of death or bonds, but since he has appealed to Caesar, he must go to Rome.

Acts 27–28. In a perilous journey, hampered by storm and shipwreck, Paul and others sail to Rome aboard a cargo ship laden with wheat from Egypt. After arriving in Rome he spends two years in a house awaiting trial. Since there is no great charge against him, Paul is optimistic of eventual acquittal. He is given freedom to have visitors but is guarded constantly by a soldier. In Rome, Paul preaches to both Jews and Gentiles that Jesus is the Christ.

Here ends the book of Acts as contained in our present New Testament. It seems that there ought to be more, as the story is unfinished. From his epistles we learn that Paul fully expected to be released soon, and that he would again visit the branches of the Church. It appears that he may have been tried twice, being released after the first time but then later being imprisoned again (see 2 Timothy 4:16–17). Paul's last epistle, 2 Timothy, does not share the expectation of release from prison that his earlier epistles did, but depicts Paul reconciled to an approaching martyrdom. Yet he is completely confident that his salvation is assured (see 2 Timothy 4:6, 7, 16 and compare with Philippians 2:23–24).

Tradition has it that Paul was beheaded outside of the city of Rome, on the Appian Way, sometime around A.D. 66–67, during a time of Roman persecution against the Christians.

Paul's three major missionary journeys and the trip to Rome are chronicled in the book of Acts. The dates and distances shown below are estimates, since precise information is not given in the scriptures. The arrangement of the epistles is likewise an estimate, based on information within the epistles, and is especially subjective with regard to the later epistles.

For maximum learning it would be advantageous to consult the maps in the supplementary sections of a Bible and trace each of these journeys, noting the cities in sequence.

Paul's Missionary Travels and Epistles

First missionary journey. Acts 13–14. Began and concluded at Antioch of Syria. Approximately 1,400 miles. Occupied at least one year, around A.D. 47–48. No known epistles.

Second missionary journey. Acts 15:36 to 18:22. Began and concluded at Antioch of Syria. Approximately 3,000 miles. Occupied at least two years, probably in A.D. 50–52. Two known epistles: 1 and 2 Thessalonians.

Third missionary journey. Acts 18:23 to 21:15. Began at Antioch of Syria and was concluded at Jerusalem with Paul's arrest. Approximately 3,500 miles. Occupied at least four years, from about A.D. 54–58. Five known epistles: 1 and 2 Corinthians, an earlier Corinthian epistle not extant today (see 1 Corinthians 5:9), Galatians, and Romans.

Journey to Rome from Jerusalem. Acts 27–28. Approximately 1,400 miles. Probably in A.D. 61. Paul was in Rome from A.D. 61–66, during which he was imprisoned two years, apparently released, and imprisoned again and executed. During this long period he wrote Philippians, Colossians, Ephesians, Philemon, Hebrews, 1 Timothy, Titus, 2 Timothy, and a lost epistle to Laodicea (Colossians 4:16).

Paul contemplated a trip to Spain (Romans 15:24, 28). It would have required an additional two thousand miles by sea alone, round trip, and would have had to be made during the interval between the two Roman imprisonments. Whether he made such a trip is not known.

CHAPTER 26

Paul and His Epistles

The epistles composed by Paul are treasures of information about Church organization, problems of the ministry, doctrine, and about Paul himself: his faith, testimony, personality, desires; his love for the Lord; his affection for the people; his future plans; and his companions in travel. It is customary to think of Acts as history and the epistles as teachings. However, as we have already seen, there is in Acts much doctrine; and as we saw in the brief excerpt from Galatians about the Jerusalem council, there is much history contained in the epistles. We learn more about Paul personally from his epistles than we do from the book of Acts.

Our present New Testament contains fourteen epistles ascribed to Paul's authorship, although it is certain that he wrote others we do not now have. We know, for example, of an earlier epistle to Corinth (1 Corinthians 5:9) and also one to Laodicea (Colossians 4:16). In almost every instance Paul's epistles were written to branches of the Church where he had already visited (the one exception is Romans), or to individuals whom he already knew. Hence these letters were not so much conversion-oriented and evangelistic as they were regulatory. Since he wrote to people who were already members of the Church, he said relatively little about baptism or about preparing themselves to become Church members. His letters were not introductory messages about the gospel of Jesus Christ but were penned to address specific problems and regulate matters among those already in the Church.

It appears that Paul did not actually do the writing with his own hand, but dictated to a scribe, although he would sign the epistle himself. Hence we find in Romans 16:22, "I Tertius, who wrote this epistle, salute you"; and in 1 Corinthians 16:21, "The salutation of me Paul with mine own hand"; and in 2 Thessalonians 3:17, "The salutation of Paul with mine own hand, which is the token in every epistle: so I write" (see also Colossians 4:18; Philemon 1:19; Galatians 6:11).

No epistles are known to have been written during the first mission. During the second journey Paul wrote 1 and 2 Thessalonians, from either Athens or Corinth after Silas and Timothy joined him from Macedonia, hence these epistles would fit in at about Acts 18:1–5. During the third journey it appears that 1 and 2 Corinthians, Galatians, and Romans were written, and are therefore within the scope of Acts 19:1 to 20:38.

The date of the Roman imprisonment is somewhat indefinite. Paul was probably imprisoned for about two years, then released for a time, and then imprisoned again. These activities possibly involved him from about A.D. 61 to about A.D. 66 and are a little beyond the scope of the book of Acts. It was during this time that he probably wrote Colossians, Ephesians, Philemon, Philippians, Hebrews, Titus, and 1 and 2 Timothy, but not necessarily in that order. 2 Timothy seems to be the last of Paul's epistles of which we have record.

At the conclusion of each of Paul's epistles in the KJV is found a short statement regarding place of origin and often also identification of the scribe. These are not part of the epistles themselves but were added by copyists or editors, and may or may not be accurate. Manuscripts earlier than the sixth century do not contain these subscriptions. Modern translations of the Bible, such as the New English Bible, Revised Standard Version, or the New International Version do not contain these subscriptions because such versions are based on manuscripts predating the sixth century.

Paul's epistles are not arranged in chronological order in

our present New Testament, but have been placed according to length, with the longest (Romans) first, in descending order to the shortest (Philemon). The book of Hebrews is longer than some of the epistles but was placed after the others because some scholars have questioned Paul's authorship. Early manuscripts of the New Testament sometimes have a different order and sequence than those of the King James Version. The earliest list of the New Testament books consisting of the same selection (but not the same order) as the King James Version was that by Athanasius in A.D. 367. He has Hebrews immediately after 2 Thessalonians.

Placing the epistles according to length is somewhat misleading as one reads the New Testament, for they are not consistent either as to subject matter, geographical destination, or chronology. Arrangement by length seems to be the least satisfactory of any system that might have been used. A chronological arrangement would have been preferable, but the sequence is not known in every instance.

The epistles reflect the problems that were current in the Church at the time they were written, and which were different at various times and places. The earlier epistles deal somewhat with problems relating to the Jews, the law of Moses, and Paul's defense of his calling against his Judaizing critics. The later epistles reflect more the problems occasioned by the influx of Greek philosophy into the Church. This distinction is not abrupt and clear-cut, but is a matter of increasing emphasis within the epistles themselves. This fine distinction is all but lost when we read the epistles in the artificial order in which they occur in the New Testament.

Excerpts from Paul's Writings

Paul and the Missionary Spirit. Paul found joy in teaching the gospel of Jesus Christ and often preferred to go where no one else had yet taken the gospel. On one occasion he wrote, "I have planted, Apollos watered; but God gave the increase" (1 Corinthians 3:6). To the Saints in Rome, where he had not visited personally, he explained:

Through mighty signs and wonders, by the power of the Spirit of God; so that from Jerusalem, and round about unto Illyricum, I have fully preached the gospel of Christ.

Yea, so have I strived to preach the gospel, not where Christ was named, lest I should build upon another man's foundation:

But as it is written, To whom he was not spoken of, they shall see; and they that have not heard shall understand.

For which cause also I have been much hindered from coming to you.

But now having no more place in these parts, and having a great desire these many years to come unto you.

Whensoever I take my journey into Spain, I will come to you. (Romans 15:19–24.)

His Extreme Hardships. Paul's missionary labors were not easy. Although he had outstanding success in converting people to the gospel of Jesus Christ, he had to endure great afflictions, persecutions, and other hardships, including several imprisonments and whippings. Among the most painful was the opposition he received from false brethren within the Church; he makes frequent reference to the trouble they caused him.

While he was on his third mission, in his second letter to the Corinthian Saints, Paul gave a partial account of the afflictions he had suffered. This account was prompted by the attempts of false brethren to defame his character. He responded in defense of his calling and his labors as an Apostle of the Lord. His listing is incomplete for two reasons: First, he did not detail every affliction; and second, he lived to endure additional problems after this epistle was written. Here is his list, most of which events are not recorded in the book of Acts:

Of the Jews five times received I forty stripes save one.

Thrice was I beaten with rods, once was I stoned, thrice I suffered shipwreck, a night and a day I have been in the deep;

In journeyings often, in perils of waters, in perils of robbers, in perils by mine own countrymen, in perils by the heathen, in perils in the city, in perils in the wilderness, in perils in the sea, in perils among false brethren;

In weariness and painfulness, in watchings often, in hunger and thirst, in fastings often, in cold and nakedness.

Beside those things that are without, that which cometh upon me daily, the care of all the churches. . . .

In Damascus the governor under Aretas the king kept the city of the Damascenes with a garrison, desirous to apprehend me:

And through a window in a basket was I let down by the wall, and escaped his hands. (2 Corinthians 11:24–28, 32–33.)

His Courage. Paul's courage is illustrated in his words: "For we preach not ourselves, but Christ Jesus the Lord; and ourselves your servants for Jesus' sake. For God, who commanded the light to shine out of darkness, hath shined in our hearts, to give the light of the knowledge of the glory of God in the face of Jesus Christ." (2 Corinthians 4:5–6.) Though the Apostles be but mortal men, they have the light of the glory of God in their souls. Paul describes this light as a "treasure in earthen vessels, that the excellency of the power may be of God, and not of us. We are troubled on every side, yet not distressed; we are perplexed, but not in despair; persecuted, but not forsaken; cast down, but not destroyed; always bearing about in the body the dying of the Lord Jesus, that the life also of Jesus might be made manifest in our body." (2 Corinthians 4:7–10.)

Paul seemed to glory in persecution. It was he who said that persecution was the natural heritage of the faithful (see Acts 14:22; 2 Timothy 3:12). As we read of his trials we are reminded of the words of the Lord to Ananias at the time of Paul's conversion, when he told Ananias that Paul was a chosen vessel, but that the Lord would "shew [Paul] how great things he must suffer for my name's sake" (Acts 9:16). Certainly Paul learned exactly what this meant before his life was through.

He also saw his life as a pattern to give strength to others who experienced suffering (Philippians 1:28–30). He even witnessed success during his imprisonment, for while in the Roman dungeon he wrote to the Saints at Philippi: "I would ye should understand, brethren, that the things which happened unto me have fallen out rather unto the furtherance of the gospel; so that my bonds in Christ are manifest in all the palace [or Caesar's court], and in all other places; and many of the brethren in the Lord, waxing confident by my bonds, are much more bold to speak the word without fear" (Philippians 1: 12–14).

His Thorn in the Flesh. In addition to persecutions from without, Paul also suffered some personal limitations, which he said the Lord inflicted upon him to help him remain humble—these he called "a thorn in the flesh." Just what this was Paul does not definitely say. He labels it "the messenger of Satan to buffet me, lest I should be exalted above measure." (2 Corinthians 12:7.) Some have thought he had reference to a physical illness of some kind. Others have supposed that a comment he makes in Galatians 4:15 indicates that his affliction was poor eyesight. However, if Paul was speaking literally, he may have meant that he was dogged and hampered by an evil spirit, "a messenger of Satan." Whatever the problem, Paul besought the Lord three times for its removal and was denied that favor, the Lord explaining that his grace was sufficient for Paul to survive (2 Corinthians 12:8–9).

Paul viewed trials with optimism and patience, believing that Jesus had placed them upon him for his own good, and that the Lord would redeem him in due time. "Most gladly therefore," said he, "will I rather glory in my infirmities, that the power of Christ may rest upon me" (2 Corinthians 12:9). He believed that he was being tried by the Almighty in the furnace of affliction.

His Regard for Timothy. Paul had greater praise and affection for Timothy than for any other of his many companions. We first hear of Timothy as a young man at Lystra when he joined Paul's entourage in about A.D. 51, near the beginning of the second mission. From that time until Paul's death about fifteen years later Timothy and Paul were very close. He often traveled with Paul and was frequently sent by him on confidential errands to various branches of the Church. In the mid-sixties, while Paul was imprisoned at Rome, Timothy seems to have been an officer in the Church at Ephesus.

Although the first mention of Timothy relates to when he joined Paul's second mission tour, Paul probably had met and converted him during his first mission at Lystra two or three years earlier. Timothy's father was a Greek and, so far as we are informed, was not a Christian. However, Timothy's mother, Eunice, and his grandmother, Lois, were both members of the Church and were of strong faith. That it was Paul who converted Timothy seems evident from Paul's affectionate greetings to him as "my own son in the faith" (1 Timothy 1:2) and also "my dearly beloved son" (2 Timothy 1:2). Paul also wrote to him of events that had occurred on the first mission in a way that suggests that Timothy might have been present when the events actually occurred: "But thou hast fully known my doctrine, manner of life, purpose, faith, longsuffering, charity, patience, persecutions, afflictions, which came unto me at Antioch [of Pisidia, not Syria], at Iconium, at Lystra; what persecutions I endured: but out of them all the Lord delivered me" (2 Timothy 3:10–11).

When Paul was at Philippi on his third mission he wrote to the Corinthian Saints that he would send Timothy to minister to them. His confidence in Timothy's ability to properly represent him is very evident: "For this cause have I sent unto you Timotheus, who is my beloved son, and faithful in the Lord, who shall bring you into remembrance of my ways which be in Christ, as I teach every where in every church" (1 Corinthians 4:17). In the same epistle he added further: "Now if Timotheus come, see that he may be with you without fear: for he worketh the work of the Lord, as I also do. Let no man therefore despise him: but conduct him forth in peace." (1 Corinthians 16:10–11.)

Later, during his first imprisonment at Rome, Paul wrote to the saints at Philippi. Since it was impossible for Paul to visit them personally at that time, he informed them that he would send Timothy, in whom he had complete confidence:

> But I trust in the Lord Jesus to send Timotheus shortly unto you, that I also may be of good comfort, when I know your state.
> For I have no man likeminded [or so dear to me], who will naturally care for your state.
> For all seek their own, not the things which are Jesus Christ's.
> But ye know the proof of him, that, as a son with the father, he hath served with me in the gospel.
> Him therefore I hope to send presently, so soon as I shall see how it will go with me.
> But I trust in the Lord that I also myself shall come shortly. (Philippians 2:19–24.)

We especially notice in the foregoing that Paul says that he has no other man quite like Timothy.

Still later, when his status as a prisoner had worsened at Rome and he expected that he would soon be executed, Paul wrote with great feeling and urgency to Timothy, who was at Ephesus:

> To Timothy, my dearly beloved son: . . .
> I thank God, whom I serve from my forefathers with pure conscience, that without ceasing I have remembrance of thee in my prayers night and day;
> Greatly desiring to see thee, being mindful of thy tears, that I may be filled with joy;
> When I call to remembrance the unfeigned faith that is in thee, which dwelt first in thy grandmother Lois, and thy mother Eunice; and I am persuaded that in thee also. . . .
> Be not thou therefore ashamed of the testimony of our Lord, nor of me his prisoner. (2 Timothy 1:2–5, 8.)

And again:

> For I am now ready to be offered, and the time of my departure is at hand. . . .
> Do thy diligence to come shortly unto me: . . .
> The cloke that I left at Troas with Carpus, when thou comest, bring with thee, and the books, but especially the parchments. . . .
> Do thy diligence to come before winter. (2 Timothy 4:6, 9, 13, 21.)

The Roman dungeon was no doubt chilly, particularly in the winter, and Paul needed a cloak. He also wanted something to read, and especially desired some writing materials. There is a note of sadness in Paul's words. He is not discouraged but is probably lonesome. There can be no mistaking the great love that Paul had for his young companion, whom he wished to have with him at the time of his last imprisonment. Paul was probably executed just outside of Rome soon after sending his letter to Timothy. We are not informed whether or not Timothy was able to reach him before Paul's death.

His Estimate of Demas and Alexander the Coppersmith. While Paul was imprisoned, some members of the Church acted in a way that disappointed him. One of these was Demas, who had been in Rome with him (Colossians 4:14; Philemon 1:24), but was there no longer. Said Paul: "For Demas hath forsaken me, having loved this present world, and is departed unto Thessalonica" (2 Timothy 4:10). Paul here makes an interesting allusion to the relative value of this world compared to the next. Persecution against Christians put their lives in jeopardy. Apparently Demas didn't want to depart from the world just yet, so instead he departed from Rome and from Paul.

Alexander the coppersmith was another disappointment to the Apostle. Paul expressed some active judgments concerning Alexander by including his name among those who had "made shipwreck" of their faith. Said Paul: "Of whom is Hymenaeus and Alexander; whom I have delivered unto Satan, that they may learn not to blaspheme" (1 Timothy 1:19–20). And further: "Alexander the coppersmith did me much evil: the Lord reward him according to his works: of whom be thou ware also; for he hath greatly withstood our words" (2 Timothy 4:14–15).

Paul's Character and Personality

In the book of Acts, Luke has given us an admirable characterization of Paul, but it is only through Paul's own writings that we gain the greatest insight into who he truly was—in his epistles we see him at work in his calling as a teacher of the gospel and as an administrator in the Church.

Paul had much to say about many things, and it was inevitable that he would be misunderstood at times. Even today, many readers misunderstand Paul. As we become familiar with his words and carefully observe him, great traits of personality and character begin to show. And, as with all complex individuals, as more is learned, understanding comes easier and some traits do not look the same as they did at the first exposure.

The purpose in citing the following passages is to briefly examine the record of events and read some of Paul's own expressions that give the clearest views of his motives and his deeds.

His Physical Appearance. Although the scripture gives no detailed physical description of Paul, he himself gives some clues in his epistles. Writing to the Corinthian Saints about those who criticized him, he said: "Do ye look on things after the outward appearance? . . . For his letters, say they, are weighty and power-ful; but his bodily presence is weak, and his speech con-temptible" (2 Corinthians 10:7, 10). And also: "But though I be rude in speech, yet not in knowledge" (2 Corinthians 11:6).

To the Galatians he wrote: "Ye know how through infirmity of the flesh I preached the gospel unto you at the first" (Galatians 4:13).

These hints of Paul's physical unimpressiveness but his power in writing seem to be reflected in a statement by the Prophet Joseph Smith, given January 5, 1841, at the organiza-tion of a school of instruction: "He is about five feet high; very dark hair; dark complexion; dark skin; large Roman nose; sharp face; small black eyes, penetrating as eternity; round shoulders; a whining voice, except when elevated, and then it almost re-sembled the roaring of a lion. He was a good orator, active and diligent, always employing himself in doing good to his fellow man." (TPJS, 180.)

His Age. No direct statement is made in the scriptures con-cerning Paul's date of birth or age at conversion. However, as with other items there exist clues and parameters within which a reasonable conclusion may be reached.

At Stephen's martyrdom Saul (Paul) is spoken of as a "young man" (Acts 7:58). The Greek word in the manuscript requires this be a man less than forty years old. Stephen's death was probably sometime around A.D. 35, give or take a year or two. While imprisoned at Rome sometime around A.D. 61–65, Paul characterizes himself as "Paul the aged" (Philemon 1:9). Both of these are relative rather than exact terms. What age must a man be to be young in A.D. 35 and aged in A.D. 65? If just a boy in A.D. 35 he would hardly be aged thirty years later. But if much more than sixty-five while in Rome, he could not be a young man at Stephen's martyrdom. I believe a commonsense conclusion would be that Saul was born sometime around A.D. 5, making him in his early thirties at Stephen's martyrdom and in his six-ties while imprisoned at Rome. Many today may wince at a man in his sixties being labeled "aged," but considering the probable life expectancy of that day and the toils of the min-istry, this conclusion does not seem unreasonable.

His Self-Characterization. Paul referred to himself as the "chief" of sinners (1 Timothy 1:15), and as "the least of the apostles, that am not meet to be called an apostle, because I persecuted the church of God" (1 Corinthians 15:9). Yet he also said he "laboured more abundantly than they all"—all the Apostles— doing so by the grace of God which was given him (1 Corinthians 15:10). He professed his own nothingness (1 Corinthians 3:5–7), but explained also that he could "do all things through Christ which strengtheneth" him (Philippians 4:13). Paul felt that of his own self he was weak, but that with the assistance of Jesus he could accomplish whatever was necessary.

His Humility. Paul was an extremely humble man, although in some of the epistles he appears proud and boastful. When we examine the context, we begin to understand his true motives. For example, he recounted to the Corinthians the many sufferings he had endured for the gospel's sake (2 Corinthians 11–12). The context of this material shows that he was reacting to the words of false brethren in the Church who had greatly influenced the Corinthian Saints against him. Upon learning that these brethren had boasted of their own labors in the Church, Paul responded:

> For such are false apostles, deceitful workers, transforming themselves into the apostles of Christ.
> And no marvel; for Satan himself is transformed into an angel of light.
> Therefore it is no great thing if his ministers also be transformed as the ministers of righteousness; whose end shall be according to their works. (2 Corinthians 11:13–15.)

Then he continued:

> Seeing that many glory after the flesh, I will glory also. . . .
> Are they [his enemies] Hebrews? so am I. . . .
> Are they ministers of Christ? (I speak as a fool) I am more [meaning more so than they are; not more than a servant of Christ. See JST]: in labours more abundant, in stripes above measure, in prisons more frequent, in deaths oft. (2 Corinthians 11:18, 22, 23.)

Then, after making a long list of his labors and sufferings, he said to his readers: "I am become a fool in glorying: [because] ye have compelled me: for I ought to have been commended of you: for in nothing am I behind the very chiefest apostles, though I be nothing" (2 Corinthians 12:11).

It doesn't appear to be a humble statement for Paul to declare that he is equal to the "very chiefest" of the apostles. But which "apostles" did he mean? The tenor of these chapters shows that he probably did not mean the true Apostles, but rather his enemies, the false apostles.

For Paul to have said (and meant it literally) that he was equal to any of the true Apostles would not be consistent with his earlier declaration that he was the "least of the apostles, and not meet to be called an apostle." But, if his words are read in context and with understanding, he is both humble and consistent. Paul probably did not feel overly confident about his own importance, but he fully intended to uphold and honor his appointment and high standing as an Apostle of Jesus Christ; he was defending not himself, but the dignity of his office.

His Integrity and Honor. One of the plainest examples of Paul's integrity was his insistence on working with his own hands for his financial support (see Acts 18:1–3). He explained that as an "apostle" he could have required support from the Saints, but that he preferred not to be burdensome (1 Thessalonians 2:5–9). Furthermore, to the Ephesians he said: "I have coveted no man's silver, or gold, or apparel. Yea, ye yourselves know, that these hands have ministered unto my necessities, and to them that were with me." (Acts 20:33–34.) And to the Corinthians he wrote: "What is my reward then? Verily that, when I preach the gospel, I may make the gospel of Christ without charge, that I abuse not my power in the gospel." (1 Corinthians 9:18.) And again: "Even unto this present hour we both hunger, and thirst, and are naked, and are buffeted, and have no certain dwelling place; and labour, working with our own hands" (1 Corinthians 4:11–12).

His Irony. Paul was frequently criticized by his enemies, who accused him of living on the liberality of the Saints, taking food and money of them for his own advantage. It was probably these accusations that caused him to emphasize so many times that he labored with his hands for his support. Paul forthrightly denied the charges (although he said he did accept some help from Macedonia), and sometimes referred to these accusations ironically. For example, to the Corinthians he wrote:

Have I committed an offence in abasing myself that ye might
be exalted, because I have preached to you the gospel of God
freely?

I robbed other churches, taking wages of them, to do you service.

And when I was present with you, and wanted, I was chargeable to no man: for that which was lacking to me the brethren
which came from Macedonia supplied: and in all things I have
kept myself from being burdensome unto you, and so will I keep
myself.

As the truth of Christ is in me, no man shall stop me of this
boasting in the regions of Achaia. (2 Corinthians 11:7–10.)

He continued:

For what is it wherein ye were inferior to other churches, except it be that I myself was not burdensome to you? forgive me
this wrong.

Behold, the third time I am ready to come to you; and I will
not be burdensome to you: for I seek not yours, but you. (2
Corinthians 12:13–14.)

Irony, of course, is always subject to misunderstanding unless the context is known. When we take note of the background and the circumstances under which Paul wrote and remember that the Saints in Corinth had been led away, to a
degree, by the false teachers, we then see the irony of Paul's
words, especially in verses 8 and 13 quoted above, when he
says he "robbed other churches," and also asks that they "forgive [him] of this wrong" of not being burdensome. He had not
literally "robbed" churches, but was speaking in a manner as
they had accused him.

Paul seems to be continually spoken against. Who is it that
makes so many accusations against him? It is primarily those
members of the Church who dislike his stand regarding the law
of Moses. These people are called "Judaizers" (not in the New
Testament, but in the writings of the church fathers in the second
century) because they want to make Jews of all the Gentiles.
Accusations also came against Paul from non-Christian Jews
who opposed his teachings about Christ. When a person has
enemies for preaching the word of God, opposition first comes

as an attempt to refute the doctrine. If the enemy is unable to refute the doctrine, the next step is to defame the character. This procedure was used against Jesus, and also against his Apostles. It was used against Joseph Smith. We see it also in the persecution against Paul.

In one instance, Paul refers to his "lie" when writing to the Roman Saints (Romans 3:7). The details of just what he has reference to are not given, but there is sufficient information to help us see that the remark is ironical in nature. The JST, as rendered by the Prophet Joseph Smith, emphasizes the figurative manner in which the word "lie" is used, and clarifies the sense of the passage (Romans 3:7–8):

KJV	JST
For if the truth of God hath more abounded through my lie unto his glory; why yet am I also judged as a sinner?	For if the truth of God hath more abounded through my lie, (as it is called of the Jews,) unto his glory; why yet am I also judged as a sinner? and not received? Because we are slanderously reported;
And not rather, (as we be slanderously reported, and as some affirm that we say,) Let us do evil, that good may come? whose damnation is just.	And some affirm that we say, (whose damnation is just,) Let us do evil that good may come. But this is false.

His Affection. We have already noted Paul's affection for Timothy. He likewise expressed his affection for entire branches of the Church. There are many such references, but one of the clearest was written to the Church at Thessalonica:

We were gentle among you, even as a nurse cherisheth her children:

So being affectionately desirous of you, we were willing to have imparted unto you, not the gospel of God only, but also our own souls, because ye were dear unto us.

For ye remember, brethren, our labour and travail: for labouring night and day, because we would not be chargeable unto any of you, we preached unto you the gospel of God.

Ye are witnesses, and God also, how holily and justly and unblameably we behaved ourselves among you that believe:

As ye know how we exhorted and comforted and charged every one of you, as a father doth his children, . . .

But we, brethren, being taken from you for a short time in presence, not in heart, endeavored the more abundantly to see your face with great desire.

Wherefore we would have come unto you, even I Paul, once and again; but Satan hindered us. (1 Thessalonians 2:7–11, 17–18.)

The foregoing passage not only speaks of Paul's affection for the Saints but also of his integrity, his graciousness, and the circumspect manner of his life.

The whole of Romans 16 speaks of Paul's affection for the Saints and his desire to know of them and to have them know of him. He had great concern for people's well-being. He cared about their situation. His many labors in sending food and welfare relief to the Saints in Jerusalem emphasizes his concern for their physical as well as their spiritual condition. (See Acts 11:27–30; 1 Corinthians 16:1–4; 2 Corinthians 9:1–15; Romans 15:24–28.)

His Industry and His Whole-souled Devotion to the Lord. All of Paul's labors and words attest to his industry. The Prophet Joseph Smith said: "He was a good orator, active and diligent, always employing himself in doing good to his fellow man" (TPJS, 180). The Prophet also said:

Though [Paul] once, according to his own word, persecuted the Church of God and wasted it, yet after embracing the faith, his labors were unceasing to spread the glorious news: and like a faithful soldier, when called to give his life in the cause which he had espoused, he laid it down, as he says, with an assurance of an eternal crown. Follow the labors of this Apostle from the time of his conversion to the time of his death, and you will have a fair sample of industry and patience in promulgating the Gospel of Christ. Derided, whipped, and stoned, the moment he escaped the hands of his persecutors he as zealously as ever proclaimed the doctrine of the Savior. And all may know that he did not embrace the faith for honor in this life, nor for the gain of earthly goods. What, then, could have induced him to undergo all this toil? It was, as he said, that he might obtain the crown of righteousness from the hand of God. No one, we presume, will doubt the faithfulness of Paul to the end. None will say that he did not keep the faith, that he did not fight the good fight, that he did not preach and persuade to the last. (TPJS, 63–64.)

Other cases could be cited giving examples of Paul's character. For example, his diplomacy is shown in the way he collected welfare relief at Corinth, saying he knew they would donate more than he asked of them (2 Corinthians 9:1–15), and in his persuasion of Philemon to graciously receive back his runaway slave (Philemon 1:1–22); we also have evidence of his practicality (1 Timothy 6:6–8; Philippians 4:10–12). There is even a sample of semi-humor found in Ephesians 5:18, where Paul makes a pun out of saying "And be not drunk with wine, wherein is excess; but be filled with the Spirit." It is as if he said, "Do not become filled and drunken with an excess of spirituous liquors, but drink all you would like of the Spirit of the Lord, and become filled, and exhilarated with that." Here, as in other instances, it is evident that Paul had extraordinary gifts of perception and literary expression.

But with all of Paul's intellectual gifts (including his ability to write, to preach, to reason, to debate, and to do so in at least three languages—Hebrew, Aramaic and Greek), and his wide experiences with various cultures and countries, enriched by the political advantage of Roman citizenship, and all of this coupled with an abundance of physical energy, the greatest assets were his whole-souled devotion, his total willingness to serve the Lord. It would not matter how many languages, how much formal education, how many skills, how much experience one had, if that person is not willing to use these in serving the Lord in the language and deeds of faith, the other traits are almost useless treasures. It was Paul's courage and whole-souled devotion to Jesus Christ that made him available as a useful instrument in the hands of the Lord.

Popular Sayings from Paul. Paul's writings contain many short, meaningful utterances that have become well-known in the Christian world, and have entered into our culture with such acceptance that many of them are used in non-religious conversation by persons who do not realize they came from Paul. A few of these are:

1. The love of money is the root of all evil (1 Timothy 6:10).
2. We brought nothing into this world, and it is certain we can carry nothing out (1 Timothy 6:7).
3. The times and the seasons (1 Thessalonians 5:1).
4. As a thief in the night (1 Thessalonians 5:2).
5. Prove all things; hold fast that which is good (1 Thessalonians 5:21).
6. Put on the whole armour of God (Ephesians 6:11–17. Note that this was earlier spoken in Isaiah 59:16–17, but Paul made it better known among readers).
7. Let not the sun go down on your wrath (Ephesians 4:26).
8. Be not weary in well-doing (2 Thessalonians 3:13).
9. Pray without ceasing (1 Thessalonians 5:17).
10. The letter killeth, but the spirit giveth life (2 Corinthians 3:6).
11. Abstain from all appearance of evil (1 Thessalonians 5:22).
12. A thorn in the flesh (2 Corinthians 12:7).
13. [A] labor of love (1 Thessalonians 1:3).
14. O death, where is thy sting? O grave, where is thy victory? (1 Corinthians 15:55).

Help from the Joseph Smith Translation. The JST makes many clarifications and corrections to the records about Paul, but two of the most useful deal with Paul's teachings about marriage (1 Corinthians 7) and about how the gospel of Jesus Christ changed his life (Romans 7:14–25). The popular myth that Paul was opposed to marriage is corrected by the JST so that his dictum that there is an advantage to remaining unmarried is limited to those on temporary mission assignments. This practice was advocated by Paul for efficiency in the temporary ministry, and is similar to the practice of The Church of Jesus Christ of Latter-day Saints today in calling young men and women, unmarried, to serve missions, and refrain from marriage while in the mission field. Paul's teachings against marriage were not for all Church members, any more than the policy for young missionaries to remain unmarried today is a permanent rejection of marriage. The JST restores the proper context.

The other topic, showing the great change that the gospel made in Paul's life, is a remarkable contribution of the JST. As rendered in the KJV, Paul is sinful, carnal, and wicked even after years in the apostleship, and knows not how to do good, or even what is good. The JST rewords the passage in such a way as to show the difference between Paul's life while under the law of Moses and his life after he found and obeyed the gospel of Christ.

Readers using the Bible published by the Church can easily find the JST corrections for these two items and many others by consulting the footnotes identified as JST.

Paul and Jesus

Any work on the life and teachings of Paul would be inadequate without a presentation of his testimony of Jesus. His utterances in this category are not only his most moving and beautiful expressions but are also his most important contributions. As one reads Paul's words about the Savior, one senses his growing feeling of love for, knowledge of, and devotion and commitment to Jesus—not a commitment born of fear or a selfish thirst for glory, but a personal attachment caused by a feeling of gratitude and indebtedness. Paul was deeply touched by the fact that Jesus cared for him personally and had rescued him from his early destructive course. He frequently said that Jesus had "given himself" for him. Paul preached repentance, redemption, and resurrection through Jesus Christ. He seemed to be amazed, but very grateful, that the Lord would have done so much for man—and especially for him. He frequently spoke of the *power* of the Atonement, the *power* of the Lord, the *power* of the Spirit. He did not preach abstract, philosophical theory, but dealt with things of power and performance, things that actually change hearts and lives. It is obvious from Paul's writings that he had an intimate relationship with Jesus. He knew him and was no stranger to his ways.

Paul expressed feelings of closeness to the Lord and gratitude for his love:

For I delivered unto you first of all that which I also received, how that Christ died for our sins according to the scriptures;

And that he was buried, and that he rose again the third day according to the scriptures:

And that he was seen of Cephas, then of the twelve:

After that, he was seen of above five hundred brethren at once; of whom the greater part remain unto this present, but some are fallen asleep.

After that, he was seen of James; then of all the apostles.

And last of all he was seen of me also, as of one born out of due time.

For I am the least of the apostles, that am not meet to be called an apostle, because I persecuted the church of God.

But by the grace of God I am what I am: and his grace which was bestowed upon me was not in vain; but I laboured more abundantly than they all: yet not I, but the grace of God which was with me. (1 Corinthians 15:3–10.)

Let this mind be in you, which was also in Christ Jesus:

Who, being in the form of God, thought it not robbery to be equal with God:

But made himself of no reputation, and took upon him the form of a servant, and was made in the likeness of men:

And being found in fashion as a man, he humbled himself, and became obedient unto death, even the death of the cross.

Wherefore God also hath highly exalted him, and given him a name which is above every name:

That at the name of Jesus every knee should bow, of things in heaven, and things in earth, and things under the earth;

And that every tongue should confess that Jesus Christ is Lord, to the glory of God the Father. (Philippians 2:5–11.)

Yea doubtless, and I count all things but loss for the excellency of the knowledge of Christ Jesus my Lord: for whom I have suffered the loss of all things, and do count them but dung, that I may win Christ,

And be found in him, not having mine own righteousness, which is of the law, but that which is through the faith of Christ, the righteousness which is of God by faith:

That I may know him, and the power of his resurrection, and the fellowship of his sufferings, being made conformable unto his death;

If by any means I might attain unto the resurrection of the dead. . . .

I press toward the mark for the prize of the high calling of God in Christ Jesus. . . .

For our conversation is in heaven; from whence also we look for the Saviour, the Lord Jesus Christ:

Who shall change our vile body, that it may be fashioned like unto his glorious body, according to the working whereby he is able even to subdue all things unto himself. (Philippians 3:8–11, 14, 20–21.)

Paul's feelings of gratitude for the redemption made by Jesus Christ are reflected in these words:

Grace be to you and peace from God the Father, and from our Lord Jesus Christ,

Who gave himself for our sins, that he might deliver us from this present evil world, according to the will of God and our Father (Galatians 1:3–4).

I am crucified with Christ: nevertheless I live; yet not I, but Christ liveth in me: and the life which I now live in the flesh I live by the faith of the Son of God, who loved me, and gave himself for me (Galatians 2:20).

Looking for that blessed hope, and the glorious appearing of the great God and our Saviour Jesus Christ;

Who gave himself for us, that he might redeem us from all iniquity, and purify unto himself a peculiar people, zealous of good works (Titus 2:13–14).

And hope maketh not ashamed; because the love of God is shed abroad in our hearts by the Holy Ghost which is given unto us.

For when we were yet without strength, in due time Christ died for the ungodly.

For scarcely for a righteous man will one die: yet peradventure for a good man some would even dare to die.

But God commendeth his love toward us, in that, while we were yet sinners, Christ died for us.

Much more then, being now justified by his blood, we shall be saved from wrath through him. (Romans 5:5–9.)

And I thank Christ Jesus our Lord, who hath enabled me, for that he counted me faithful, putting me into the ministry;

Who was before a blasphemer, and a persecutor, and injurious: but I obtained mercy, because I did it ignorantly in unbelief.

And the grace of our Lord was exceeding abundant with faith and love which is in Christ Jesus.

This is a faithful saying, and worthy of all acceptation, that Christ Jesus came into the world to save sinners; of whom I am chief.

Howbeit for this cause I obtained mercy, that in me first Jesus Christ might shew forth all longsuffering, for a pattern to them which should hereafter believe on him to life everlasting. (1 Timothy 1:12–16.)

The Testimony of St. Paul. In Part II of this work we observed that the books of Matthew, Mark, Luke, and John are not so much histories or biographies but are testimonies concerning Jesus Christ, with emphasis on who he is, what he said, what he did, and why those things are important. It was also observed that the JST corrects the titles from "The Gospel According to St. Matthew," Mark, and so on, to "The Testimony of St. Matthew," Mark, and so on. An analysis of the pattern or style of these four testimonies shows that they contain certain historical events and doctrinal concepts from the Savior's life, including birth accounts, genealogies, preaching of John the Baptist, Jesus' teachings, the Last Supper, the Crucifixion, the Resurrection, and the Ascension. An analysis of Paul's writings shows that he discussed many of the same events and concepts, but not in organized chronological form. However, the following topics and reference show that a "Testimony of St. Paul" could be arranged from his words.

1. Jesus is the eldest of the Father's spirit children, and is the firstborn among many brethren (Romans 8:29; Colossians 1:15).
2. Mankind, as premortal spirits, had a relationship with Jesus, and received promises from him (Ephesians 1:3–4; 2 Timothy 1:9; Titus 1:1–2).
3. Jesus created our earth and many others (Ephesians 3:9; Colossians 3:10; Hebrews 1:2, 10).
4. Jesus is the Son of God in the flesh, and heir of the Father (Romans 1:4).
5. Jesus came to earth through the lineage of Abraham, the tribe of Judah, and the house of David (Acts 13:22–23; Romans 1:3; 15:12; Hebrews 7:14).

6. John the Baptist prepared the way for Christ, and testified that the people should believe on him who would give them the Holy Ghost (Acts 13:23–25; 19:1–7).

7. Jesus was a high priest after the order of Melchizedek (Hebrews 3:1; 4:14; 5:10; 7:18–21).

8. As a mortal, Jesus was subject to temptation but refused to sin (Hebrews 2:17–18; 4:14–15).

9. All mankind can become the children of Abraham and inherit the promises of eternal life, by baptism and faith in Jesus Christ, thus becoming joint-heirs with Jesus (Romans 8:16–17; Galatians 3:26–29; 4:1–7).

10. Jesus said, "It is more blessed to give than to receive" (Acts 20:35).

11. The night he was betrayed, Jesus instituted the sacrament of bread and wine. We partake in remembrance of him (1 Corinthians 11:23–26).

12. Jesus purchased man's redemption, by the shedding of his own blood (Ephesians 2:13; Colossians 1:14, 20).

13. As in Adam all die, so in Christ shall all be made alive (1 Corinthians 15:22).

14. Jesus died on the cross for our sins (1 Corinthians 15:3; Galatians 2:20; Philippians 2:8).

15. The law of Moses and the service in the tabernacle, animal sacrifices, and performances, prefigured, and were symbolic of the true Messiah who is Jesus Christ (1 Corinthians 5:7; Hebrews chapters 7–10).

16. Jesus accomplished for us what the law of Moses could not do. Man can be justified only by the grace of Jesus Christ (JST Romans 3:24; Romans 8:3, 4).

17. Jesus rose from the dead in the resurrected condition and appeared to more than 500 brethren at one time (1 Corinthians 15:5).

18. Because Jesus is resurrected, all mankind will also be resurrected in their proper order and time (Acts 17:18, 31–32; 26:23; 1 Corinthians 15:22–57).

19. Jesus ascended into heaven, but he will return. When he comes the dead in Christ shall be resurrected first and rise to meet him (Ephesians 4:8–10; 1 Thessalonians 4:14–17).

20. Jesus' name is above every name; the whole family in

heaven and earth is named for him. Every knee shall bow, every tongue confess that he is Christ (Ephesians 3:14, 15; Philippians 2:9–11).

21. Jesus is a God with all the fulness, wisdom, knowledge, and power of the Father (Colossians 1:19; 2:2, 8, 9; Philippians 2:5–6).

22. Jesus will judge all mankind (Romans 2:16; 2 Corinthians 5:10; 2 Timothy 4:8).

It is evident from Paul's enthusiasm, his testimony, and his absolute certainty that he had indeed beheld the Messiah.

Scripture Index

BOOK OF MORMON

PEARL OF GREAT PRICE

Subject Index

— I —

Iconium, 330
Idolatry, 304, 313–14
Immortality, 15
Irony, used by Jesus, 218, 223–26
    used by Paul, 335–37
Isaac, 16
Isaiah, 16, 75, 89, 280
    prophecies concerning Jesus, 78, 84, 254
    prophecies concerning John the Baptist, 44
    prophecy concerning Mary, 77

— J —

Jacob (Old Testament patriarch), 16
Jacob (son of Lehi), 89
    on miracles of Jesus, 129
    on the Atonement, 100
    on wickedness of Jewish rulers, 271
Jairus, 145–46, 148
    daughter of, 145–46, 272, 284
James (brother of Jesus), at Jerusalem council, 303–4, 306, 307
James (brother of John), 104–5, 134, 135, 145–46, 165–66, 227
    appearance of resurrected Christ to, 286
    martyrdom of, 300, 303
    missionary record of, in Acts, 290, 291
    See also Peter, James, and John
James (son of Alphaeus), 104–5
Jaredite prophets, 16
Jehovah, 16, 69, 73–74, 75, 89, 232, 273
    See also Jesus Christ
Jeremiah, 89, 226
Jericho, 163
Jerusalem, 107, 162, 265
    council in, 287–88, 290, 292–302, 302–9, 310–11, 324
    early Church in, 295, 297, 298, 300, 307–8, 314–15, 317–18, 323, 338
    Jesus in, 92–93, 138, 159, 162, 267–70, 290
    temple in, 24, 30, 80–82, 92–93, 95, 186–87, 247, 318
Jesus Christ, Apostles special witnesses for, 103
    appearance after resurrection, 108–9
    appearances after resurrection (chart), 286
    appearances of, to Joseph Smith, 17, 200
    arrest and trial of, 269–70
    ascension of, 70, 71, 73, 285, 286, 292–93, 345

at wedding in Cana, 188–89
atonement of, 3–4, 12–13, 15, 69–70, 71, 73, 76, 99–102, 194, 201–2, 214, 217, 224, 254, 257, 273, 301–2, 341–45
authority of, 204–5
baptism of, 43, 187, 216
baptisms performed by, 191, 264
birth of, 30, 77–80
brothers and sisters of, 84–86
carpenter, 84
childhood and youth of, 80–86, 92–94, 185–87, 202–3
children blessed by, 194
Church established by, 72–73
circumcision of, 83
color of robe of, 198
compassion of, 128, 129, 131–32, 135–44, 146–49, 152–55, 158–63, 165, 193, 257
conversation with woman at the well, 221–22
creator of the earth, 214, 344
creator of many worlds, 15–16, 75, 344
crucifixion of, 210–11, 270, 276
eldest of Father's spirit children, 344
example of, 235
Firstborn, 73, 75, 214
followed in path of Father, 209–10
foreordination of, 5, 8, 203
forty days in wilderness, 47, 187–88, 216, 255
genealogy of, 31
high priest after order of Melchizedek, 345
instructions to the Twelve, 32, 72, 73, 112–21, 220, 262
Jewish leaders rebuked by, 217, 233, 258–59, 260–64
John the Baptist praised by, 41, 44
judge of all mankind, 214, 345
known only by revelation, 90–92
law of Moses fulfilled in, 308, 313
Lord of the Sabbath, 189
meekness and lowliness of, 204
Millennial reign, 213
ministry in spirit world, 70, 73, 211–12, 277
missionary methods of, 316
money changers cast out of temple by, 95
Nephite ministry, 5, 32, 129, 256, 277
obedience of, 204
on Mount of Transfiguration, 205, 242, 250
Only Begotten of the Father, 75, 284

on Mount of Transfiguration, 39,
    242–43, 248
on mysteries as cause of crucifixion of
    Jesus, 210–11
on obedience of Jesus, 204
on ordination by John the Baptist, 65–66
on parables, 178–80, 225
on Paul, 333, 338–39
on perfection of Jesus, 203
on power of Jesus over death, 209–10
on rock of revelation, 240
on the salt of the earth, 114
on salvation of animals, 205–6
on second coming of Christ, 212–13
on spirit of Elias, 51
on suffering of Jesus, 255
on understanding the scriptures, 128
on why Jesus associated with sinners,
    208
on why Jesus spoke in parables, 206–8
on wickedness of his generation, 271
restoration through, 291
revelation to, 6, 19–20, 65, 200
Teachings of the Prophet Joseph Smith, 172,
    179–81
vision of glorified earth, 39
See also Bible, Joseph Smith Translation
    (JST)
Snow, Erastus, 281, 282
Soldiers, 47–48, 197–98
Solitary places, 193
Spain, 291, 323
Spirit world, 3, 280
    ministry of Christ in, 70, 73, 211–12, 277
Spiritual death, 11–13, 100–102
Stephen, 64, 294–97, 333
Syria, 311

— T —

Talmage, James E., *vii*
    Jesus the Christ, 4–6, 106
    on Jesus as heir to throne of David, 78
    on John the Baptist, 54
    on male and female spirits, 8
Taylor, John, on eternal principles, 1
Teaching, 215–38

by the Spirit, 214–16, 219, 234–35
Temple at Jerusalem, 24, 30, 80–82, 92–94,
    95, 186–87, 247, 318
Ten Commandments, 117
Thaddaeus, 104
Theophilus, 29, 289
Thessalonica, 313, 332, 337–38
Thomas, 31, 104–5, 165, 268, 277–78, 286
Three Witnesses, 181
Timothy, 307, 311–15, 325, 329–31, 337
Titus, 305–6
Tongues, 293
Tradition, 290, 307–9
Transfiguration. *See* Mount of
    Transfiguration
Troas, 311, 317
Turkey, 291, 307, 311
Tyre and Sidon, 152, 153, 193

— U —

United order, 295

— V —

Visual aids, 228–29

— W —

Washing of feet, 31, 34, 107
Welfare program, in early Church, 295,
    296–97, 300, 317, 338–39
Whitmer family, 291
Wise men, 28, 92, 184–85, 250
Witnesses, law of, 198–99, 249–52
Women, 30
Wonderful Flood of Light, A, (book), 10

— Y —

Young, Brigham, on keys of resurrection,
    281–282

— Z —

Zacharias, 30, 34, 52–53, 64, 250